Shi'ism and Royalty in Safavid Poetry

Haddad Hamdi

Table of Contents

TRANSLITERATION

The transliterations used in this work follow a system adopted by the *International Journal of Middle Eastern Studies* in accordance with Persian sub category, except the Arabic and Persian words which end with *tā' marbūṭa*. They are rendered with *eh*. The names of well-known places are not written in transliteration. Titles such as Shah, Sultan, and Amir are not transliterated as well.

ABSTRACT

My research concerns intertwined issues of religio-political legitimacy and panegyric poetry during the Safavid dynasty (r. 1501 – 1722). I explore ways that ideology and dominance were enacted and reproduced through the Safavid panegyrics in *qaṣīdeh* and *masnavī* form. This research specifically examines how court poets responded to Safavid ideology for legitimizing kingship. Panegyric poetry has been one of the chief forms of political propaganda in praise of rulers and other holders of political authority from pre-Islamic times until modern days. Panegyric poems, especially *qaṣīdeh* and *masnavī,* were the production of a court system and they were dominantly produced when a king was in power. By considering the nature of panegyric, as written for receiving a reward, the poets' portrayal of kings is traditionally "assumed" to be the closest to the kings' self-image. The Safavid Persian panegyric, especially the *qaṣīdeh* form, has heretofore received little scholarly attention. Scholars have usually investigated the literary value of this poetic genre and dismissed the role it could play in the promotion of Muslim rulers. This dissertation explores the ways in which religio-political legitimacy was produced and transmitted through the *qaṣīdeh* and *masnavī* forms during the Safavid period and emphasizes the significance of investigating the panegyric genre of poetry not only from a literary perspective, but through a historical lens. While other cultural materials of the time emphasized the role of Safavid kings in the propagation of Twelver Shiʿism and portrayed the kings in a subservient position to the Shiʿi Imams, I demonstrate that the

Safavid court poetry highlighted the idea of "sacred" in Sufi discourses and in notions that invoke pre-Islamic forms of Persian kingship to legitimize the Safavid rulership. From the time of Shah 'Abbās I (r. 1588 – d. 1629), these two forms of representation were established more profoundly in Safavid panegyrics and stood in contrast to traditional notions of Shi'ism that were predominant in other cultural materials that issued in the name of the Safavid rulers.

This dissertation, on the one hand, serves historians of the Safavid period, who investigate the Safavid courts and ideology in kingship. It demonstrates how the poets worked differently from the other sources through which the legitimization of the Safavid kingship was established. On the other hand, my study serves scholars of religion, who study Safavid religious treatises in order to shed light on the development of Shi'ism, Sufism, and other religious traditions of the time. By demonstrating the differences between the representation of a Shi'i Safavid king in cultural materials of the time and panegyrics, my research invites these scholars to examine non-religious sources more extensively to investigate Safavid ideology because these sources give a sense of how the religio-political ideology of the kings was perceived among the public and how it developed through time.

INTRODUCTION:
PERSIAN LITERARY CULTURE AND SHI'ISM

I. Poetry of Monarchs

There is usually a disciplinary division when inquiring into monarchy's significance in the world. Political theorists and literary critics pay less attention to monarchs to demonstrate who they were and how they defined themselves, and historians of kingship usually focus on monarchy's chronology rather than the political theories of monarchy and social structures in which a monarch practiced power. The court poetry of monarchs does not usually attract the attention of historians. Considering praise as an activity that cannot be rated highly, the Persian literary scholars and critics usually look down at panegyrics. Neither literary critics nor historians have focused on panegyrics to study ideas of kingship. This is specifically the case for Safavid court poetry, which belongs to an era whose literature has raised comparatively less excitement among scholars.

It is the prime goal of this dissertation to achieve more engagement with the panegyric form of poetry of the Safavid period. What this poetry presents helps us to understand Safavid kingship and the process through which these self-styled Sufi kings became known and legitimized as Muslim leaders during the absence of Imam Mahdī, the twelfth Shi'i Imam. Studying the literary representation of religion and spirituality in Safavid panegyrics as well as their relationship with images of kingship explains the "sacred" and "spiritual" concepts affiliated with the position of kingship for followers of Twelver Imami doctrines.

Persian poetry of praise was composed in different forms. However, the *qaṣīdeh,* which is heavily influenced by Arabic models, is the major genre for writing panegyrics. Arabic panegyric *qaṣīdeh* had ceremonial functions, as did the Persian *qaṣīdeh*. Both Arabic and Persian *qaṣīdeh* were written in a prescribed manner to offer praise and allegiance to the holders of political authority and nobles. While the structure of the Arabic *qaṣīdeh* and the role of kingship in panegyric have been the subject of several studies in recent years, this topic has not been fully explored by historians and literature scholars in its Persian context. Julie Scott Meisami, in her 1987 work *Medieval Persian Court Poetry,*[1] sheds light on different aspects of Persian panegyrics since its early formation at the court of Samanids (r. 819 – 999 CE) and its further development through the court of Ghazneh (r. 977 – 1186 CE). She explained the features of writing panegyric in different forms of poetry, including *qaṣīdeh, ghazal,* epic and romance. Citing from Jerome Clinton, Meisami argues that the works of praise cannot be perceived as historical texts which construct the portrait of a specific king. The image of a king in Persian panegyrics, or Arabic panegyrics, is "a successful presentation of an idealized monarch," an image which is mostly a praise of "Islamic monarchy", but not "an Islamic monarch."[2] Earlier, in a 1977 article covering similar ground about Arabic panegyrics, Sperl mentioned that the Arabic *qaṣīdeh*s of

---

[1] Julie Scott Meisami, *Medieval Persian Court Poetry,* (N.J: Princeton University Press, 1987).

[2] Ibid, 43.

early ninth century praised the "basic values and political ideals" of the Abbasid state, and not a specific king. Based on this idea Sperl writes:

> "It is clear that the panegyric does not attempt to portray the character of individual monarchs. Instead, it extolls the role of Kingship which an individual assumes. Its thematic development, its liturgical formalism, and the expression it gives to essential social values all suggest that the public recitation of panegyric poetry was an act of ritual."[3]

Sperl, in the same paper, argues that the result of his analysis on form and function of early ninth century Arabic panegyrics dedicated to the Caliphs can also be applied to other poetry of praise and even poems written earlier than the ninth century. In the same paper, he discusses that the image of a sovereign in Arabic poems is rooted in the visions of political authority celebrated traditionally in the Ancient Near East rather than specific features describing an individual monarch.[4] It is assumed that the panegyric writers did not intend to praise a specific king, but they pointed to "the timeless nature of the virtues considered to [be inherent] in the occupant of the given position."[5] While this statement could be valid about praising Sunni Caliphs, its validity should be investigated in the case of non-Sunni rulers such as the Safavid kings. While the Safavid poets usually praise a king by investing him with similar virtues and personalities, the effect of Shi'i identity of new kings on poetic discourses should be investigated to draw a conclusion about the relationship between poets, Shi'ism, and kingship. What was the influence of Shi' discourse on poetic discourses?

---

[3] Stephen Sperl, *Mannerism in Arabic Poetry: a Structural Analysis of Selected Texts:3rd Century AH/9th century AD-5th Century AH/11th Century AD*, (Cambridge; New York: Cambridge University Press. 1989), 34.

[4] Ibid, 35.

[5] Meisami, *Medieval Persian Court Poetry*, 43.

Did the image of a Safavid king undergo change over time? What was Shi'ism and a Shi'i king in the eyes of poets who may not have been Shi'i? Did the Safavid ideology appear fully in the poems? Or did some of its elements outweigh the others? What is the effect of conventional images of kingship in this poetry? If the image of a Sunni and Shi'i king stays the same regardless the religio-political changes, could we assume that the function of praise was different, and could we assume that panegyric work differently in its legitimization of power in comparison to the other legitimizing tools of the time?

II. Shi'i Kings, non-Shi'i Poets

That Shah Ismā'īl (b. 1487 – d.1524) recruited Shi'i religious scholars of Lebanon to educate people with Shi'i ideas indicates that many people, including the poets, were unfamiliar with different aspects of this new faith. Shah Ismā'īl had little, if any, Shi'i theological training and his advisers were not even aware of the meaning of the central Shi'ite concepts. According to Rula Abisaab, Shah Ismā'īl's understanding of Islam drew upon ancient Asian rituals and the cult of 'Alī, but his followers were not able to distinguish between a dervish and a shaman.[6] Turning to Shi'ism and the Shi'i clerics of Jabal 'Āmil, was done in order "to institute proper, court-sanctioned religious socialization for both educated and common Persians," Abisaab argues.[7] The interest in Twelve Imami doctrines, according to Andrew Newman, had no precedence in early Safavid history. The early leadership of Safavids

---

[6] Rula Abisaab, *Converting Persia: Religion and Power in the Safavid Empire*. (London [u.a.]: Tauris, 2015), 10.

[7] Ibid, 12.

did not demonstrate any interest in Twelver Shi'i or other religious discourses. Also, claiming connections with the family of 'Alī or the prophet's family was not part of the early claims of the Safavids.[8] The reason for turning to Twelver doctrines, Newman argues, was the setting it could provide for the "culmination of the messianic radicalism adopted under Junayd"[9] and further "encouraging and cementing the profound sense of separation from, and hostility among the order's followers to the exciting socio-economic and political structure as dominated by Sunni Muslims."[10] Shah 'Abbās I (b. 1571 – d. 1629) further reinforced the ideas of kingship based on Twelver Shi'i doctrines. He had a desire to be known as the defender of divine law and the servant of Imām 'Alī (or Imām Riżā), and, in general, to be in a devoted position to the Shi'i Imams; thus, he practiced public acts of piety assiduously to portray himself as the servant of Shi'i doctrines.

In contrast to what is known in regard to how becoming Shi'i was important for the Safavid polity, the Safavid panegyrics (in *qaṣīdeh* and *masnavī* form) did not address this interest of their patrons. Despite the desire of Safavid kings to be publicly known as servers of the religion, the panegyrics dedicated to them are not colored for the most part by Shi'i terms and expressions. Depending on the genre and form of the poetry, for most of the Safavid period and after Shah 'Abbās I's time, the poets did not apply Shi'i terms and expressions in order to praise the Safavid kings. Although references to the return of Imām Mahdī (the last Shi'i Imam) are to be found along

---

[8] Andrew Neman, "The Myth of Clerical Migration to Safavid Iran", *Die Welt des Islams*, New Series, Vol. 33, Issue 1 (Apr. 1993), 68.

[9] Junayd (d. 1460) was the father of Shaykh Ḥaydar and the grandfather of Shah Ismā'īl. It is assumed he had the leadership of the Safavids from 1447 – 1460.

[10] Ibid, 69.

with a few references to the incident of Karbala, the ideas related to Twelver Shiʻi

doctrines are absent from the panegyrics. Instead, the poets depicted Safavid kings as

sovereigns whose virtues and mystic power are emphasized. This image is similar to

the image of pre-Islamic kings of the Persian empire such as Jamshīd and Firīdūn.

Special features similar to traits of famous Sufi saints were also associated with the

Safavid kings via the language that usually predominated in lyrical and *ghazal* writing.

This image links the title of Shah and Imam, and further allows the kings to claim

power of Muslim leadership in the absence of a qualified Imam. This idea, as Newman

argues, would reinforce the Safavid power among the peasants and tribal nomads,

while appealing to the community of Twelver Shiʻism throughout the region.[11]

III. Aim and Scope of the Dissertation

In this research, I have examined the two most important genres of praise,

qaṣīdeh and *masnavī,* while paying attention to the literary representation of notions of

kingship and Shiʻism. This does not mean that other forms of poetry did not serve to

legitimize the kingship or did not praise a king as there are many *ghazal*s and *qitʻeh*s

which are dedicated to the praise of kings. However, since *qaṣīdeh* and *masnavī* are

mostly known as the dominant genres of praise, and were mostly written on the order

of monarchs, I investigated these two forms of poems in this research, and I left the

examination of other forms for future projects.

My research is concerned with intertwined issues of religio-political legitimacy

and poetry during the Safavid period. I look at discursive verbal enunciations of power

in public places such as mosques and palaces, as well as in the poems in which power

---

[11] Newman, "The Myth of Clerical Migration," 72.

declares itself. My goal in reconstructing the patterns of legitimacy in historical and cultural material of the time provides a comparative tool for studying the Safavid *qaṣīdeh*s and *masnavī*s and the compatibility of their ideological discourses with what has been considered as a dominant Safavid ideology tied mainly to Twelver Shi'ism. To this end, my study examines the patterns of religio-political legitimacy in Persian *qaṣīdeh*s and *masnavī*s written during the Safavid period and dedicated to the Safavid kings. Studying these patterns helps to portray the trajectory of Safavid ideology from one court to the next and further demonstrates the development of ideas related to Shi'ism and kingship throughout history.

By contextualizing the Persian panegyric in its culture and history and by choosing Safavid ideology as an analytical lens, this dissertation offers insights relevant to fields outside of literary studies such as history and religion, I hope to catalyze a pattern for future studies concerned with Safavid Persian *qaṣīdeh*s and *masnavī*s. For example, my analysis serves the historians of the Safavid period who investigate the Safavid courts and ideology in kingship. I demonstrate that the Safavid poets combined the ideas of Persianate kingship with attributes of Sufis within the Shi'i frame. This combination resulted in an image in which the Safavid kings looked similar to the Shi'i imams in terms of having a spiritual and sacred personality. This research demonstrates that poetry, along with historical chronicles and other texts, are central for understanding history because they provide information and data for writing histories of the 16th and 17th century. Further, I hope my study will serve scholars of religion, who assiduously study Safavid religious treatises in order to shed light on the development of Shi'ism, Sufism, and other religious traditions of the time as this research demonstrates how Shi'ism and kingship was perceived within non-religious circles. Examining the patterns of Safavid legitimacy and the trajectory of Safavid ideology over two and a half centuries in cultural materials and panegyric poems demonstrates that Shi'ism at the beginning of the Safavid dynasty was perceived differently from the final years of this dynasty. Shi'ism and its framework were changing concepts that stabilized only during the middle years of the Safavid reign. The instability of the religio-political ideology was evident in the use of kingly titles and benedictions in different cultural materials of the time until Shah 'Abbās I. After him, the inheritors of his kingship followed his choice of titles, benedictions, and system of ruling.

This dissertation is a study of the Safavid Persian literary culture because the literary representation of kingship and religion in these poems sheds light on the economics of writing panegyrics. It demonstrates how adapting new ways of writings or continuing the conventional ways of praise shaped the literary sphere of the time. I demonstrate that the Safavid panegyrics, while not appreciated in terms of literary value, contain themes and ideas that make the poetic culture of the time unique, specifically in that they speak of multiculturalism that influenced the 16th and 17th century literature as a result of the cultural interrelations between the Safavid and Mughal courts. That I chose Safavid Persian literature for my study does not mean that I see the Safavid and Mughal literary cultures as separate. The mobility of poets between the two domains produced new literary images and ideas that affected both literatures. Specifically, the influence of Mughal literary culture on the Safavids demonstrates itself in urban descriptions and the images of gardens and palaces that became a source of legitimacy for the Safavid kings by end of 17th century. Sunil

Sharma in *Mughal Arcadia* extensively studied the representation of gardens and

palaces among the Mughal poets who wrote in Persian. He argues that focusing on

topoi of palaces and gardens, the way that they were presented and praised in their

poetic and historical texts of Safavid, Mughal, and Ottoman empires in a comparative

mode, provides a useful matrix for a comparative study of the cultural history of these

polities.[12] Paul Losensky in *Welcoming Fighani* admits that "our critical understanding

of the [early modern] period remains hampered by an inadequate conceptual

framework."[13] Both Losensky and Sharma focused on a set of related themes in

representative texts of the period through comparison of literature of Islamicate

empires to examine the shared culture among the three polities of the Safavids,

Mughals, and Ottomans, and to portray the developments of social and political

culture of each polity. This dissertation by focusing on representation of kingship and

Shi'ism in Safavid panegyrics as two important elements of Persian panegyric poetry,

hopes to expand this subject of study to a comparative study of the other two dynasties

in future.

Furthermore, translating the Safavid panegyrics dedicated to the Safavid kings

will hopefully encourages further studies of the overlapping literature of these

dynasties and of the representation of Muslim kingship through times. These

panegyrics have not been translated previously. In translation, my primary goal was to

present the images of kingship and religion closely as possible to their originals. The

---

[12] Sharma, *Mughal Arcadia,* 13.

[13] Paul Losensky, *Welcoming Fighani: Imitation and Poetic Individuality in the Safavid-Mughal Ghazal,* (Costa Mesa, Calif: Mazda Publishers, 1998), 3.

attempt is to keep the images of kingship and religion within the Safavid and its Persian and Shi'i context. However, in some cases, since the dominant language of kingship in English is rooted in medieval Europe, the translations do not seem to fully comprehend the Safavid idea of kingship. The best example is the terms *vilāyat* and *sulṭeh,* usually translated in English as "sovereignty," which does not invoke the religious and social connotations of Muslim kingship. The other obstacle in translation was to explicate fully the meaning of complicated metaphors in a web of images in which they were employed. In many cases, translating these metaphors was not possible. Therefore, I preferred only to mention one aspect of a metaphor and explain the second meaning and the interrelation of images within a line in footnotes in order to demonstrate the line's literal value. I hope that by developing the translation of these works, I provide more data for historians and scholars of religion.

IV. Key Concepts

Before analyzing the texts, there are some expressions and key concepts that need to be discussed. In the following pages, I explain how these terms are defined in scholarly writings about Safavid ideology and how these concepts factor into my analysis of Safavid poetry.

A. Ideology within the Safavid Context

Although it is difficult to apply western and modern definitions of ideology produced during Europe's 19th century with reference to the medieval society of the Safavids, there is no way to discuss Safavid legitimacy without applying the word "ideology." There is a general methodological confusion in applying purportedly universal and general theories. This means that although an explanation of a phenomenon can be valid, there will be still places in which the theory does not apply. The theories of European societies, such as theories of ideology by Marx, Foucault, and Althusser, should not be applied as if they are automatically suitable only because they investigate ideology and power relations. Rather, their suitability for the Iranian context should be justified. Nevertheless, to discuss political authority and legitimacy during the reign of the Safavids, I need to employ terms such as "discourse" to speak of a cluster of ideas that was imposed on people to legitimize Safavid kingship. In using the term "ideology," I refer to discourses that existed in the verbal representations of power. By ideology I mean the central ideas of the Safavid dynasty that worked toward reinforcing the kingship – the ideas that appeared in different forms and shapes to support the monarchical dynasty. The forms were not necessarily verbal; sometimes they took the form of particular dress, ritual movements, and spatio-temporal dispositions of bodies.[14] The paintings remaining from this period are good examples that could elaborate more about the ideas of Safavid kingship. However, given that the main focus of this dissertation is poetry, I eliminated from my study the sources which presented non-verbal forms of power, such as paintings, miniatures, and pottery. Instead, I focused on poetry because by applying a metaphoric language and using of specific forms of images, poetry could play an important role in promoting a specific ruler or undermining a specific ruler.

---

[14] Aziz Al-Azmeh, *Muslim Kingship: Power and the Sacred in Muslim, Christian and Pagan Polities*. (London: I.B. Tauris, 1997).

B. Sacred Kingship and Safavid Legitimacy

Azfar Moin has called the religious history of pre-Safavid Iran during the

Timurids a "messianic age" because it was rooted in the norms and rituals of Sufi

movements which allowed the presentation of the king to be a heaven-ordained savior

and the embodiment of divinity.[15] The Sufi movements of this period had two key

elements in their central discourse: temporality and a reviver. While Moin studied the

similarities of different sacral forms of kingship among the three empires of the

Safavids, Mughals, and Ottomans, Matthew Melvin-Koushki has examined the

scholarship about different forms of sacral kingship. Melvin-Koushki studied

astrology, lettrism, and geomancy as the bases of the occult-scientific methods of

Post-Mongol Islamicate imperialism, which represented a sacred king in the leading

position of the Muslim society. Melvin-Koushki demonstrated that sacral forms

provided religio-political legitimacy for the empires from the 13th century onward.[16]

Jonathan Brack by considering the Mongol kings as "Philosopher-King"s focused on

the process of sacralization of Muslim kings from the 13th century.[17] Further, the

works of Kathryn Babayan and Sholeh Quinn examined the role of different religious

groups and tribes in shaping Safavid sacred power and constituting the Safavid

---

[15]Azfar Moin, *The Millennial Sovereign: Sacred Kingship and Sainthood in Islam,* (New York: Columbia University Press, 2015), 1-22. Also see Kathryn, Babayan, *Mystics, Monarchs and Messiah: Cultural Landscape of Early Modern Iran.* (Cambridge, Mass: Harvard University Press, 2003).

[16] Matthew Mevlin-Koushki, "Astrology, Lettrism, Geomancy: The Occult-Scientific Methods of Post-Mongol Islamicate Imperialism", *The Medieval History Journal*, Vol 19, Issue 1, pp. 142 – 150. First Published March 1, 2016, https://doi.org/10.1177/0971945815626316

[17] See Jonathan Brack. "Mediating Sacred Kingship: Conversion and Sovereignty in Mongol Iran." PhD diss., University of Michigan, 2016.

ideology. This sacred power usually was claimed through connecting the rulers to the

House of the Prophet and the Sufi *shaykh*s of Ardabil.[18]

When I use the term "sacred" to refer to the Safavid dynasty and its rulers, I

am referring to the fleeting tendencies and behaviors of each groups that formed

together to present the king as the God's representative on earth. Although it is

difficult to draw a distinct line between the ideas involved with Safavid form of

kingship, they mostly reflect upon the Sufi, Shi'i, and concepts such as *farr* that

represent divinity of pre-Islamic kings of Persian Empire. The image of Safavid

kingship that is represented in poems is not rooted in one culture but borrows its

power from different socio-cultural groups and traditions that formed the Safavid

identity, a combination of material and spiritual/other-worldly ideas including the

ideas related to power, genealogy of the rulers, religious practices, and national myths.

The king that is represented through this consolidation is not only a mighty king

whose palace and retinue are magnificent but is a representative of the divine, whose

nature is made of non-material ideas such as *farr* and *karāmat* of Sufis.[19] The

legitimacy that their connection to the Alid family provides allows them to seek and

further maintain the power they required to separate their kingship from other sources

of power. Like Imām 'Alī, who in a popular Shi'i believe did not seek to fight over for

power the prophet's death and only reluctantly accepted by request of the Prophet's

friends and family, the Safavid kings were represented as leaders with no material

---

[18] See Kathryn Babayan *Mystics, Monarchs and Messiah: Cultural Landscape of Early Modern Iran.* (Cambridge, Mass: Harvard University Press, 2003), and Sholeh Quinn, *Historical Writing During the Reign of Shah 'Abbas: Ideology, Imitation, and Legitimacy in Safavid Chronicles,* (Salt Lake City: University of Utah Press), 2000.

[19] For definition of *karāmat* see this chapter page 23.

intention in mind for seeking power. Lack of interest in political authority for the sake of power allows Sufi aspects of the king's character to be foregrounded.

C. Iranian Kingship and Its Symbols

Divine Glory or *farr-i īzadī,* which in Old Persian was known as *khvarenah,* is usually invoked to project the legitimacy of rule and divine sanction.[20] This term was central to discussions of power and authority within the Iranian kingship discourse. Abolala Soudavar in *The Aura of Kings* studies the symbolism of *khvarenah* from the Parthian to the Sasanian period. Soudavar studied documents from the pre-Islamic period to shed light on the formulation and development of the symbolism of kingship in Iran and relevant geo-cultural neighbors. He argues that *farr,* as the consistent pattern of power and authority in the Iranian world, was profoundly affected by the Mithraic legacy, which linked Sasanian iconography to Achaemenid and Median symbols of *farr.*[21] Touraj Daryaee argues that early Sasanian kingship was mainly a reworking of the Avestan, Old Persian, and Hellenic notions of kingship. By paying special attention to frequent expressions of kingship during the Sasanids— *bayān, chihr az yazdān, shahān shah,* and their roots—Daryaee argues that the early Sasanian kingship was a hybrid idea drawing strength from Zoroastrian, Persis, Parthian, and Hellenic traditions to justify its rule over *Īrānshahr.*[22] References to *Īrānshahr* (the

---

[20] To read about *farr,* its derivations and various forms in Old and New Persian, as well as in other languages see Gherardo Gnoli, "FARR(AH)", *Encyclopædia Iranica,* online edition, available at http://www.iranicaonline.org/articles/farrah.

[21] Abolala Soudavar, *The Aura of Kings: Legitimacy and Divine Sanction in Iranian Kingship,* (Costa Mesa, Calif: Mazda Publishers, 2003).

[22] Touraj Daryaee, "Kingship in Early Sasanian Iran", in *The Sasanian Era: The Idea of Iran.* III ed. Curtis Vesta Sarkhosh and Sarah Stewart, (2010), 60-70.

realm of the Iranians/Aryans) connected the Achaemenid tradition to Zoroastrians, who supported Ardashīr religiously and politically. The term *Īrānshahr* refers to both the provinces of Iran and non-Iranian places such as Syria, Cilicia, Armenia, Georgia, Albania, and Balasgan, which were under the control of Ardashīr.[23] Daryaee also argues that while in the early Sasanian period the kings were perceived as the seed/image of gods, later and in the fourth century, during the Shāpūr II's reign and under the influence of the Zoroastrian religious hierarchy, the king became a *cosmocrator,* a mediator between gods and men.[24]

The kings of the Persian empire were endowed with *khvarenah,* "glory," which made them invincible. In the early iconography of pre-Islamic cultures, *khvarenah* was presented through different symbols, including a lotus flower, a jug of water, a pomegranate, and a pearl.[25] The other famous forms of *khvarenah* were the sign of crescent-sunburst, sun-moon, and star-moon symbols. The regal headgear of the Sasanid kings with the Parthian tiara is another such symbol. Soudavar saw a connection between the Safavid red scarlet baton-headgear that was wrapped in a turban and the Parthian tiara and concluded that the headgear played the role of a crown for the Safavids.[26] He also considered the Safavid *dastārcheh,* famously known

---

[23] Ibid, *Sasanian Persia: The Rise and Fall of an Empire*, (London: I.B. Tauris & Co. Ltd in association with the Iran Heritage Foundation, 2014), 6.

[24] Ibid, 69.

[25] See Abolala Soudavar, *The Aura of Kings: Legitimacy and Divine Sanction in Iranian Kingship*, (Costa Mesa, Calif: Mazda Publishers, 2003). Abolala Soudavar, "FARR(AH) ii. ICONOGRAPHY OF FARR(AH)/XᵛARƎNAH," *Encyclopædia Iranica*, online edition, 2016, available at http://www.iranicaonline.org/articles/farr-ii-iconography (accessed on 19 May 2016).

[26] Soudavar, *The Aura of Kings*, 71.

by its Turkish name as *sārūq*, to be a symbol of authority.[27] Iranian *dastār* (turban),

dayhīm, headband, and flying ribbons were among the other symbols that represented

the *farr*.

Khvarenah is defined by its transient nature. It does not have a fixed status; by

victory and doing good, *khvarenah* can be increased, and in case of defeat, it will

decrease and ultimately be lost, as seen in the story of Jamshīd. The possession of

God's grace (*farr-i īzadī*) legitimized the position of ancient Iranian rulers. As

depicted in *Shāhnāmeh,* this grace was bestowed on the person of the ruler, and it was

not necessary for the person be the first in the line of succession. In most cases, the

farr was acquired by succeeding or by performing supernatural acts to win power. The

term *farr* was also used to confirm the divine legitimacy of post-Islamic rulers and

asserts itself in titles such as "shadow of the Almighty."[28] This phrase had a similar

expression in the Sasanid period: *keh chihr az yazdān* that followed the kings' names.

The translation of this phrase has always been a source of conflict among scholars of

the field. While some scholars, by considering the Greek translation of *chihr*, ascribe

to it the meaning of "the king whose seed is from God," other scholars such as

Soudavar believed that *chihr* denotes the reflection of God in power and authority.[29]

The expressions "the king whose seed is from God," "the king whose face is from

God," "the king who reflects God's power," and "the shadow of God's glory on earth"

all indicate that the Shah was God's viceregent on earth. The titles *Shah-i Shahān-i*

---

[27] Ibid, 12.

[28] Homa Katouzian, *Iranian History and Politics: The Dialectic of State and Society.* (Routledge: 2007), 44.

[29] Soudavar, *The Aura of Kings*, 47.

Īrān, and its variation, *Shahanshah,* were part of the Achaemenid tradition of kingship.[30]

"Persianate form of kingship" in my dissertation refers to Sasanid ideas of kingship and its origins within other cultures, which referred to the kings of the Persian Empire. Ascribing *farr* to the Safavid kings, and the appearance of falcons as the symbol of Sasanid kingship, are among the most dominant symbols used to refer to the Safavid kings. Also, titles such as *shāh-i shāhān,* as well as *pādishāh-i pādishahān* (the king of kings) and its variations, represent the idea of Persianate kingship within the Safavid context. The litany of names of pre-Islamic kings of Iran is another way to color legitimacy sought by the Safavid kings who held Persianate ideas of pre-Islamic times. Usually, the pre-Islamic kings of Persia become a source of comparison for the Safavid kings in regard to their form of kingship or for having specific features such as justice, wit, or bravery. Firīdūn, Alexander, Darius, Kāvūs, and Jamshīd are some examples. The Persian heroes of *Shāhnāmeh* and the objects or animals close to them—for instance, Rustam, his horse (*Rakhsh),* and Isfandīyār— were among the other images in poems that I examine as elements connecting the Safavid kings and their sacred form of kingship to the Persian forms of kingship from the pre-Islamic period.

---

[30] Ardashīr was the first ruler who claimed to be the "king of kings" of Īrān. Before defeating Ardavān, Ardashīr followed very closely the Persis tradition of being MLKA, or simply the "kings". However, after defeating Ardavān, his title changed to "king of kings," which may be due to the change in the power relations between the kings of Persis and their Parthian overlords. Touraj Daryaee argued that this title makes its appearance from the Parthian period in the middle of the first century BCE and the claim to descend from the Achaemenids resulted from successive victories over Romans. (Vesta Sarkhosh Curtis, *The Sasanian Era,* 2010).

D. Ṣāḥib-qirān

The most important symbol of imperial kingship of Tīmūr, known as
Tamerlane, Tīmūr the Lame, or Amir Tīmūr, was the title *ṣāḥib-qirān* (Lord of
Conjunction). Although this title was originally known in Middle Persian and was
used before Tīmūr, it signifies the Timurid model of kingship as it became pivotal to
Tīmūr 's imperial-sacral persona. After him, *ṣāḥib-qirān* became a central title of all
following dynasties developed in the Turko-Mongol and Perso-Islamic world.[31]

The implication of the term varied from one culture to another and from its
first use onwards. While in pre-Islamic Iran the title was meant for commenting on
drinking rituals, in Pahlavi literature it came to refer to the charisma and eulogistic
ideas of certain rulers as "world-conquerors" or kings with "great personalities."[32]
During the 13th century, the term referred to Iranian concepts of justice and kingship,
while in pre-Safavid periods the title was used to speak of legends such as Amīr
Ḥamzeh, the prophet's uncle, who was famous for his war skills.[33]

While *ṣāḥib-qirān* is purely astrological and implies the conjunction of Saturn
and Jupiter (as the date of Tīmūr's birth), the title indicates "something from
heaven."[34] Tīmūr applied the term to mystify his roots and genealogy. He claimed
direct contact with angels, prophetic visions, and access to the ladder of the sky. He

---

[31] Matthew Melvin-Koushki, "Early Modern Islamicate Empire", in *The Wiley Blackwell History of Islam,* ed. Salvatore, Armando, Roberto Tottoli, and Babak Rahimi (Hoboken, NJ : Wiley-Blackwell, 2018), 351-375.

[32] Naindeep Chann, "Lord of the Auspicious Conjunction: Origins of the *Ṣāḥib-qirān.*" *Iran and the Caucasus* (2009), 13: 94, http://www.jstor.org/stable/25597394

[33] Ibid, 95.

[34] Ibid, 98.

used the term to forge a synthesis between Turko-Mongolian conceptions of authority and the Perso-Islamic connotation of the royal glory which it still possessed.[35] Sometimes *ṣāḥib-qirān* found a messianic meaning and referred to a reviver, *mujadid*, or *mahdī*. For example, the Ottoman Emperor Sulaymān (b. 1494 – d. 1566), was perceived as the awaited Mahdī.[36] In the early 15th century, Shah Ismāʿīl was also called *ṣāḥib-qirān* and the awaited Mahdī by Khwandmīr. Although during the time of Ismāʿīl the *ṣāḥib-qirān* edged towards Mahdism, in Shah ʿAbbās's time this term, which had been long Islamicised, was used to celebrate the king's charisma and to portray him as victorious and to associate him with divine providence.[37]

While the use of the term *ṣāḥib-qirān* is widespread in historical writing during the reign of Shah ʿAbbās and there was a constant attempt to make connections between Shah ʿAbbās and Tīmūr, the term *ṣāḥib-qirān* is not very popular in the court poetry of the time when speaking of the kings. *Ṣāḥib-qirān* in Safavid poetry appeared in different contexts, and it does not offer a messianic meaning as it connoted for Tīmūr or later for Akbar Shah (b. 1556 – d. 1605). It is sometimes an alternative for the name or titles of kingship, and it can come as an adjective after *shah*. In some instances, the term refers to the fortune (*bakht*) of the king with respect to being born in the conjunction of Saturn and Jupiter.[38] The term in poems of Ṣāʿib (b. 1592 – d.

---

[35] Ibid.

[36] Ibid, 101.

[37] Ibid, 104.

[38] The tale of Amir Ḥamzeh is a very famous one of pre-Safavid periods. Famous for his bravery, his characteristic was an amalgamation of Ḥamzeh bin ʿAbdul Muṭallib, the prophet's uncles who was killed in Uḥud war in the ninth century, and Ḥamzeh bin ʿAbdullāh, who belonged to the Kharijite sect and rebelled against Hārūn al-Rashīd. Amīr Ḥamzeh is one of the first people who was described as the *ṣāḥib-qirān*. See Chann. "Lord of the Auspicious Conjunction," 95-97.

1676) is used along with any objects that are associated with light and brightness, for example the stars and the sun. In this case, the term also evokes the divine glory of Persianate kings and *farr*.

E. Spirituality

The terms "spirituality" and "spiritual" have long been the concern of human beings among different cultures and religions. Each religion has a characteristic way of living in the world and develops a set of disciplines to assist their community in pursuing their relationship with the cosmos. "Spirituality" and "spiritual," historically, were perceived as being an integral part of religion and its disciplines. The spiritual and religious usually overlap; however, as I will argue further in this section, I do not see these two concepts as the same and integrated in terms of what spirituality means in the context of the Safavid legitimacy. Scholars, such as Babayan and Quinn, have applied the term "spiritual" to refer to the Safavid king as a religious/Sufi leader. This Sufi leader was perceived as *"insān/murshid-i kāmil"* (the perfect being). The relationship between the Sufi leaders and their devotees was based on the absolute obedience to the follower to the leader, as the Sufi *shaykh* possessed virtues that not all people could have. The relationship between Shah Ismā'īl and his Qizilbāsh followers was known as a *pīr-murīd* relationship. Shahzad Bashir's study of Safavid forms of punishment after triumph in wars investigated some aspects of this relationship.[39]

---

[39] Shahzad Bashir, "Shah Isma'il and the Qizilbash: Cannibalism in the Religious History of the Early Safavid Iran", in *History of Religions,* Vol. 45, No.3 (February 2006), 234-256. DOI: 10.1086/503715

Accepting Shah Ismāʻīl as a Sufi leader was not only about his charisma but attributed to his Sufi lineage as well. Descending from a mystic Sufi *shaykh* "infused" him with an "aura of saintliness," which in the early modern period was intimately associated with the Sufi culture.[40] Babayan compared the Muslims' views of Imams with the Qizilbāsh's understanding of Ismāʻīl. She mentioned that, in the same way that the Muslims knew the Imams as scions of Muḥammad's divinity, the Qizilbāsh saw Ismāʻīl "as the godly heir to the spiritual throne of the Safavid order."[41] Babayan investigated the "spiritual" roots of the Safavid claim in Sufism and the belief in transmission of charisma through descendants of the particular family. This belief came about due to the effort of Shah Ismāʻīl's grandfather, Junayd (d. 1460), in generating the basics of the Safavid ideology. Junayd crystallized the Safavid ideology around myths and symbols derived from Sufi, 'Alid, *ghulāt,* and Turco-Mongol cultures. A unique cosmological feature of *ghulāt* was their rejection of the concept of resurrection.[42] The idea of reincarnation (*tanāsukh)* was also crucial to this culture.

---

[40] Kathryn Babayan, "The Safavi Synthesis: From Qizilbash Islam to Imamite Shiʻism", *Iranian Studies,* Vol 27, number 1-4, (1994), 136, http://www.jstor.org/stable/4310890.

[41] Ibid.

[42] *Ghulāt* refers to the group whose ideas were considered as *ghuluvv. Ghuluvv* is derived from the Arabic root "gh-l-w", means "to exceed the proper boundary." The use of the term is problematic. It has been used pejoratively to refer to individuals with extreme and unorthodox views on the nature of intercessors between man and God. "The Ghulāt envisaged divinity as incarnated in human, with each believer an earthly god who is able to connect with the holy personally through prophetic inspiration, illumination, or permeation. They believed in the dual and yet integrated existence of spirit and matter and in the human potential to transcend matter and access the divine while on earth". "Exaggeration refused to separate heaven from earth; in fact, for some, heaven exists on earth, and it is to earth, they believed, that we keep returning in different forms, thus Muḥammad, 'Alī, Jesus, or Moses could be reincarnated in an individual at any given historical time. This cosmology and ontology embedded in *ghuluww* represents their essential differences from normative Islam and accounts for their being considered heretics by Muslim orthodoxy." (Babayan, *Mystics, Monarchs and Messiah*, Introduction). To see more information about *Ghulāt* and their relationship with the Safavids see Michel Mazzaoui, "The Origins of the Safavids: Shiʻism, Sufism, and the Ghulāt," Vol. 3, Freiburger Islamstudien, (Wiesbaden: Steiner), 1972.

Tanāsukh would interpret the death of a human being as the return of the soul to the world in a new form within a new body. Based on this idea, the soul of the Prophet Muḥammad and the earlier prophets could transmigrate into different human beings, including the Safavid *shaykh*s, at any given time.[43]

In their prefaces, the chronicles usually included a narrative of the Safavid rise through the world of dream. These dreams, which usually predict the future of the dynasty and its political direction, are considered a political prophecy.[44] These dreams, which are not only from the Safavid culture but a common concept between Safavid-Mughal-Ottoman empires, provide a spiritual (non-physical) space, open to different socio-cultural interpretations, which seeks to place the political/material power of the king in non-materialism. The reality of dreams can hardly be questioned; therefore, they were safe spaces to make political claims and for justifying important religio-political decisions. Shah Ṭahmāsb (b. 1514 – d. 1576) had a special relationship with the Imams through the world of dream. He talked to and was addressed by Imams through his dreams concerning important events.[45] Talking to Imams in the world of dream or being confirmed in reign through the world of dream by important political and Sufi leaders of the past were "non-ordinary" acts and actions but compelling

---

[43] Babayan, "The Safavid Synthesis", 135-161.

[44] Sholeh Quinn, "The Dreams of Shaykh Safi Al-Din and Safavid Historical Writing". *Iranian Studies.* 29, no. 1-2: 127-147, http://www.jstor.org/stable/4310973. Babayan also paid attention toward the use of dream for legitimizing purposes, especially in the case of Abū Muslim. See Kathryn Babayan, "The Waning of the Qizilbash." Ph.D diss., Princeton University, 1993.

[45] A series of dreams in *Tazkireh-yi Shah Ṭahmāsb* have been narrated through which Shah Ṭahmāsb was helped by Imam 'Alī before going into battels. See Shah Ṭahmāsb, *Tazkireh-yi Shah Ṭahmāsb beh Ghalam-i Khudash,* (Chāpkhāneh-yi Kāvyānī: 1964), see pages 15, 23, 30.

factors in creating a quasi-divine nature for kings to help them construct their material

power.

To conclude, when I use the term "spiritual" in the Safavid context, I mean

those divine qualities similar to Muḥammad's and the Imams, a charisma that is

bestowed on Muslim saints freely by God's will. *Karāmat* in singular form and

karāmāt in plural form are the qualities available to *awlīyā* (friends of God). *Karāmat*

is an action or a quality which contravenes the norms *(nāqiż-i 'ādat)* of ordinary life[46]

and it is available for those who are *ṣādiq* (truth-teller/honest).[47] *Karāmat* may be

enacted by those who are known as *valī* (guardianship/intimate friend).[48] Receiving

food upon request from God, passing through the boundaries of place and time,

finding water where it was not available before, or hearing a voice from the unseen

realm are among the most common *karāmāt* ascribed to the friends of God. The

Safavid poets frequently, and especially in the epic *maṣnavīs*, depicted the ancestors of

the Safavid kings with such qualities. In poems, the Sufi Safavid *shaykhs* were usually

portrayed in connection with the other world, because they transgress the temporal and

spatial dimensions, and they talk to Imams in dreams. The great ancestors of the

Safavid kings could predict their times of death, and their bodies would become doves

to fly to the other world. Their tombs were sacred places where angels hovered and

talked to them. These tombs resembled the heaven pictured in the Quran. By ascribing

---

[46] 'Alī ibn 'Uṣmān Hujvīrī, *Kashf al-Maḥjūb*, ed. Mahmud 'Abidi (Tehran: Surūsh, 2004), 327-329.

[47] 'Abd al-Karīm ibn Hawāzin Qushayrī, *Tarjumeh-yi Risāleh-yi Qushayrīyyeh*, trans. Badi' al-Zaman Furuzanfar, (Tehran: Markaz-i Intishārāt-i 'ilmī va Farhangī, 1982), 622.

[48] *Karāmat* is for *awlīyā,* and *mu'jizāt* is for the prophets and it demonstrates their authenticity of *wilāyat.*

these divine qualities, Safavid poets helped to legitimize the Safavid kings as Sufi-leaders and to give them an aura of divinity.

V. Approaching the Safavid Poetry Texts

Among scholars who have investigated Safavid ideology, only Quinn has focused her attention on the transition of religio-political ideology of the Safavids among a social group, i.e. chronicle writers. Quinn's re-examination of the chronicles indicates that textual changes occurred in the chronicles, which reflect ideological shifts of the Safavids.[49] On the basis of Quinn's study of ideological shifts of the Safavids in chronicles, I study the *qaṣīdeh*s and *masnavī*s which are dedicated to the kings of the time. By applying Sperl's thematical and structural analysis of Arabic *qaṣīdeh*s and Meisami's approach towards the relationship between panegyric writing and court ethics, I examine the Safavid panegyrics that were dedicated to the kings. I demonstrate that these two forms of writing, *masnavī* and especially *qaṣīdeh* starting from Shah 'Abbās I's time, did not promote the Safavid king as a Shi'i king. In most of the Safavid *qaṣīdeh*s that are dedicated to the kings, the structure of *qaṣīdeh*, the choice of opening lines, the connection between the opening lines and the body of poems stayed similar to the early *qaṣīdeh*s of Persian literature; therefore, no major difference in structure of poetry is detectable between a *qaṣīdeh* which is written for a Sunni ruler or a Shi'i king. The steady structure of the *qaṣīdeh* did not allow a structural change in the images of kingship. However, the features of their praise helped to endorse the Safavid king as a pious individual similar to Imams. "The

---

[49] Sholeh Quinn, *Shah 'Abbās: The King Who Refashioned Iran*, (England: Oneworld Publications, 2015).

Safavid kings initially promoted their legitimate right to rule by presenting themselves

as (1) the representative of the Hidden Imam, (2) the shadow of God on earth, and (3)

the head of the Safavid Sufi order."[50] These three pillars of thought respectively, if not

entirely, present Shi'i-Persian-Sufi concepts of Safavid kingship. By studying the

poetic representation of legitimizing ideologies in Safavid panegyrics, I categorize the

Safavid kings' portraits into four groups, which offer Shi'i, Persian, Sufi and Timurid

legitimacy to the kings. In the first group, I consider any references to the doctrines of

Shi'ism and Shi'i lineage. Expressions of servitude, displays of humility at the shrines,

and public displays of religious devotion which especially hold the kings in a

subservient position in relation to the first and last Imam are also considered in this

group. References to incidents at the Battle of Karbala, whose primary function is to

claim lineage and similarity with Shi'i Imams, are also categorized in the first group.

In the second group, I consider Persian legitimacy according to any references to

Persian notions of kingship, such as *farr* and the symbol of the falcon. I also

considered the comparisons made between the Safavid kings and pre-Islamic kings of

the Persian empire such as Firīdūn and Darius as instances of Persian legitimacy. The

expression, "the shadow of God on earth" as well as references to the light of

---

[50] Sholeh Quinn, *Historical Writing During the Reign of Shah 'Abbas: Ideology, Imitation, and Legitimacy in Safavid Chronicles,* (Salt Lake City: University of Utah Press. 2000), 5. Of course this is a simplified version of the Safavid ideology. The roots and origins of the Safavid thoughts are a combination of different and various religious systems and cultures. It is difficult, or better to say impossible, to categorize the representation of each of these systems of thought as they appear to be fully attached together. However, for making a workable framework, I presented this ideology in a simplified manner. For further reading on the origins of the Safavid ideology see Sa'id Amir Arjomand, *The Shadow of God and the Hidden Imam: Religion, Political Order, and Societal Change in Shi'ite Iran From the Beginning to 1890* (Chicago: University of Chicago Press, 1984). Also see Michel Mazzaoui, "The Origins of the Safavids: Shi'ism, Sufism, and the Ghulāt," Vol. 3, Freiburger Islamstudien, (Wiesbaden: Steiner), 1972.

kingship, despite being a mutual concept between different cultures is also considered in this second category because it also refers to pre-Islamic Persian concept of divine right of kingship. In the third category, I consider Sufi legitimacy according to references to the kings' *karāmat* (miraculous acts of Sufis and Imams, not of the prophets as their miracles are known as *mu'jizeh*). Seeing the future and prescience of one's own time of death, as well as titles such as *murshid-i kāmil* (the perfect guide) are part of the Sufi legitimacy sought by the Safavids. The fourth category concerns images related to Timurid legitimacy, which is exclusive to the application of the term *ṣāḥib-qirān*. As mentioned in the section above about the title *ṣāḥib-qirān*, there was a tendency of the Safavid kings to associate themselves and their careers with this world conqueror by applying this title closely associated with Timur. Through this emulation, the Safavid kings could benefit from his prestige as a world conqueror.[51]

Table 1. Categories of kings' images in Safavid *qaṣīdeh*s and *masnavī*s

Categories	Examples
1) Shi'i legitimacy	• References to Imām Mahdī's return • Shi'i lineage • Expressions of servitude displaying humility at the shrines • Public displays of religious intentions • Reference to Shi'i Imāms or events such as Karbalā
2) Persian legitimacy	• *Farr* • Falcon • The shadow of God • Comparisons to pre-Islamic Persian kings • Light and epiphany
3) Sufi legitimacy	• Sufi lineage • Seeing the future • Awareness of one's own time of death • Titles such as *murshid-i kāmil* (the perfect guide)
4) Timurid legitimacy	• *Ṣāḥib-qirān*

---

[51] Quinn, *Shah 'Abbās*, 40-42.

Some of the descriptors can be included in any of the first three categories. For example, the kings' characteristics and attributes, such as justice and magnanimity or glory and pomp, can be placed in any of these groups. Therefore, I do not include them in any of the categories, but I analyze their effect on the general structure of the poems.

VI. Organization

Chapter One provides an overview of some of the major themes, shifts and developments in the 16th and 17th century Persian poetry of Iran. This chapter attempts to demonstrate that by the beginning of the 16th century new venues for presenting poetry had been shaped. There were more practitioners of poetry as well who did not necessarily need court patronage to write and to be heard. I argue in this chapter that as a result of the changes within the superstructure and infrastructure of the society, the traditional lenses for examining the literature of this period and determining its literary value do not respond to the needs and requirements of poetry at this time. This chapter frames the changes and developments in Safavid poetry and, by focusing specifically on the *qaṣīdeh* and *masnavī*, attempts to demonstrate the significance of this literature from both literary and historical aspects. Chapter One demonstrates that in Safavid poetry new themes emerged while being written in older, traditional forms. Also, some classic themes, which were previously limited to specific forms, became widespread in various forms of Persian poetry. The chapter, by going through the chronicles and *tazkireh*s, attempts to construct which factors were essential to the success of a poet. In general, my study suggests that religious poetry, did not have literary or social value for scholars of the time to include in their works, although poets intended to write religious poems in praise of Shi'i Imams. The chapter ends with the biographies of the most important poets of the Safavid period. In this part, I attempt to frame the diversity among the poets (familial background, religion, and education) to argue that this diversity caused different forms of poetic representation; therefore, this poetry needs another analytical tool beyond writing style. I offer theme or concept analysis for examining the Safavid poems which have features in common, including the form in which they presented; time in which the work is produced, and the background of its poets.

Chapter Two deals with the cultural material of the Safavid period that was used to present the Safavid ideology of kingship in public. The primary purpose of this chapter is to reconstruct the patterns of religio-political legitimacy to capture the trajectory of Safavid ideology and to demonstrate which elements of the Safavid ideology were fixed and which were transient. I also identify the appearance or disappearance of concepts from each source throughout history. By analyzing coins, royal decrees, inscriptions of mosques and palaces, as well as the documents remaining from ceremonies of royal investiture, I demonstrate the instability of Safavid ideology until the reign of Shah 'Abbās I. I argue that when Shah 'Abbās I came to power, he marginalized the dominant, orthodox representations of political authority in Sunni Islam to define his unique form of kingship, which was based on the declaration of servitude towards the Shi'i Imams. This chapter demonstrates that Shi'i titles and expressions remain among the most common discourses in public, while towards the end of the Safavid dynasty, the titles and expressions of the Persianate form of kingship became more popular.

Chapter Three analyzes the *qaṣīdeh*s which dedicated to the Safavid rulers starting from Shah Ṭahmāsb to Shah Ṣafī II, famous as Sulaymān (b. 1611 – d. 1642). The chapter examines the Safavid *qaṣīdeh*s to show the trajectory of Safavid ideology and to investigate how poets portrayed the Safavid kingship and kings in their works. The chapter argues that while the Safavid poets were committed to the conventional form of poetry of praise, they attempt to legitimize the Safavid kings by invoking attributes of Sufis and pre-Islamic Persian kings.

The chapter argues that, in contrast to the cultural materials examined in chapter two, the Safavid *qaṣīdeh* did not turn to ideas related to Shi'ism to legitimize kingship. I demonstrate that especially from Shah 'Abbās I's reign, the kings were praised for their kingly features and their Sufi charisma. In other words, the poets did not give explicitly Shi'i legitimacy to these kings despite the fact that in public cultural materials they were presented in a subservient position to the Shi'i Imams. The poems focused on the two other pillars of the Safavid legitimacy, Sufism and Persianism, without focusing on ideas that reinforced the idea of a Shi'i king. The Sufi-oriented images revolve around the concept of *karāmāt*, and the titles of the pre-Islamic kingship and the symbols of Persianate kingship speak of the poets' intentions to link the Safavid kings and the Persian kings of the pre-Islamic period. My study further demonstrates that the patterns of legitimacy in *qaṣīdeh* is dissimilar to the other means of legitimizing power because the poets did not show tendency to apply Shi'i terms and expressions in poem. Whether ignoring the Shi'i aspects of kingship was due to the power of poetic convention or was for ideological interference, attention to ideas of pre-Islamic kingship and Sufism provided an ideal opportunity the Safavid kings to be presented similar with Imams.

Chapter Four is dedicated to the *qaṣīdeh*s of Ṣā'ib Tabrīzī (b. 1592 – d. 1676). He provides a counterexample against the dominant discourse of the Safavid court poetry. While I argue in Chapter Three that the poets did not create an affiliation between the Safavid kings and Shi'ism, in this chapter, I study Ṣā'ib's poems which did not follow the dominant form of panegyrics for kings. While poets such as Salīm (d. 1647) and Faṣīḥī (d. 1639), who wrote for the same patrons, did not depict a Shi'i king, Ṣā'ib took the other direction and wrote many *qaṣīdeh*s in praise of Shah Ṣafī I (b. 1611 – d. 1642) and Shah 'Abbās II (b. 1632 – d. 1666) to advocate for them religiously and politically in their role as the disseminator of Twelver Shi'ism. While most of the Safavid poets turned towards Sufi-oriented images, Ṣā'ib intensively applied the dominant terms and expressions of Shi'i discourse into his *qaṣīdehs,* which transform his poems to religio-political manifestations of Safavid kingship. By examining the poetic and political discourses of his poems, I demonstrate that Ṣā'ib applied structural changes into his *qaṣīdeh*s in order to make his poetry a medium for presenting the multi-culturalism of Safavid ideology. The forms of *radīf* (repeated rhyming words at the end of each line) in his poems and the connectivity of those *radīf*s to specific themes that he applied in each line in relation to the Safavid ideology worked together to portray the Safavid kings as sacred and spiritual, and subsequently legitimate in their role as the kings of Muslim lands.

In Chapter Five, I continue my analysis of Shi'ism and kingship in the works of the *mas̱navī* genre. Many poems in this form were also dedicated to legitimizing

Safavid rulers. Starting from the Safavid period, the number of *masnavīs* increased

enormously and the section of praising the kings was also developed more broadly.

The Safavid kings supported the writing of this genre and directed poets to write

masnavīs in praise of the Safavid kings as well as the Imams. I argue that in this genre,

the representation of Safavid kingship varied from one period to another. I studied the

trajectory of this representation from Shah Ṭahmāsb to Shah Ṣafī II to demonstrate

that the Safavid kings, and especially the Shiʾi aspects of the kingship, were limited to

the works of Ṭahmāsb's period. After Shah Ṭahmāsb, the Shiʿi depiction of kingship

was omitted from *masnavīs*; instead, special attention was given towards the

descriptions of palaces, which depicted the political authority of the kings through the

spaces they inhabited.

VII. Sources[52]

A. Biographical Dictionaries and Historical Sources

Although biographical dictionaries (*tazkireh*) are mainly focused on the lives

and vocations of poets along with painters, calligraphers, and religious scholars, these

are not the only sources of biographical information. These biographies also speak of

people's tastes in poetry. Although the structure and forms of narration of the

*tazkireh*s are not my main concern in this dissertation, I relied on *tazkireh*s of the

Safavid period to argue for the prevalence of different forms of poetry during this

period. In discussing the most important forms of poetry which represented the

Safavid ideology, I benefited from various *tazkireh*s. *Tuḥfeh-yi Sāmī* (written by 1550)

by Sām Mīrzā, *Tazkireh-yi ʿArafāt al-ʿĀshiqīn va ʿAraṣāt al-ʿĀrifīn* (written between

---

[52] For more information about the manuscripts see the bibliography.

1613 –1615) by Awḥadī Balyānī, *Tazkireh-yi Meykhāneh* (written by 1619) by ʿAbd al-Nabī Fakhr al-Zamānī Qazvīnī, *Tazkireh-yi Naṣrābādī* (written by 1662) by Muḥammad Ṭāhir Naṣrābādī (b. 1618 – d. 1677), *Khuld-i Barīn* (written by 1668) by Vāleh Iṣfahānī, and *Majmaʿ al-Fuṣahā* (written by 1868) by Riżā Qulī Khān Hidāyat helped me to identify poets who were mentioned in relationship with a Safavid court or as who wrote poetry for a Safavid king. I also studied *Tazkireh-yi Riyāż al-Shuʿarā'* (written by 1748) by Vāleh Dāghistānī and *Tazkireh-yi Ḥazīn* (written by 1752) by Muḥammad ʿAlī Ḥazīn, which supported my argument about the poets' and literary scholars' lack of interest in religious poetry.

To gain a more critical understanding of the formation of specific themes and images in the poetry of the time and the relationship between the poets and their patrons, I also benefited from *Tārīkh-i ʿĀlam Ārā-yi ʿAbbāsī* written by Iskandar Beyg (Beg) Munshī (begun by 1616), which covers the incidents of 1600 until 1680. This chronicle is one of the most significant historical sources of the Shah ʿAbbās period because Iskandar was an eyewitness to the events he described, or he was at least in a good position to obtain and assert the truth. He was with the Shah on many of his expeditions and was close to the Shah's vizier, Ḥātim Beyg Urdūābādī (d. 1610). The historical chronicles, although mainly reporting the lives and times of the Safavid kings, wars and their affairs, provide information on the socio-religious life of the Safavid period. They portray the relationship between the kings, *ʿulamā* and poets and the patronage system of their courts; *ʿĀlam Ārā-yi ʿAbbāsī* narrates the life of the Safavid viziers, nobles, Persians poets and musicians as well.

B. Works of Poetry

This dissertation mainly draws upon works of poetry. I mostly relied on the

best edited and published manuscripts of those poets who dedicated poetry to the

Safavid kings of their time. I primarily examined books of poems by Vaḥshī Bāfqī (d.

1583), Muḥtasham Kāshānī (d. 1588), Shānī Takallū (d. 1614), Salīm Tihrānī (d.

1647), Faṣīḥī Hiravī (d. 1639), Muḥsin Taʾsīr Tabrīzī (d. 1717), Ṭarzī Afshārī (d.

1679), and Ṣāʾib Tabrīzī. I also studied Hātifī Kharjirdī (b. 1454 – d. 1521), Qāsimī

Gunābādī (d. 1574), ʿAbdī Beyg Shīrāzī (d. 1590), Zulālī (b. 1607 – d. 1627/8), and

Mullā Rafīʿ (d. 1678) for their works of *masnavī*. For some of these poets, I had to

consult various manuscript versions, since the poems varied from one edited volume

to another. This problem mainly concerned Ṣāʾib's *dīvān*. In some cases, when I found

the meaning and interpretation of a text problematic, I preferred to check other

editions which I could find in the National Library of Iran and Majlis-i Shurā-yi Islāmī

Library. I would like to add that these works are not the only *dīvān*s that I scrutinized.

I chose the aforementioned poets after reading the works of many other poets of the

16th and 17th century who were either in Iran or India or moved between the courts of

the Safavid and Mughal emperors in the 16th and 17th centuries. ʿUrfī Shīrāzī (b. 1555

– d. 1591), Kalīm Kāshānī (b. 1581 – d. 1651), Naẓīrī Nīshābūrī (b. 1560 – d. 1612),

Shāpūr Tihrānī (d. 1621), Ṣaydī Tihrānī (b. 1616 – d. 1659), and Fayżī of Deccan (b.

1547 – d. 1595) as well as Jān Qudsī Mashhadī (d. 1646) were among the poets whose

works I read but finally decided to not incorporate in my dissertation as these poets

mostly lived in India. Reading these works helped me to understand the poetics of

writing about kingship and Shiʿism within the Safavid context.

C. Coins, Ṭughrās, Inscriptions, Royal orders, *Waqfs*

There is significant scholarship on Safavid coins in both Persian and English.

In several studies, Rudi Matthee and Willem Floor inspected the Safavid to Qajar

monetary systems.[53] A comparative analysis of Safavid and Mughal monetary patterns

was also conducted by Sayyid 'Ijāz Hussayn.[54] Sughra Isma'ili and Farzaneh Qa'ini

both conducted extensive research on Iran's monetary system during the Safavids and

commented on the patterns of the coins, the centers involved with the monetary

system, the coins' material, and the developments within the coinage system of Iran

during the 16th and 17th century.[55] Therefore, my study of the patterns of the Safavid

coins is mostly based on secondary sources: the works of scholars who previously

identified the coins of different periods and examined their patterns. However, I also

was able to see some collections of the Safavid coins during my visit to Iran in

summer 2016. Malek Museum in Tehran presented a small number of Safavid coins

which were mostly minted in Tehran and Lar during the 16th century. The museum

also uploaded images of some of these coins on their website; my images in this

dissertation are taken from there. I also visited a collection of coins in Qazvin

Museum, where I could identify more Safavid coins. In addition, in Isfahan, I had

access to a unique and personal collection of these coins, which ranged from the Shah

Ṭahmāsb period to the time of Sultan Ḥusayn (b. 1668 – d. 1726).

---

[53] For more information see Rudolph Matthee, Willem Floor, Patrick Clawson, *The Monetary History of Iran: From the Safavids to the Qajars,* (London; New York: I.B. Tauris, 2013).

[54] For more information see Stephen Jeyaseela, *The Indian Trade at the Asian Frontier,* (Gyan Publishing House, 2008).

[55] See Sughra Isma'ili, *Sikkeh hā wa Muhr hā-yi Dawreh-yi Ṣafavī,* (Tehran: Sāzmān-i Mīrāṣ Farhangī, 2006), and Farzaneh Qa'ini, *Sikkeh hā-yi Dawreh-yi Ṣafavī* (Tehran: Pāzineh,2009).

The same approach applies to my analysis of royal orders, charters of charitable trusts, inscription, and enthronement orations. While some scholarship on each of these sources partially presented the ideas related to my dissertation, I revisited the archives (National Library of Iran and Majlis-i Shurā-yi Islāmī Library), as well as palaces and mosques in Isfahan and Qazvin to complete what was partially narrated to provide more information on these inscriptions. The texts of royal orders and the inscriptions are much inspired by Lutf Allah Hunarfar's work on Isfahan's historical sites.[56]

D. Miscellaneous

There are other sources that I made use of to gain knowledge about Safavid history and ideology. European travelogues provide useful information about Safavid socio-political, economic, and religious institutions. They also contain information about the attitudes and manners of the Shahs in ceremonies and when receiving the regular people and the nobles of time, which helped to construct the image of a Safavid Shah in the eyes of a foreign visitor. Chardin's travelogue is among the important sources of Safavid history. Jean Chardin (d. 1713) covered ten years of his stay in Isfahan during the 1660s and 1670s in this travelogue, where he gave much information about the population, libraries, mosques, educational institutions, as well as people of the time and king's manner.

---

[56] Hunarfar, Lutf Allah. *Ganjīneh-yi Ās̱ār-i Tārīkhī-i Iṣfahān: Ās̱ār-i Bāstānī Va Alvāḥ Va Katībeh hā-yi Tārīkhī dar Ustān-i Iṣfahān*, Isfahan: Kitābfurūshī-i Saqafī, 1965.

From the anthologies and books of polemics, I mostly focused on the works of the famous and powerful Shiʻi cleric and the chief religious leader of Isfahan during the reign of Shah Sultan Ḥusayn, Muḥammad Bāqir Majlisī (b. 1616 – d. 1698), especially his famous work on Shiʻi hadiths *Biḥār al-Anwār* (completed between 1695 – 1670). In this book, Majlisī attempted to preserve the heritage of Shiʼism by narrating thousands of Shiʻi hadiths.

E. Secondary Sources

Many important works on Shiʼi intellectual history, the Safavid dynasty, and kingship, have been published recently. For the study of the life and role of Safavid scholars and the socio-political circumstances of the time, I benefited from the works by Saʻid Amir Arjomand, Devin. J. Stewart, Rula Jurdi Abisaab, Roger Savory, and Andrew J. Newman. The works and personal writings of Rasul Jaʻfarian in his weblog and his Telegram channel also supported me in finding sources and developing my research.[57] To study the area of Safavid cultural history, I investigated the exemplary works of Kathryn Babayan, Sholeh Quinn, and Azfar Moin. I also benefited from the works of Melvin-Koushki, who focused on the representation of "sacred" in the three dynasties of Timurids, Safavids, and the Mughals. In studying the relationship between works of art and architecture and their relationship to the Safavid ideology, I relied on the works of Susan Babaie and Kishwar Rizvi. In reference to the works of poetry, I examined the research of Safavid and Mughal literature scholars including Paul Losensky, Sunil Sharma, Muhammad Qahriman, Mazahir Musaffa, and

---

[57] For his weblog see : https://www.khabaronline.ir/weblog/jafarian. For his Telegram channel see: https://t.me/jafarian1964

Amirbanu Karimi, although not all of them are mentioned in the text. The primary

reason is that most of these scholars are focused on the *ghazal* form and the poets'

style of writing. As mentioned previously, the Safavid *qaṣīdeh* has not held much

appeal for literary scholars or historians. To study the history of Safavid literature and

Indian/Isfahani style, the works of Muhammad Riza Shafi'i Kadkani, Sirus Shamisa

and Zabih Allah Safa were my primary sources.[58]

VIII. Conclusion

This project highlights the many ways in which *qaṣīdeh*s and *masnavī*s as

court poetry contribute to our understanding of the literary, social, and cultural history

of the Safavid period. By bringing new sources into the field of Safavid legitimacy,

my research shows that panegyrics helped to legitimize the Safavid kingship by

implying that the Safavid rulers led the empire in the absence of an Imam. While the

Safavid dynasty attempted to disseminate the idea of Shi'ism as a necessary feature for

the leadership of the Muslim society in the public domain, the poets did not invoke

themes and concepts related to Shi'i doctrines to legitimize the kingship. The Safavid

court poets did not usually make a connection between kingship and ideas of Twelver

Shi'ism in the panegyrics, while most of the cultural materials of the time broadly

commented on Shi'i aspects of the Safavid kingship. This dissertation elaborates how

the poets emphasized "sacred" kingship by making connections between the Safavid

kings and the pre-Islamic Persian kings, as well as associating the Safavids with the to

---

[58] See the bibliography for full citations of these scholars' writings.

allow the Safavid kings to claim possessing features similar to attributes of Imams to legitimize their leadership in the absence of the last Shi'i Imam.

<h1 style="text-align:center">CHAPTER ONE:
SITUATING SAFAVID POETRY</h1>

I. Introduction

This chapter provides a literary historiographical overview for some of the major themes, shifts, and developments in Iran's 16th and 17th century Persian poetry. By exploring the general historiographical matrices of Persian literary culture during this period, this chapter sheds light on the dynamics of the poetic environment of the period. At this time new literary trends formed and new genres emerged. New subject matters introduced to poetry and nobles' houses or public places such as coffeehouses arose as venues for poetry reading. The number of poets significantly increased during the reign of the Safavids. Not only the Safavid courts, but Mughal and Ottoman courts were literary circles for reciting Persian poetry and literary criticism. In general, poetry writing since the 16th arose in unique circumstances, which made its discourse—if not completely different—vibrant and dynamic. Poetry pushed boundaries and experienced new themes as its subjects. Love, kingship, the description of nature, and virtues of kings and the nobles of time were not the only subjects that poets represented in their works. The poets of 16th and 17th century paid attention to the detail in their surrounding; any object could be a subject for poems.

To demonstrate the diversity of this literature, Part II, titled "Safavid poetry: themes, forms and genres," sheds light on the formation of new poetic genres that were used for poetic expression. In Part II, I survey the most dominant genres and themes that served the courtly system and were widely practiced by contemporary poets. I discuss the similarities and differences between the most dominant forms of and the intended subjects of Safavid poetry against that of earlier periods. In my analysis, I avoid looking at forms separately from the themes and genres because different forms can apply for the same themes. For example, love-related themes appeared in multiple forms: *qaṣīdeh, ghazal,* and *maṣnavī.* Similarly, praise of kings is not specific to *qaṣīdeh* and *maṣnavī* can relate to love or religion. Using the *qaṣīdeh* for writing about Imams, writing new forms of *maṣnavī,* and embracing poetry in the *qiṭ'eh*[1] form through applying acronyms or writing chronograms are reflect shifting aspects of socio-political changes in society.

In Part III, titled "What do sources of the period tell us about poetry?", I study the poet-patron relationship through chronicles and contemporary *tazkireh*s. In this section, I attempt to answer questions such as, what elements did define the poet-patron relationship? What factors did result in an outstanding reward? On what occasions did the patron reward the poet? My discussion of Safavid poetry ends by giving an overview of the major poets of the time in Part IV. The main focus in this part is introducing the most famous poets of each Safavid court and reporting on their family background and style of writing. I also discuss the genres and forms they used for praising the king. The goal, beyond introducing the most famous poets of time, is demonstrating the diverse circumstances of poetry writing during the 16th and 17th century.

---

[1] *Qiṭ'eh* is a traditional form of poetry that was derived from *qaṣīdeh.* Only the even lines are with the same rhyme.

II. Safavid Poetry: Themes, Forms and Genres

A. *Masnavī*

Since the 16th century writing *masnavī* in traditional genres found momentum and became dominant. For example, the number of epics in this period is markedly higher than in the other periods. *Shāhnāmeh*-yi Ḥayratī (written by 1546), *Ghazvnāmeh*-yi Asīrī (written by 1560), and *Ḥamleh-yi Ḥaydarī* by Bāzil Mashhadī (d. 1711) are the works written in *masnavī* form and were supported by the court system. Qāsimī Gunābādī's *Shāhnāmeh* in praise of Shah Ismāʿīl (d. 1487 – d. 1524) and Shah Ṭahmāsb (b. 1514 – d. 1576), and *Shāhnāmeh*-yi Hātifī Kharjirdī (b. 1454 – d. 1521),[2] also in praise of Shah Ismāʿīl, are among the other "book of kings" epics that were written in imitation of *Shāhnāmeh*'s Firdawsī and that narrate the story of Safavid's rise to power.[3] Writing *Khamseh* in imitation of Niẓāmī (b. 1141 – d. 1209 CE) and writing *masnavī* poems in the form of *sāqīnāmeh*, as well as shorter *masnavī* pieces in praise of kings, mark a difference between literary culture of the Safavid period and that of earlier periods. These *masnavīs*, through description of the heroics of the Safavid kings and depiction of the palaces and gardens related to these kings, present different aspects of the Safavid kingship in all different genres and shed light on the religio-political circumstances of the period.

While these *masnavīs* follow the conventions of *masnavī* writing in terms of poetic themes, they are different in terms of structure and development of subjects

---

[2] For the full sources on life and work of Hātifī see Michele Bernardini, HĀTEFI, ʿABD-ALLĀH, *Encyclopædia Iranica,* Originally Published: December 15, 2003, http://www.iranicaonline.org/articles/hatefi

[3] Chapter Five pays special attention to this genre of *Shāhnāmeh.*

from the earlier *masnavī*s. The major difference is in development of sections in praising Imams. While earlier *masnavī*s only praised Prophet Muḥammad and Imam 'Alī, some Safavid *masnavī*s, after praying to God and praising the Prophet Muḥammad and Imam 'Alī, praise the other Shi'i Imams as well. There is also a difference between *Shāhnāmeh* of Firdawsī (b. 935 – d. 1020 CE) and the Safavid *Shāhnāmeh*s. The Safavid *Shāhnāmeh*s, unlike Firdawsī's *Shāhnāmeh*, dismiss description of nature, virtue, and love. Instead, they focus on the king's personality and his claims to power.

Safavid ideology in *masnavī*s written in imitation of *Khamseh* of Niẓāmī (b. 1141 – d. 1209 CE) distinguish these *masnavī*s from the conventional writing in this genre. For example, a *Khamseh* of 'Abdī Beyg (d. 1590), does not narrate a story. Instead, it portrays the special character of the king by describing the closest objects to the king and his power (palace, gardens, and cities).[4] In 'Abdī Beyg's *Jannāt-i 'adn*, the description of nature is a rhetorical device displaying the king's power and his Sufi character. The beautiful world is depicted in response to the king's special character; a king who is a true follower of the Prophet Muḥammad. By comparing the king's character to Imams, some sections of 'Abdī Beyg's *masnavī*s are good examples of *manqabat* (praising the Imams) of all twelve Shi'i Imams—a theme that is absent from traditional *masnavī*s. *Manqabat* of all Shi'i Imams also became a widespread practice in writing *qaṣīdeh*. However, the non-court poets usually wrote in this genre. The

---

[4] Jannat al-Asmār more than other *Khamseh*s of him include these images. See Zayn al-'Ābidīn 'Abd al-Mū'min Navīdī, *Jannat al-Asmār; Zīnat al-Awrāq; Ṣaḥīfat al-Ikhlāṣ*. (Moskva: Izd-vo "Nauka, " Glav. red. vostochnoĭ lit-ry, 1979). For reading more on his life see "Abdi Sirazi," Encyclopædia Iranica, I/2, pp. 209-210; an updated version is available online at http://www.iranicaonline.org/articles/abdi-sirazi-1513-80-poet (accessed on 21 January 2014).

court poets mostly wrote *qaṣīdeh*s in praise of Imam ‘Alī, Riżā, and Mahdī and not the

other Imams. For example, Vaḥshī wrote six *qaṣīdeh*s for Imam ‘Alī, one *qaṣīdeh* for

Imam Riżā and one *qaṣīdeh* for Imam Mahdī. Ṣā‘ib also wrote two *qaṣīdeh*s in praise

of Imam ‘Alī and one for Imam Sajjād, the fourth Shi‘i Imam.

B. *Sāqīnāmeh*

Sāqīnāmeh[5] (Book of the Cupbearer) is a poetic genre in which the speaker

seeks relief from his hardship, losses, and disappointments by repeatedly asking the

sāqī to bring him wine or the *mughannī* (musician) to provide songs for him. In this

form of poetry, the images of celebration and the drinking parties of the nobles and

cultural elites of the time has its roots in the traditions of early Arabic and Persian

poetry. The thematic features of the *sāqīnāmeh* began to take shape in the works of

Niẓāmī of Ganjeh. In the many responses that poets wrote to Niẓāmī's works over the

following centuries, the theme of the cupbearer continued to serve the poets. Hāfiẓ of

Shiraz (d. 1392 CE) developed this genre into an independent form of writing but it

was not until a century later that *sāqīnāmeh* became recognized as an independent

genre. It was with the rise of the Safavid dynasty in the early 16th century that the first

independent poem of *sāqīnāmeh* was written by Ḥakīm Partuvī (d. 1522).[6] The poem

opens with a lament on the collapse of social, psychological, and cosmic order. The

---

[5] Paul Losensky, "SĀQI-NĀMA,*" Encyclopædia Iranica,* online edition, (accessed on 19 May
2016)., available at http://www.iranicaonline.org/articles/saqi-nama-book . For more information and
examples of this genre see Sunil Sharma, "The City of Beauties in Indo-Persian Poetic Landscape" in
Comparative Studies of South Asia, Africa and the Middle East 24, 2004, no. 2: 73-81. For the origins
of this genre, see Sunil Sharma, "Hāfiz's Sāqīnāmah: The Genesis and Transformation of a Classical
Poetic Genre," *Persica 18* (2002): 75-83. DOI: 10.2143/PERS.18.0.493

[6] ‘Abd al-Nabī Fakhr al-Zamānī Qazvīnī, *Taẕkireh-yi Meykhāneh.* ed. Ahmad Gulchin Ma‘ani
(Tehran: Shirkat-i Nisbī-i Ḥāj Muḥammad Ḥusayn Iqbāl va Shurakā', 1961), 124.

speaker then calls on the cupbearer and singer to deliver him wine to release him from

this despair; the poem concludes with a eulogy to "the cupbearer of both worlds,"

Imam ʿAlī, the first Shiʿi Imam.[7]

The same structure is evident in other early Safavid *sāqīnāmeh*s by Ṣidīq

Astarābādī (d. 1545) and Mīrzā Sharaf Jahān Qazvīnī (d. 1561). The main difference

between these two forms of *sāqīnāmeh* is that the latter finish with a royal panegyric,

while the former lacks this section. Similar to *qaṣīdeh* and its three sections known as

nasīb, raḥīl, and *madīḥ,* some *sāqīnāmeh*s have three sections. Similar to traditional

role of *nasīb* in *qaṣīdeh,* poets move from self-alienation to a new communal identity

in introductory lines. The middle section is a psychological quest, in which wine and

music help the speaker to affirm his affiliation with the patron and to relieve old

obsessions. *Sāqīnāmeh*s also could finish with wishing long life for the patron at the

end.[8] The poet-patron relationship was also important in generating the form of

sāqīnāmeh as a new poetic genre. In the Safavid period, sometimes a *sāqīnāmeh* ends

by praising the patron. In this period, there are *sāqīnāmeh*s that not only describe

nature and seeking relief from worldly sadness, but they are panegyrics for the

legitimation of the Safavid king. For example, Mīrzā Qāsimī Gunābādī, in his famous

sāqīnāmeh, after describing the chaotic world during the autumn and calling for a *sāqī*

and his fiery wine, continues by praising Shah Ṭahmāsb, and he attempts to show the

Shah's spiritual and religious character. He compares the king with Qubād and

---

[7] The association between Imam ʿAlī and wine bringing was not unusual at that time.

[8] Losensky, "SĀQI-NĀMA," *Encyclopædia Iranica,* 2016.

Firīdūn. He calls the king "the sign of God's mercy on earth" and claims that his kingship brings back peace and security to the world:

بیا ساقی ای خضر راه مراد
سکندر به دانش سلیمان به داد

ثریا سریر فلک بارگاه
گل باغ اقبال طهماسب شاه

فلک پای تختش ز اقبال و بخت
گدایان او صاحب تاج و تخت

قباد احترام و فریدون حشم
سفال سگان درش جام جم

Come and give me wine you! The *Khiżr* for the path of salvation!
You! Who are similar to Alexander in knowledge and you similar to Solomon in justice!

Your throne is Pleiades and the skies are your palace
In the garden of fortune, Ṭahmāsb Shah, you are the best flower

The heaven is lucky and fortunate to serve at his throne,
The owners of thrones and crowns look like beggars

He has the same respect as Qubād, and the same army as Firīdūn,
His dogs will drink from the cup of Jamshīd[9]

In another example, Masīḥ S̱ānī, after praising Shah 'Abbās I (b. 1571 – d. 1629) for being an extraordinary warrior, claims that the king is God's shadow on earth through which understanding God becomes possible:

نبی حق، ولی نیستی ز او جدا
ره از تو توان برد سوی خدا

ترا سایه حق جهان خواند و بس
ز سایه توان برد ره سوی کس

You are not the God, but you are not separate from him
Through you one can find way to God

You, only, were called the shadow of God
From the shadow one can reach to the person[10]

---

⁹ Qazvīnī, *Taẕkireh-yi Meykhāneh*, 176.

¹⁰ Ibid, 513.

C. Māddeh Tārīkh (Chronogram)

Māddeh tārīkh is among the other genres that developed extensively for the purpose of legitimizing kings. *Māddeh tārīkh* incorporates dates into Persian texts in disguised form, especially by applying the letters of the alphabet which have numerical value, to validate the Safavid kingship. Invention of poetry of chronogram was not the invention of Safavid poets; however, it became a very popular genre since the 15th century and throughout the Safavid dynasty. Incorporating dates into texts had various functions. A good chronogram could demonstrate the poet's professional skill in writing. Chronogram also had a reference function; it could reference the dates for important occasions (e.g. the birthdate of a king or construction of a royal or religious place like a palace or a mosque).

In rhetorical theory, there are different versions of chronograms. One of the most famous is explicit dating, famous as *tārīkh-i ṣūrī*, in which the date is mentioned directly. It was also possible to combine the names of months or seasonal festivals from different calendars to reference a date in poems. Another group is *tārīkh-i ma'navī* (meaningful date), in which the date must be calculated from a word or a phrase with the help of numerical values of the Arabic letters famous as *abjad*. Usually these chronograms take the form of short phrases or single words. In poetry, these chronograms usually occur in the final half-verse of a poem. Quatrains and *qiṭ'ehs* were particularly suitable poetic forms for this purpose. They might record dates of birth or death, the date of the accession of a ruler, the completion of buildings like mosques and *madraseh*s, or other important events. Chronograms also appear in the form of a riddle or *mu'ammā. Mu'ammā* applies intricate rules for riddles.

Muʿammā became prominent in Persian poetry during the Timurid period and continued into the reign of Safavids. The most famous poets who wrote *muʿammā* were Qāżī Mīr Ḥusayn Maybudī (d. 1506) and Vafāʾī (d. 1534). *Taẕkireh-yi Naṣrābādī* documented a few chronograms and the biographies of the chronogram writers. The rising number of poems in this genre demonstrates the significance of this genre in court culture. These poems could reference the dates of important events in the form of praise for the kings and the royal family.[11]

III. What Do Safavid Primary Sources Tell Us About Poetry?

The poet-patron relationship during the Safavid period is a source of controversial debate amongst scholars. During the 17th century there was an influx of poets from Safavid Iran to Mughal India and the Deccan.[12] Scholars of Persian literature provide different explanations for this move. Mīrzā Muḥammad Qazvīnī explained the lack of Safavid patronage for non-Shiʿi poetry as the main reason of the

---

[11] De Bruijn, "Chronogram", *Encyclopædia Iranica*, online edition 2011, available at http://www.iranicaonline.org/articles/chronograms-pers For more example on the best poems written in chronogram see, Gernot L Windfuhr, "Spelling the mystery of time". *Journal of the American Oriental Society Journal of the American Oriental Society* (1990, 110, no. 3), 401. Safa in full length studied different forms of chronograms during the Safavid reign. See Zabih Allah Safa, *Tārīkh-i Adabīyāt dar Īrān.* (Tehran: Intishārāt-i Firdawsī, 1984), v5/1, 625 – 628.

[12] It is difficult to estimate exactly how many poets left Iran and the court of Safavids for neighboring courts. It was during the reign of Akbar Shah that India received the most poets from Iran comparatively to any other courts in the 16th century. Two hundred and fifty-nine poets left Iran for India in the 16 and the beginning of the 17th century for different reasons. This time falls between the last twenty years of Shah Ṭahmāsp's rule, and the period of Ismāʿīl II (b. 1537 – d. 1577), Khudābandeh (b. 1532 – d. 1595), and 24 years of Shah ʿAbbās I's reign. Jahāngīr Shah (b. 1605 – d. 1627), despite its short period of ruling, after Akbar Shah was the second Mughal king who received the most poets from Iran. During his reign, which coincided with the last twenty-four years of Shah ʿAbbās I's reign, one hundred and seventy-three poets left Iran. The emigration process slowed down by the time of Shah Jahān (b. 1627 – d. 1658). During his reign, one hundred and fourteen poets left Iran. This period coincided with the last two years of Shah ʿAbbās I's rule, Shah Ṣafī (b. 1611 – d. 1642), and 16 years of Shah ʿAbbās II's reign.

move.[13] Rypka and Browne both wrote that the cultural interests of the Safavids were confined to the dissemination of Shi'i doctrine; therefore, the literary circles suffered from the kings' "lack of interest in the poets, their works and their burial places."[14] Noting the Persian poets' endeavors to reach to Mughal courts in India, Minorsky identified a link between the different quality of Safavid poetry and the lack of patronage. He justified the lack of patronage by mentioning a decline in mysticism in Iran, a point which was rejected by Aziz Ahmad, who indicated that mysticism was also in decline in the literature of India; however, this did not affect poet-patron relationships.[15] As Ahmad writes, the economic situation of the Middle East after the disappearance of Italian colonies in the Black Sea and the development of a sea route to India by the Portuguese played a significant role in shaping Safavid literature.

Systematic and comprehensive reconstruction of the poets' emigration to India and the Deccan is not possible. Some poets left the country on their own accord and some were forced to leave. Literary and historical sources including chronicles, travelogues, and *tazkireh*s show more interest in the move itself rather than providing insight about the causes. In many cases, it is indicated that poets not succeeding in securing court patronage, they decided to go to India in hope of finding better patronage. Biographical sources mention the names of a few poets for receiving monthly income from the Safavid kings. This monthly income, known as *suyūrghāl,*

---

[13] Browne, *A Literary History of Persia,* V5, 26.

[14] Ibid, 293.

[15] Aziz Ahmad, "Safavid Poets and India", *Iran,* vol 14, (1976), 117. DOI: 10.2307/4300548.

usually varied but in most cases was twelve *tumān*.[16] For example, Shah ʻAbbās I

assigned Niẓām al-Dīn Aḥmad-i Sharmī Qazvīnī, who was a tailor, an annual income

to move from Qazvin to Isfahan to become his court poet.[17]

The money which poets usually received from the kings was not always in the

form of monthly income, but it was a reward for improvising a poem or reciting a

good poem at the presence of kings. Shah Ṭahmāsb challenged the poets by requesting

a poem as good as Muḥtasham's panegyric in praise of Imam Ḥusayn. He declared he

would pay 50 *tumān* to someone who write such a poem.[18] Hilālī Hamidānī received

12 thousand *tumān* for a panegyric *qaṣīdeh* in praise of Ismāʻīl Mīrzā.[19] Ḥuznī

Iṣfahānī received 50 *tumān* for a piece he read in the presence of Shah ʻAbbās I.[20]

Amīnā Najafī received 50 *tumān* when he visited Shah ʻAbbās I in Isfahan and read

his poem for him.[21]

Although it was not mentioned in any of these examples that the poet was

rewarded for writing a religious piece, scholars usually agree that the Safavid kings

encouraged writing religious poetry more than other forms. Ahmad, however, warns

against analyzing the reasons of patronage seeking in India for the religious beliefs of

---

[16] Muḥammad Ṭāhir Naṣrābādī, *Tazkireh-yi Naṣrābādī: Mushtamil bar Sharḥ-i Hāl va Āsār-i Qarīb-i Hizār Shāʻir-i Aṣr-i Ṣafavī*, ed. Vahid Dastgardi, (Tehran: Kitāb furūsh-yi Furūghī, 1973). See Muqimā-yi Maqsūd, 355.

[17] Taqī al-Dīn Awḥadī Balyānī, *Tazkireh-yi ʻArafāt al-ʻĀshiqīn va ʻAraṣat al-ʻĀrifīn*, ed. Muhsin Naji Nasrabadi (Tehran: Intishārāt-i Asāṭīr, 2009), 378.

[18] Ibid, 618.

[19] Iskandar Beyg Munshī, *Tārīkh i ʼĀlam Ārā-yi ʻAbbāsī*, ed, Iraj Afshar, (Tehran: 1955), 57.

[20] Mīr Taqī al-Dīn Kāshānī, *Khulāṣat al-Ashʻār va Zubdat al-Afkār: Bakhsh-i Kāshān*. ed. Adib Barumand, Muhammad Husayn Nasiri Kahnamuyi, (Tehran: Mīrās-i maktūb, 2005.), 59.

[21]Awḥadī Balyānī, *Tazkireh-yi ʻArafāt al-ʻĀshiqīn va ʻAraṣat al-ʻĀrifīn*, 666.

the kings, or the economic situation of the time. Not all the poets who wrote religious poetry found patronage at the Safavid court. Although Ahmad believes that the patronage resources from Shah Ṭahmāsb to Shah 'Abbās II (b. 1632 – d. 1666) in comparison to the courts of Akbar (d.1605), Jahāngīr (d. 1627) and Shah Jahān (d. 1666) were inadequate; he mentions this should not be recognized as the only reason which made the poets to go to India, the Deccan, and other nearby territories. For example, Ghurūrī Kāshī went to India to escape 'Abbās I's displeasure due to his plagiarizing of a *qaṣīdeh* of Anvarī.[22] There are a few cases of persecution of poets in Iran for their "heresies". Qāsim Amīrī was blinded and then executed.[23] Kāmī Qazvīnī also left Iran to India because of the persecution of his family by Ṭahmāsb. Qāẓī Aḥmad also went to India; he was accused to be a Shāfi'ī. Ghazālī Mashhadī, the poet laureate of his time, escaped to Akbar's court because there were charges of heresy against him.[24]

There are questions about the significance of religious poetry for the time. Against all the arguments about Safavid kings' interest in writing religious poetry, the biography writers of the time rarely cited religious poems. Sām Mīrzā (b. 1518 – d. 1567) in *Tuḥfeh-yi Sāmī*, in which he recorded the name and life of more than seven

---

[22] His birth is unknown. He was born in Kashan and received his literary training in Shiraz. Because of his overbearing attitude he was not popular among the community of poets. It is said he read a *qaṣīdeh* of Anwari for his patron in Lār, who did not understand it was not his poem. Before the truth was disclosed, he fled to India, before Lār was occupied by Shah 'Abbās I. See Nabi Hadi, *Dictionary of Indo-Persian Literature*, (New Delhi: Indira Gandhi National Centre for the Arts: 1995) 207-208. Naṣrābādī, *Tazkireh-yi Naṣrābādī*, 291. 'Abd al-Nabī Fakhr al-Zamānī Qazvīnī, *Tazkireh-yi Meykhāneh*. ed. Ahmad Gulchin Ma'ani (Tehran: Shirkat-i Nisbī-i Ḥāj Muḥammad Ḥusayn Iqbāl va Shurakā', 692-703.

[23] 'Alī Qulī Khān Vāleh, *Tazkireh-yi Riyāż al-Shu'arā'*, ed. Muhsin Naji Nasrabadi (Tehran: Intishārāt-i Asāṭīr, 2005).

[24] Ahmad, "Safavid Poets and India", 122.

hundred poets who lived under Shah Ismā'īl and Shah Ṭahmāsb, rarely included

religious poems. The cited poems were mostly love poems or poems containing witty

remarks on the relationship between humans and the world. Moreover, these poems

commented on existential concepts such as life, death, and morality.[25] *'Arafāt al-

'Āshiqīn* and *Majma' al-Fuṣaḥā* also did not include religious poetry of the period.

Muḥammad Ṭāhir Naṣrābādī (b. 1618 – d. 1677), the author of *Tazkireh-yi Naṣrābādī*,

cited more religious poems in comparison to other biographical dictionaries. The most

cited religious works in *Tazkireh-yi Naṣrābādī* are for the poets whose names were

mentioned under the section "viziers, *mustawfī*s, and the writers of chancellery,"[26]

which demonstrates that religion was more appreciated among the nobles of time.

Naṣrābādī also cited some religious poetry in the section titled as "nobles and

'*ulamā*".[27] The lack of interest in religious poetry marks *Tazkireh-yi Ḥazīin* in which

Ḥazīin Lāhījī (b. 1692 – d. 1766) recorded the names and works of one hundred poets

of his time, of whom only a few belonged to the court or were from a religious

background. Those chronicles that included the names and works of some court poets

also did not show interest in citing religious poetry. Naṣrullāh Munshī in *Tārīkh-i

'Ālam Ārā,* and Vāleh-yi Iṣfahānī in *Khuld-i Barīn* included less than ten poems with

religious themes.

    *Tazkireh*s and other biographical sources of the time did not show much

---

[25] See Sām Mīrzā, *Tuḥfeh-yi Sāmī: Mushtamil bar Asāmī va Āsār-i Qarīb Haftād Shā'ir az Shu'arā-yi Nāmdār va Gumnām*, ed. Hasan Vahid Dastgirdi, (Tehran: Kitābfarūshī-i Furūghī, 1976). See Shāhāb al-Dīn 'Abd Allāh Bayānī, 63, Jāmī, 86, and Mawlānā Niāmī Mu'ammāī, 101.

[26] See *Tazkireh-yi Naṣrābādī* for Mīrzā Mu'īn al-Dīn 'Alī,76, Muḥammad Bāqī Beyg, 86, and Khalīl Beyg, 88.

[27] Ibid, see Mīrzā 'Abd al-Razzāq Lāhījī, 56. Vā'iẓ Qazvīnī, 72. Amīnā Farāhānī, 183.

interest in citing *qaṣīdeh*s as well. The most mentioned poems are in *ghazal* or *rubāʿī* form, and the cited poems do not usually represent religio-political ideology of the period. The cited poems are mostly love poems commenting on the relationship between humans and nature. Although some of the cited poems are in praise of Imam ʿAlī and Twelver Shiʿi doctrine, most of the poems contain Sufi ideas and are about love, nature, and praising morality. Against the attempt from Shah ʿAbbās I's time to suppress Sufi doctrines, the poetry of his time and subsequent poetry show significant interest in applying Sufi terms and expressions for legitimizing the king as a head of Sufi orders, a concept that emphasize the relationship between Shah ʿAbbās and his great Sufi ancestors. Ḥazīn Lāhījī shows this interest in compiling his *Tazkireh.* The poets whom Ḥazīn included in his work had the least affiliation with the court. Most of the cited poems in this book are in *ghazal* form or are one unique special verse in describing nature, love, and Sufi ideas.

As mentioned before, the literary culture of the Safavid and Mughal time is more dynamic in terms of poets and the territories they were writing from. This feature makes it difficult to construct the dynamic of poetry, poet-patron relationship, and the audience of poetry during the Safavid dynasty, yet we can be sure about the formation of poetry in non-court circles. During this period, more people intended to write poetry without relying on the court for publication. Non-court poetry was diverse in themes, was produced under different circumstances, and contained different images and motifs. This diversity suggests that poetic literary approaches, namely style of writing, cannot be used alone to interpret and evaluate all poetry written during this time; therefore, limiting the scope of analysis to a specific form, for example *qaṣīdeh,* and considering the poets' purposes in writing, for example praise of the kings, allows

focusing on the literary and historical value of the work.

IV. The Major Poets

In this section, by narrating the biographies of some major poets, I shed light

on the diversity of life and works of the poets which were diverse in comparison to the

literature of past. The poets whose names I mention here are not necessarily the best

poets of their time. I chose the ones who were either court poets or who were

patronized by a king, or who at least wrote a panegyric for the ruler of his time.

Muḥtasham of Kashan (b. 1500 – d. 1588), who was of a mercantile family,

was the main poet of Shah Ṭahmāsb and his daughter, Parīkhān Khānum (b. 1548 – d.

1578). Although, Muḥtasham never resided in the Safavid court, he was a professional

poet throughout his life for Shah Ṭahmāsb as well as contenders for the throne. For

example, he wrote panegyrics for Shah Ṭahmāsb's successors Ismāʿīl II (r. 1576 –

1577) and Muḥammad Khudābandeh (r. 1578 – 1587). Muḥtasham constantly

attempted to stay in touch with the Safavid court. He was concerned with the transition

of power and addressed Ḥaydar Mīrzā (b. 1554 – d. 1576), Ḥamzeh Mīrzā (b. 1568 –

d. 1586), administrators of the Safavid court, and a variety of Qizilbāsh leaders. It was

due to his concerns about attachment to the courts that he also addressed the

ʿĀdilshāhīs who ruled the sultanate of Bijapur (r. 1490 – 1686), the Niẓāmshāhīs who

ruled over sultanate of Ahmadnagar (r. 1490 – 1636), and Akbar Shah (r. 1556 –

1605) from the Mughal court.[28]

---

[28] ʿAlī ibn Aḥmad Muḥtasham, *Haft Dīvān-i Muḥtasham Kāshānī*. ed. ʿAbd al-Ḥusayn Navāʾī (Tehran: Mīrās̱-i Maktūb, 2001), 84-91. (cited hereafter in text and footnotes as Muḥtasham)

Though Muḥtasham was not living at the centers of political power, namely Tabriz and Qazvin, he had a central role in the poetic life of the 16th century. During his lifetime, he managed to earn fame and respect to the extent that Shah Ṭahmāsb's daughter, Parīkhān Khānum, required other poets of Kashan to submit their work to him for inspection before sending it to the royal court.[29]

Muḥtasham is regarded as the most important poets of his time. His fame mostly surrounds a single poem—his elegy on the martyrdom of Imam Ḥusayn at Karbala that includes twelve strophes (*davāzdah-band*). The power of this poem has colored the perception of Muḥtasham's career, his other works, and even the Safavid literary patronage system.[30] The anecdote that Iskandar Beyg Munshī submitted in *ʿĀlam Ārā-yi ʿAbbāsī* about Muḥtasham's seven-strophe poem in praise of Imam ʿAlī played an important role in complicating scholars' understanding of the dominant poetic discourses of time. Citing De Bruijn, Losensky argued that Browne and subsequent scholars, mistakenly believed that Muḥtasham read the twelve-strophe poem for Shah Ṭahmāsb when the king reproached the poet for polluting his tongue with the praises of temporal rulers.[31] Shah Ṭahmāsb requested that a poem be written on the virtues of Imams. The poem Muḥtasham then rehearsed was a seven-strophe poem in praise of Imam ʿAlī. That poem received an outstanding reward and poets started to imitate it afterwards.

---

[29] Ibid.

[30] Paul Losensky, "MOḤTAŠAM KĀŠĀNI," *Encyclopædia Iranica*, online edition, available at http://www.iranicaonline.org/articles/mohtasham-kashani (accessed on 20 September 2016).

[31] Ibid.

The main themes of Muḥtasham's poems do not support the idea that the Safavid kings sought religious poetry. Muḥtasham's book of poetry includes a variety of themes, including erotic themes and images. Muḥtasham wrote many panegyrics in praise of the Safavid kings on various occasions in various forms and genres from *qaṣīdeh* to *qiṭ'eh* and from chronograms to love poetry without describing the king with Shiʻi terms and expressions. His style of writing in *ghazal* form are similar to the language of poets in *maktab-i vuqū'*, as Muḥtasham portrayed his romantic affections in detail. In *Nuql-i 'Ushshāq* (The Lovers' Confection) and *Risāleh Jalāliyyeh* (The Glorious Treatise) are also among the famous works of him in representing romantic affections. Muḥtasham in *Nuql-i 'Ushshāq* expressed love towards a female beloved and in *Risāleh Jalāliyyeh* he showed affection toward a boy named Jalāl.[32]

Vaḥshī Bāfqī (b. 1532 – d. 1583), the other most famous poet of the Safavid period, was born to a middle-class family with no merchant background.[33] Considering that Bāfq is an agricultural town, his father probably worked as a farmer. Although there is not much information about his early life, it is known that he received his training in poetry from his older brother and the local literary luminary Sharaf al-Dīn ʻAlī Bāfqī. He moved to Kashan in the early Safavid period, and soon he was welcomed by many local poets of his time, because they saw him as the only poet who could compete with Muḥtasham. Although he is known for his poverty, he

---

[32] To read about this work see Paul Losensky, "Poetics and Eros in Early Modern Persia: The Lovers' Confection and the Glorious Epistle by Muhtasham Kāshānī." *Iranian Studies* 42, no. 5 (2009), and Losensky, "MOḤTAŠAM KĀŠĀNI," 2016, Maryam Salihiniya, Muhammad Javad Mahdavi, "Rasāʻil-i Muḥtasham-i Kāshānī", *Naqd-i Adabī,* no 15, (Fall 2011), 187-210.

[33] For bibliography on Muḥtasham's life and work see Paul Losensky, "VAḤŠI BĀFQI," *Encyclopædia Iranica*, online edition, 2004, available at http://www.iranicaonline.org/articles/vahshi-bafqi (accessed on 20 September 2016).

enjoyed a prominent position as the foremost poet at the court of Yazd's ruler, Ghīyās̲

al-Dīn Mīr-i Mīrān.[34] He wrote many panegyrics for Mīr-i Mīrān, and dedicated

poems to the governor of Kerman, Baktāsh Beyg Afshār. Having these two great

patrons of his poetry, he did not see any reason to send more panegyrics to the court of

Shah Ṭahmāsb and his sons beyond the two *qaṣīdeh*s he had written. He also wrote

two short chronograms on the enthronement of Ismāʿīl II.

Vaḥshī has composed devotional poems in honor of the Shiʿi Imams. The

*qiṭʿeh*s he wrote primarily served him as a tool for panegyric. In writing these forms

and genres, although he applied the cultural terms of Shiʿism, he hardly associated

kingship with Shiʿi Imams. His praise for kings was limited to the same imagery as his

earlier poets. Vaḥshī's style, like that of Saʿdī, for its simplicity, has been described as

a style that its simplicity is inimitable.[35] His *ghazal*s, *ma̲s̲navī*s, and his sole *tarjīʿ-

band* is an extended celebration of mystical intoxication. In his *ghazal*s, he also

depicted the full range of emotions for earthly love.[36]

The other famous poet of the time was the poet laureate of Shah ʿAbbās I's

court, Vajīh al-Dīn famous as Shānī (d. 1614). Born in Tehran and living in Isfahan

and Hamadan, he was embraced by Shah ʿAbbās I because of the line he wrote about

Imam ʿAlī.[37] He attempted writing in different forms of Persian poetry, and his *divān*

---

[34] Ghīyās̲ al-Dīn Mīr-i Mīrān and his son, Khalīl Allāh, were descendants of the Sufi shaikh
Shah Niʿmat Allāh Valī and in-laws of the Safavid royal house. Both rulers patronized many poets
during the reign of Shah Ṭāhmāsp.

[35] Gulchin Maʿani, *Maktab-i Vuqūʿ dar Shiʿr-i Fārsī*, 238-40.

[36] Paul Losensky, "VAḤŠI BĀFQI," 2016.

[37] To read the full story of the event see Chapter Three, p. 130, fn 46.

includes more than nine thousand poems in the *qaṣīdeh, tarkīb-band, ghazal,* and

maṣnavī forms. He wrote panegyrics for Imams, some nobles of his time, and Shah

'Abbās I. Although Vāleh Dāghistānī did not have a positive appraisal of Shānī's style

of writing, he did nevertheless mention that the poet had eloquent *ghazal*s. Shānī

demonstrated familiarity with poets such as Ḥāfiẓ and Sa'dī, but in *qaṣīdeh* his style

was close to Khāqānī's (b. 1120 – d. 1190 CE) style of writing.

Salīm Tihrānī (d. 1647) was born in Tarasht and raised in Lahijan. He did not

have a systematic education. During his stay in Lahijan he wrote panegyrics to

dedicate to the rulers of Lahijan. When he left Lahijan for Isfahan, he dedicated poems

to both Shah 'Abbās I and Ṣafī I but did not receive the attention he desired from

either king. The biographers of his time believed he left Isfahan for Shiraz before his

final departure to India, where he entered the circles of power in Agra and Lahore. He

passed away in Kashmir and was buried there.[38] His *dīvān* is a combination of all

forms of poetry. His language is simple and with no intricate metaphors or other

literary devices. As Safa mentions, Salīm's language was closer to the "language of

ordinary people" because his lack of education. Despite this fact, Salīm included

images which are sources for inspiration for the very famous poets of his time such as

Kalīm (b. 1581 – d. 1651) and Ghanī Kashmīrī (d. 1668).[39] At the same time,

Naṣrābādī mentioned Salīm as someone who borrowed his themes from the other

poets as well.[40] As is mentioned in Chapter Three, his *qaṣīdeh*s in praise of the kings

---

[38] To read about his life and work in India, specially his works on description of gardens see Sunil Sharma, *Mughal Arcadia: Persian Literature in an Indian Court*, (Harvard University Press, 2017), 125-156.

[39] Safa, *Tārīkh-i Adabīyāt-i Īrān.* v5/2, 1162.

[40] Naṣrābādī, *Tazkireh*, 227.

are different from the works of poets such as Muḥtasham and Ṣā'ib who served the court. His *qaṣīdeh*s are written in a simple language and contain different themes including nature and notes about his mastery in poetry. Poets of the Safavid era rarely spoke boldly of their poetic skills in their poems, which they wrote to present at the court stage.

Faṣīḥī Hiravī (b. 1579 – d.1639) was born and raised in Bukhara. In *qaṣīdeh*, he is inspired by Khāqānī and Anvarī (b. 1126 – d. 1189 CE) while he followed Sa'dī and Ḥāfiẓ in *ghazal*. His grandfather was a poet and his father was well educated in philosophy and religion.[41] Raised in a noble family and showing his poetry skills, he was with Shah 'Abbās I when the king undertook his occupation of Herat. "Faṣīḥī had a very limited world and perspective since he never left Herat and the court of Ḥusayn Khān-i Shāmlū", Dehqani wrote.[42] Indeed, Faṣīḥī, similar to his peers during that period, was interested in traveling to India. Once he left Herat and went to Qandahar where he received an outstanding reward from the ruler. However, because he did not ask for Ḥusayn Khān-i Shāmlū's permission for leaving, he was arrested and sent back to Herat by Ḥusayn Khān's order. In 1622, the poet met with Shah 'Abbās I and presented his work to him. Shah 'Abbās praised his work and asked him to travel to Mazandaran with him. There is no other information available about Faṣīḥī after this event; it is only known that he passed away in 1639.[43]

---

[41] Muhammad Dehghani, "Shā'ir-i Shu'leh hā: Pajūhishī Darbāre-yi Faṣīḥī Hiravī va Shi'r-i Ū", *The Department of Literature and Humanities of University of Tabriz*, #189, (Winter 2002), 82.

[42] Ibid, 86.

[43] Ibid.

Faṣīḥī wrote many *qaṣīdeh*s and *ghazal*s, which form the majority of his work.
He was familiar with the great poets from the 13th to 15th centuries and imitated many
of their works but never mentioned his sources. He can be considered as among the
pioneers of *maktab-i vuquʻ*. He was interested in applying similes and personifications
in writing; therefore, his poetic language is closer to writing lyrics. Similar to writers
in the Indian/Isfahani style of his time, he showed more interest in writing *ghazal*. His
*qaṣīdeh*s are also famous because of their metaphoric language and very emotional
*tashbīb*s. This degree of emotional expressions in panegyric' *tashbīb*s is unusual for
the poetry of this period. Dehqani described the poet's extra attention to emotive
expressions of language with the poet's intention in praise "as if the praise was
secondary to the poem."[44]

Mīrzā Rafīʻ al-Dīn Muḥammad ibn Fatḥullāh Qazvīnī (d. 1678), famous as
Mīrzā Rafīʻā, was of the religious scholars of the 17th century who experienced the
reigns of Shah ʻAbbās I to Shah Ṣafi II. In Qazvin, he acted as a preacher, and his
treatise *Abvāb al-Jinān* (The Doors of Heaven) on ethics is among the most important
writings on Shiʻi scholarship. His *dīvān* includes *qaṣīdeh*, *ghazal*, *rubāʻī*, and *masnvaī*.
He wrote many panegyrics in praise of the twelve Shiʻi Imams and Shah ʻAbbās II.
Many of his *rubāʻī*s refer to historical incidents of his time from the king's
enthronement to erecting buildings.[45] His most famous poem is a *masnavī* piece about
the war between Ismāʻīl I and Shaybak the Uzbek king, which I discuss in Chapter
Five. His poems cover topics such as ethics, morality, and love for God. Although his

---

[44] Ibid, 103.

[45] Safa, *Tārīkh-i Adabīyāt-i Īrān.* v5/2, 1032.

language is very simple and free from the regular intricate metaphors of his time, his poems never competed with those of his contemporary poets.

Muḥsin Ta'sīr Tabrīzī (b. 1650 – d. 1717) was the accountant-poet of Shah Ṣafī II. He spent most of his time at the court of Shah Ṣafī II in Isfahan and as his accountant. Also, he worked for the local governor of Yazd until Shah Sulṭān Ḥusayn dismissed him from the position. He was well educated in the religious centers of Isfahan. He learned theology, Quran, and hadith from Āqā Ḥusayn Khwansārī (d. 1688) and was well trained in Shi'i legacies. This familiarity with Shi'i learning highly influenced his poetry, and he wrote many *qaṣīdeh*s in praise of the prophet and Shi'i Imams. Inspired by Muḥtasham, he wrote a piece on the incident of Karbala, which is one of the best examples of the genre. His *ghazal*s are occupied with Sufi expressions and concepts and are exhortations to stay away from the material world. In *qaṣīdeh* he was inspired by Sa'dī, Khāqānī and Anvarī. From the Safavid poets he followed the style of Muḥtasham and Naẓīrī (d. 1612). He is famous for his *qaṣīdeh*s in praise of Shi'i Imams, but he also wrote some *masnavī*s, most of which are in praise of Shi'i Imams.[46]

As mentioned above, some famous poets of the time pursued their professional career abroad. The first major poet who left Ṭahmāsb's court after being accused of heresy was Ghazālī Mashhadī. He first visited the Deccan and later went to Mughal India where he became the poet laureate of Akbar's court. The other poet who left Iran to the Deccan was 'Urfī Shīrāzī (d. 1591); however, he did not prosper there. In

---

[46] Muḥsin Ta'sīr Tabrīzī, *Dīvān-i Muḥsin Ta'sīr Tabrīzī*, ed. Amin Pasha Ijlali (Tehran: Markaz-i Nashr-i Dānishgāhī, 1994). For reading on his life also see Husayn Nakhjavani, "Mīrzā Muḥsin Tabrīzī", *The Faculty of Humanities and Literature of Tabriz*, no 1, (March 1948), 47-52.

Mughal India, his patron Fayżī helped him to gain better success but their friendship soon changed to rivalry—an incident that forced him to change his patronage to Abū al-Fatḥ al-Gīlānī[47] (d. 1588) and later to Khān-i Khānān (d. 1592).[48] Although he wrote panegyrics for Akbar, he never find success in Mughal court. Naẓīrī Nīshābūrī (d. 1612) was a famous poet-merchant who stayed at the Safavid court for some time before seeking patronage in India. He was already a famous poet when Khān-i Khānān decided to patronize him. Two years before death, Jahāngīr called him to his imperial court. Ṭālib Āmulī (b. 1538 – d. 1627), who was born and raised in Mazandaran, was another great poet of time who, due to lack of access to the court of Shah 'Abbās, decided to seek better opportunities for his career in India. He served at the courts of Lahore, Qandahar, and Gujurat, where Diyānat Khān from Gujurat introduced him to Jahāngīr. He did not impress the king at this first presentation, but he was successful when he presented a poem for I'timād al-Dawleh. In 1619, he was appointed as poet laureate of Jahāngīr's court. Muḥammad Jān Qudsī Mashhadī (d. 1646) was another famous Safavid poet who migrated to India. He gained the attention of Shah Jahān and wrote the famous *masnavī, Pādshāhnāmeh.* However, he could not become the poet laureate, as the position went to Kalīm of Kāshān.[49] Kalīm also tried his chances first in the Deccan before joining the court of Shah Navāz Khān Shīrāzī, the vizier of Ibrāhīm 'Ādil Shah II, and then the court of Mīr Jumleh Shahristānī. After years of residency in India, he went back to Iran for a period of two years. However, he had

---

[47] He was the Persian poet of Akbar Shah's court.

[48] He was the last king of Kārkīyā dynasty in Gilan who ruled from 1538 to 1592. For more information see his name in Dehkhoda and *Tazkireh-yi Naṣrābādī.*

[49] Ahmad, "Safavid Poets and India", 123.

been happier in India, where he later returned. This time he joined the court of Shah

Jahān and was appointed poet laureate. Similar to Jān Qudsī (d. 1646), he also wrote a

masnavī for the king famous as *Pādshāhnāmeh*. He is the most successful Persian

immigrant poet, and more than any other emigrant Persian poets of Persian origin, he

was adapted to Indian culture.[50]

The other famous poet of time who is much praised for his *ghazal*s and the

refined and abstract imagery of his style is Sā‘ib of Tabriz.[51] Ṣā‘ib, similar to his peer

Muḥtasham, was a child of the mercantile elite. His father was a successful merchant,

who was evacuated with his family from Tabriz by ‘Abbās I in response to Ottoman

incursions. Like many aspiring Persian poets of the age, he felt the Mughal courts

offered him better prospects for his literary career. Upon his arrival in Kabul, Ṣā‘ib

met the governor of the city, Ẓafar Khān, and this young governor patronized the poet

for the next several years. Upon his father's request, he wrote a *qaṣīdeh* and asked for

Ẓafar Khān's permission to leave India in 1632. His seven-year residence in India

established his reputation as the foremost poet of the age. He had a well-established

relationship with Shah ‘Abbās II, until Shah Sulaymān's reign. Ṣā‘ib's diwan did not

only consist of *ghazal* and *qaṣīdeh*. He also wrote *masnavī*s. His most famous *masnavī*

is *Qandahārnāmeh,* or *‘Abbāsnāmeh,* which describes ‘Abbās II's conquest of

Qandahar in 1641. These descriptions usually associated the beauty, peace, and

---

[50] Ibid.

[51] Paul Losensky. ṢĀ’EB TABRIZI," *Encyclopædia Iranica*, online edition, 2003, available at http://www.iranicaonline.org/articles/saeb-tabrizi (accessed on 20 September 2016). For reading more about Ṣā‘ib see Chapter Four of this dissertation.

security of the palaces with the personality of a king whose character had the most similarity with the Shi'i Imams.

The other famous contemporary poet of Ṣā'ib's time was Muḥammad Ṭahir Vaḥīd the secretary and chronicler under Shah 'Abbās II, Shah Ṣafī II, and Shah Ḥusayn for a half century. He wrote *masnavī*s that provide significant information on the life and times of the kings under whom he worked. His works shed light on the intellectual and literary life of 17th century. He has a *masnavī* that describes the various kinds of weapons used by Safavids and his *fathnāmeh* describes Shah 'Abbās II's occupation of Qandahar. But war is not the only subject Vaḥīd discussed in his works. He also praised the royal gardens and palaces of his time in addition to portraying courtly love relationships.[52]

V. Conclusion

In the following chapters I analyze Safavid court poetry composed in panegyric *qaṣīdeh* and *masnavī* form. Safavid court poetry has potential to be an important source for understanding the history of Safavids, which has been left unexamined in existing literature. I argue that such a great lack of emphasis on the literary value of poetry in the Safavid period resulted in the downplaying of the socio-historical significance of Safavid panegyrics. While scholars such as Babayan, Quinn, Babaie and Rizvi examined the role of ideology in shaping the historical and cultural circumstances of the Safavid period, I am drawing attention towards poets to

---

[52] Sunil Sharma provides more information on life and poetry of Vaḥīd Qazvīnī in his latest work, *Mughal Arcadia*. See 189-195.

specifically study the involvement of this community with the doctrines of Shi'ism during this period.

What kings' perceptions of Shi'ism and how was it defined for different social groups? How many forms of Shi'ism existed? Was Shi'ism presented in the same way in public and courtly venues? To what extent was the propagation of Shi'ism a top-down process? Which groups of the society took part in this process and which groups did not? What was the role of poets in the production and dissemination of Shi'i knowledge? Were the poets themselves the subject of this ideology? How did changing religion affect their position at the court stage and how did it influence their work? Did it change their relationship with the monarchs and the system that usually constructed their identity? How did they negotiate their power at this stage?

These questions guide my work throughout this dissertation. To explore Safavid ideology and its manifestations in public places, I study the means of communication that the Safavids used for legitimizing purposes in the next chapter. Chapter Two reconstructs public discourses of kingship in order to further examine the court poetry of the time and its utility within the political dynamics of the Safavid reign.

CHAPTER TWO
VERBAL REPRESENTATION OF POWER:
PUBLIC AUTHORITY AND SAFAVID LEGITIMACY

I. Introduction

The many cultural products in Isfahan today are mostly remnants from the Safavid periods. These products provide scholars with an opportunity to investigate the Safavid dynasty from different vantage points, for example, their contribution to the political ideology of the time or how they demonstrate the dynamics of economy and society during that period. The primary purpose of this chapter is to reconstruct the patterns of religio-political legitimacy in a series of Safavid cultural products to learn how the state applied these terms to legitimize their rule and what concepts were significant for their legitimacy. This analysis builds a foundation for future chapters, which investigate the relationship between the court poets and the Safavid kings.

In this chapter, by analyzing the verbal representations of power in different Safavid cultural products, I argue that the core ideology of the Safavids did not consist of a monolithic idea. It was a changing concept moving between the different polemics that were initiated by Ismāʿīl I (b. 1487 – d. 1524) but expanded differently through time. Ismāʿīl I came to power by declaring himself as a reincarnation of the Prophet, the Messiah, and God's representative power on Earth.[1] These ideas held

---

[1] Kathryn Babayan, *Mystics, Monarchs and Messiah: Cultural Landscape of Early Modern Iran.* (Cambridge, Mass: Harvard University Press, 2003).

sway until the reign of Shah ʿAbbās I (b. 1571 – d. 1629), who was mentioned as "a master of public displays of religious devotion" by Quinn.[2] During Shah ʿAbbās I's reign, demonstrating public servitude towards Shiʿi Imams overshadowed other forms of political claims. From Shah ʿAbbās I's time, instead of grandiose titles such as al-Sultan or al-Khaqan, the expressions of servitude towards the Shiʿi Imams, namely the "guard dog of the threshold of ʿAlī," held the king in a subservient position in relation to the first Imam and gave the king a pious image, which along with the king's other public demonstrations of servitude towards Shiʿism, made him different from the Sunni rulers of his time and the times of his forefathers.

In this chapter, I identify the verbal representations of various ideologies and concepts that exist in cultural materials. While Quinn and Babayan mostly demonstrate the origins and elements of the Safavid ideology, I investigate how each of these elements were represented in these materials as they speak of the kings' self-image in public. Finding these patterns and their variations, transformations, appearance and disappearances can help to identify the arc of Shiʿism in society. Analyzing the patterns of legitimacy in different cultural materials from different times demonstrates that while Twelver Shiʿism was part of the system of political propaganda from the very beginning of the Safavid periods, it was not a coherent and well-defined concept until Shah ʿAbbās's time. Although Shah Ismāʿīl announced Shiʿism as the religion of state, it was from Shah ʿAbbās I's time, especially after moving the capital to Isfahan in 1598, when serving Shiʿism and the Shiʿi Imams

---

[2] Quinn, *Shah ʿAbbās: The King Who Refashioned Iran*, (England: Oneworld Publications, 2015), 77. For reading on the life and times of Shah ʿAbbas I see Encyclopedia Iranica "'Abbās I" and its bibliography; see also the annotated bibliography of "Safavid Dynasty".

became pivotal to the Safavid public discourse. This idea had previously been promoted by Shah Ṭahmāsb's constant effort to connect himself through the world of dreams with Imam ʿAlī and his descendants,[3] but it did not become established until Shah ʿAbbās's time, when some of the cultural materials, especially coins, marginalized the dominant, orthodox representations of political authority offered by Sunni caliphs to claim a similarity between the Safavid kings and the Shiʿi Imams.

My analysis demonstrates that after Shah Ismāʿīl I seized power, Safavid ideology experienced changes in terms of employing the ideas of kingship dominated in Persian Empire before advance of Islam, and the amalgamation of Sunni and Shiʿi expressions throughout the time period. During the reign of Shah ʿAbbās I, the titles associated with pre-Islamic forms of kingship were gradually dropped, and Twelver Shiʿi discourse became dominant. However, the last two Safavid kings were again usually presented in ways similar to the Persian kings of the pre-Islamic period. Studying these products demonstrates that by end of the reign of Shah Sultan Ḥusayn (b. 1668 – d. 1726), the patterns of political legitimacy of Shah Ismāʿīl's period had come back into practice. The emphasis on different forms of kingship and Shiʿim implies the interest in making connections between these two forms of sovereignty in order to make a connection between kingship and imamatship for legitimizing purposes during the reign of the Safavids.

The expressions of Shah ʿAbbās's servitude, for example *muravvij-i maẕhab-i ḥaqq-i aʿimmeh-yi eẕnā ʿasharī* (the propagator of the religion of the twelve Imams),

---

[3] A series of dreams in *Taẕkireh-yi Shah Ṭahmāsb* have been narrated through which Shah Ṭahmāsb was helped by Imam ʿAlī before going into war scenes. See Shah Ṭahmāsp, *Taẕkireh-yi Shah Ṭahmāsb beh Ghalam-i Khudash*, (Chāpkhāneh-ye Kāvyānī: 1964), see pages 15, 23, 30.

ghulām-i beh-ikhlās-i amīr al-mu'minīn (the true servant of the king of believers), *kalb-i āstān-i 'Alī* (the dog of Ali's threshold), or *nuvvāb-i kalb-i āstān-i 'Alī* (the servants of the dog of Ali's threshold), along with expressions that revolved around the notions of the Safavid lineage such as *ṣāḥib al-nasab al-ẓāhir al-nabavī* (the owner of pure prophetic lineage), were widely used from Shah 'Abbās I's time to depict the king in a manner far from regular portraits of a worldly lord. These expressions, along with Shah 'Abbās's avoidance of being known as an absolute king in public and his regular visits in disguise to the people of the city, built Shah 'Abbās the reputation as a humble and modest king who did not see distance between himself and regular people.[4] This mindset gave a coherent footing to the political arrangements of the Shi'i system of rule in the future. The expressions of servitude and display of religious devotion, nevertheless marked the position of a sovereign king represents Safavid kings similar to Shi'i Imams who guide the people to path of salvation. The new Shi'i king did not publicly perform rulership for the maintenance and enjoyment of power but rather expressed love for the people. The well-established relationship between the Shah and *'ulamā* allowed the Safavid king to take further steps to religiously infuse his reign. The *'ulamā* argued that the Safavid kings are the promised leaders chosen to hand over rule to Imam Mahdī. This has been done by emphasizing the importance of enjoining good and forbidding

---

[4] Tales of his visits to the lower quarters of Isfahan exemplify his style of justice. The French traveler, Tavernier, narrated the incident in which the Shah punished a baker who sold him short to be baked in his own oven. There is also a narration about a cheating butcher whom the shah ordered to be roasted to show his justice towards the people whom the butcher did not treat well. There were also stories that framed the king as a hero and a helper. (Jean-Baptist Tavernier, cited in Roger M. Savory, Iran under the Safavids, (Cambridge University Press:1980). To read more of the stories surrounding Shah 'Abbās and his attention toward regular people, see Ulrich, Marzolph, *Ṭabaqeh bandī-i Qiṣṣeh hā-yi Īrānī,* trans, Kaykavus Jahandari (Tehran: Surūsh, 1992), under *947 A, 945, 930, *922, 841, *844, 40, 724). As defined in these stories, the shah usually buys the product of poor businesspeople (467) to help them, marries the daughter of a poor family, or a dervish promises the poor wife of an unfaithful man that she may bring him back to the path of guidance (844 B).

wrong, which, in some hadiths and narrations, have been understood as the characteristic of a just and legitimate king.

Shah 'Abbās's public performances of piety were accompanied through the religious endeavors of clergy members to assign more power to their institution. During 'Abbās's reign, the practice of public Friday prayers became a tradition again, and mosques were built specifically for this practice.[5] *'Ulamā* were controlling the affairs of mosques and coffeehouses, and the Shah himself appointed religious scholars for each coffeehouse and required them to report to him any unusual circumstances that may have transpired. Shah 'Abbās specifically showed a consistent intent toward practicing acts of piety, which presented him as an obedient Muslim leader and a servant of the religion.[6]

In general, as we move from the early beginning of the Safavid dynasty to Shah 'Abbās's time, it is clear that the Safavid dynasty was developing into a pious Shi'i ruling system in which the Safavid king was accepted similar to an Imam in a leading position. However, by the time of 'Abbās I, some of the initial religious

---

[5] For reading about Friday prayer and its establishment as the continuation of a Shi'i tradition, see Stewart Devin J, "Polemics and Patronage in Safavid Iran: The Debate on Friday Prayer During the Reign of Shah Tahmasb". *Bulletin of the School of Oriental and African Studies,* University of London. 72, no. 3 (2009): 425-457. http://www.jstor.org.ezproxy1.library.arizona.edu/stable/40379028. On the role of Arab 'ulamā and their ideas about Friday prayers, see Rula Abisaab, *Converting Persia: Religion and Power in the Safavid Empire.* (London [u.a.]: Tauris, 2015). There, Abisaab explains how and why the Arab *'ulamā* was brought from ottoman Syria to Iran. She explains how these émigré scholars changed the face of religion in Iran and furnished source of legitimacy for the Safavid monarchs. For more information, also see Andrew Newman, *Safavid Iran: Rebirth of a Persian Empire,* (I.B. Tauris, 2012).

[6] Quinn, *Shah 'Abbās,* 61-64. For reading on Shah 'Abbās' acts of piety see Kishwar Rizvi, "Architecture and the Representations of Kingship during the Reign of the Safavid Shah 'Abbās I" in Mitchell Lynette, C.P Melville. *Every Inch of a King: Comparative Studies on Kings and Kingship in the Ancient and Medieval Worlds,* (Brill:2013), 371- 97.

impulses of the Safavids, such as Sufism and *ghuluvv*[7] religiosity, had started to

fade—even though traces were still apparent. Shah 'Abbās himself showed interest in

these unorthodox religious movements at the beginning of his reign, only to suppress

them later.[8] Although he suppressed these groups and their practices, he was

nevertheless much inspired by their pious activities, which were highly influenced by

Shi'i ideas. It was during Shah 'Abbās's reign that the Persian Empire became

increasingly orthodox in its Shi'i religious character and identity. Constructing the

new capital in Isfahan also helped facilitating that transformation.[9] Based on

information recorded by travelers during his reign, Shah 'Abbās's style of kingship in

Isfahan was very personal and informal. The chronicles of his time, like the formal

and luxury buildings he made, depicted him as a powerful, pious king in control of his

own public image, the economy, and the religious establishment.

This chapter is written in five parts. In Part II, I study the benedictions and

titles preserved on coins, royal orders, and *tughrā*s of the Safavids. The expressions

printed on coins speak to the early ideology of each king sitting on the throne at the

time. Some images of coins are provided at the end of the chapter. In Part III, I study

the documents which remained from the ceremonies of royal investiture to shed light

on the images of a king in such a crucial event where many people witnessed the

enthronement. In Part IV, I investigate mosques and *madrasehs*' inscriptions, as well

as the charities of charitable trusts. These places were available for public use, and

---

[7] See Introduction, fn 42.

[8] Quinn, *Shah 'Abbās*, 31.

[9] Ibid, 36, and Babayan, *Mystics, Monarchs and Messiah*, 90-108.

they played an important role in the daily life of the people. The four analytical sections of this chapter serve to recognize the shifting aspects of political legitimacy as expressed in these materials.

By reconstructing the legitimizing patterns of kingship in Safavid cultural materials, this chapter portrays the trajectory of Safavid ideology through the Safavid history.[10] While this chapter pays special attention to the elements of Shi'i ideology and its formation within the Safavid discourse, it demonstrates that the main elements of the Safavid ideology – ruling as the shadow of God on earth, ruling as the head of Sufi order, and ruling as the representative of the hidden Imam – were not simultaneously emphasized in various sources throughout Safavid history. From the reign of Shah 'Abbās I, the Sunni titles of kingship, which dominated during the reign of the first four Safavid kings, were gradually replaced by titles and patterns that demonstrated the king in subservient position to Twelver Shi'i Imams. However, the materials remaining from the last two Safavid kings demonstrate that by end of the reign of Shah Sultan Ḥusayn (b. 1668 – d. 1726), the patterns of political legitimacy of Shah Ismā'īl's period came back in position with an emphasis on the similarity between the Safavid kings and pre-Islamic Persian kings. The materials of Shah Sultan Ḥusayn's time emphasized the pre-Islamic forms of kingship within the political framework of Shi'i doctrines. This form of representation allowed the Safavid kings to declare power based on Islamic imamatship. Part V is the concluding section and sets the stage for the next chapter.

---

[10] The translations of mints on coins and the inscriptions are by the author unless otherwise noted.

II. Coins, Royal Seals, *Ṭughrās*[11]

Coinage systems are an important historical source for studying the core

ideology of any dynasty, including the Safavids. Coins manifest elements of power

that introduce the principles of the relevant rulership. The titles, benedictions, and

images on coins illustrate how each king was perceived at the time and indicate the

main ideas that was associated with him. Safavid coins were impacted by the change

of state religion. However, this change did not have a great impact on the coins until

the reign of Shah ʿAbbās I. Investigation of the mints demonstrates the instability of

Safavid ideology until the reign of Shah ʿAbbās I (see Table 2).[12]

At first, Shah Ismāʿīl adopted the Āq Qūyūnlū (r. 1378 – 1501)[13] prototypes

with comparable titles and benedictions. Before coming to the throne, Shah ʿIsmāʿīl

minted the phrase: "who shelters with the righteous will be saved." However, after

coming to the throne, the inscriptions gradually changed to comprise the word of the

Shahādat, the phrase *ʿAlī valī Allāh* (ʿAlī is the vicegerent of Allah), the names of

twelve Shiʿi Imams on the obverse, and the name and benediction of the Safavid king

on its reverse. To already existing titles such as al-Sultan (the sovereign), *al-ʿādil* (the

---

[11] For coins, see Malek National Library and Museum Institution's website. The Safavid coin collection in there is endowed by Haj Husayn Agha Malak to the museum. The images at the end of the chapter are mostly taken from this website.

[12] For more information on the Safavid coinage system, see Sughra Ismaʿili, *Sikkeh hā va Muhr hā-yi Dawreh-yi Ṣafavī,* (Tehran: Sāzmān-i Mīrās Farhangī, 2006), and Farzaneh Qaʿini, *Sikkeh hā-yi Dawreh-yi Ṣafavī* (Tehran: Pāzineh,2006).

[13] This dynasty also called the White Sheep Turkomans was a Persianate Sunni Oghuz Turkic tribal federation that ruled from 1378 to 1501 at regions which in present day is the countries of Armenia, Azerbaijan, Eastern Turkey, and the majority of Iran and Iraq. Their power was undermined by the Safavids by the final years of the fifteenth century when finally, Shah ʿIsmāʿīl I defeated them in the battle of Nakhjivan and seized the throne.

just), *al-kāmil* (the complete), *al-hādī* (the guide), and *al-vālī* (the vicegerent), which were previously used for rulers with an important Shi'ite religious order, Shah Ismā'īl added titles such as *bahādur* (courageous) and *al-muẓaffar* (victorious) to underscore his physical power. Further, *al-ḥusaynī* and *al-ṣafavī* were added to the royal inscriptions on his coins to accentuate the religious background of the king (See Figure 1).

The coinage system under Ṭahmāsb revolved around his important goal, which reinforces the idea of ruling in the absence of Imam Mahdī as well as servitude toward him. While titles such as *Sultan al-'ādil* were still available, phrases such as *ghulām-i Imam Mahdī* (the servant of Mahdī) and *ghulām-i Imam 'Alī* were used to demonstrate the king's servitude and commitment to the persons of Imams, emphasizing loyalty to the 'Alid family. The reverse side continued with the names of twelve Shi'i Imams (see Figure 2).

Safavid ideology was altered during the reign of Shah Ismā'īl II (b. 1537 – d. 1577). The king ordered the elimination of all Shi'i expressions and the names of Shi'i imams from coins. Ismā'īl II was accused of attempting to re-establish rule in accordance with traditional Sunni practices. He banned the practice of cursing the caliphs and dedicated a source of income to those families who had never been disrespectful to the caliphs (see Figure 3).[14] References to the Shi'i Imams on coins

---

[14] Regarding coin design changes, Iskandar Beyg Munshī in *'Ālam Ārāy-i 'Abbāsī* mentioned that Ismā'īl II believed if a non-Muslim touched a coin, especially the words of *shahādat*, they would become untouchable and equal in status to excrement. He ordered the replacement of the expression *'Alī Valī Allāh* (Ali is the representative of Allah) with the Persian verse ز مشرق تا به مغرب گر امام است/ علی و آل او ما را تمام است (if there is one Imam from west to east/It is 'Alī and his family who are enough for us) in order to show his attachment to the primary causes of his Sufi background, i.e. commitment to the Alid family. (Kazim Musavi Bujnurdi, Hasan Riza'i Baghbidi., Mahmud Ja'fari-Dehaghi, Sadiq Sajjadi, *Tārīkh-i*

reappeared again during the rule of Shah Muḥammad Khudābandeh (b. 1532 – d. 1595). They were modeled on the coins of Shah Ṭahmāsb's reign. Expressions such as *ghulām-i Imam Mahdī* (the servant of Imam Mahdī) became common again during Khudābandeh's reign (see Figures 4 and 5).

Shah ʿAbbās gradually formed his political framework. He established his position between the people, the state, and religious scholars. Piety and subservience to the "true" religion were the best ways for the king to compel ordinary people, the elite, and religious scholars to accept him as the righteous ruler, similar to Imams, and follow his commands. Shah ʿAbbās's system of reign was very similar to Shah Ṭahmāsb's. By placing distance between himself and the regular symbols of power in public, and further by announcing his servitude toward the Shiʿi Imams, Shah ʿAbbās moved the monarchy away from the Safavid past and took serious steps in increasing the orthodox character of the Safavids as a Shiʿi state in which religious discourse was dominant and the king was to rule based on religious directives.[15]

Bandeh-yi Shah-i vilāyat (the servant of the king of sovereignty)[16] was the dominant script on his coins. Rhythmic sentences on the coins became common from Shah ʿAbbās I's reign and never faded thereafter. ʿAbbās I minted *az bahr-i khayr īn sikkeh rā kalb-i ʿAlī ʿAbbās zad* (for [the public] good, the guard dog of ʿAlī, ʿAbbās, minted this coin). These titles and expressions foreground the Shiʿi aspects of the

Jāmiʿ-i Īrān (Iran: Markaz-i Dāʾirat al-Maʿārif-i Buzurg-i Islāmī, Markaz-i Pizhūhish hā-yi Īrānī va Islāmī, 2014.

[15] Quinn, *Shah ʿAbbās*, 43 and Babayan, *Mystics, Monarchs and Messiah*, 90-106.

[16] This is a dominant term for referring to Imam ʿAlī. This was a unique title for a Safavid shah that depicted commitment and modesty towards the Shiʿi cause.

kingship. The titles that introduce Shah 'Abbās as a mere servant of Shi'ism linked the Safavid king to Shi'i doctrine and implied obedience to the one and true caliph after the Prophet, i.e Imam 'Alī, who indeed was not interested in Muslim leadership and did not himself claim the power after the prophet's death. On the one hand, by connecting himself to Imam 'Alī, Shah 'Abbās I and his courtiers were presented as pious retainers of Imam 'Alī's instructions and legacies. On the other, they presented new views of power and sovereignty, which distinguished them from the other Muslim kings of time. Shah 'Abbās was known for his friendly manners with the people of the society and as a king who supported the poor against the unfair tradesmen of the time. Emphasizing the king's justice through minting the expressions of *'adl* (justice) and *'adl-i shahī* (kingly justice) helped Shah 'Abbās I to retain the image of a pious king in the eyes of the people (see Figure 6).

Although historians of his time tend to make connections between Shah 'Abbās and the Muslim world conqueror Tīmūr (b. 1336 – d. 1405 CE) in regard to legitimization, Safavid coins did not demonstrate this tendency during the reign of Shah 'Abbās I. Nevertheless, the title *ṣāhib-qirān* (Supreme Lord of the Auspicious Conjunction), along with the king's name and lineage, appeared on the coins starting from the reign of Shah Ṣafī (see Figure 7).[17] Unlike *farr*, *ṣāhib-qirān* augured predestined and everlasting success for its fortunate possessor.[18] The expression *sikkeh-yi ṣāhib-qirān-ī* (The coin of the Lord of the Conjunction) was used within a

---

[17] The concept of *ṣāhib-qirān* was based on a projection of everlasting good fortune due to an auspicious birth, when two auspicious stars had gathered in one constellation. This event was referred to as *qirān al-Sa'dayn*. The concept has been explained in the introduction of this work.

[18] Quinn, *Shah 'Abbās*, 64-67. See Introduction to read about *farr*.

Persian verse on the reverse side of the coinage during Shah Ṣafī's term. Titles of

servitude were still minted on the coins after him (see Shah ʿAbbās II's coins in

Figures 8 and 9). Similarly, in other periods, the coins' reverse, had the names of

imams. *Ṣāhib-qirān* stayed on coins during the reign of Ṣafī II, famous as Shah

Sulaymān (b. 1646 – d. 1692). Sulaymān did not change the expression *sikkeh-yi*

ṣāhib-qirān-ī, and by bringing forth his father's name, he brought his father's

legitimacy and power to his own kingship (see Figure 10).[19] Ḥusayn continued to call

himself *bandeh-yi shah-i vilāyat* to show his Shiʿi intentions (see Figures 11 and 12).[20]

The royal seals[21] also presented similar ideological patterns by expressing titles

of servitude. The seals were declarative of Safavid power within the state and abroad.

Unlike coins, the seals were not displayed in public daily; nevertheless, seals served a

---

[19] Some of the verses include:

به گیتی بعد شاه عباس ثانی

صفی زد سکه صاحبقرانی

    After Shah ʿAbbās II in the world
    it was Ṣafī who minted *sikkeh-yi Ṣāḥib-qirānī*

[20] Another example:

سکه مهر علی تا زدم بر نقد جان

گشت از فضل خدا محکوم فرمانم جهان

زد از توفیق الله سکه صاحبقران

صاحب دوران سلیمان جهان

    as I minted the coin for ʿAlī from my soul
    By God's kindness the world came under my power

    By God's help he minted the *sikkeh-yi ṣāhib qirān*
    the owner of the world, Sulaymān

[21] The Safavid monarchs wrote official orders to address other kings as well as to send
messages to nobles and regional leaders under their reign. The seals of differing shapes served different
functions. The most common nine seals of the Safavid courts were *nishān, khalʿat, kūchak, khatm,
musavvada, innā fatahnā, ṣabt, sharaf, nifāz̲* and *julūs*. For more on this, read Jahangir Qaʿim Maqami,
"Muhr hā-yi Nowyāfteh-yi Pādishāhān-i Irān az Īlkhān tā Pāyān-i Qājār", *Barrasī-yi Tarīkhī*, 7th year,
no. 2, 95-108.

public function. They were used on letters and official orders and they contained special features that worked towards legitimizing the Safavid kingship based on making associations between the Safavid kings and the Shi'i Imams. The seals had inscriptions that declared the political and religious role of each Safavid king. Love and respect for the family of the prophet, which were factors that played a significant part in the Safavid legacy, appeared on the seals. Ismā'īl I made a special seal for himself with the motto, *ghulām-i shah-i mardān, Ismā'īl ibn Ḥaydar* (the servant of the king of all men, Ismā'īl the son of Ḥaydar).[22] Shah 'Abbās I had the name of the fourteen infallibles[23] on his seals. From Shah 'Abbās II, the seals applied more Persian verses in praise of Imam 'Alī and his family. The seals of Sultan Ḥusayn also applied Persian verses and expressions. *Kalb-i kamtarīn-i amīr al-mu'minīn* (the least guard dog of Imam 'Alī) and *bandeh-yi farmānbar-i mawlā-yi haq sultan Ḥusayn* (the obedient servant of righteous leader Sultan Ḥusayn) were among the titles chosen by the king.[24] The end result displayed the kingly features of the ruler mixed with the religious discourses for the public presentation of power.

---

[22] There are other examples of Ismā'īl's seals, such as حفظهما على العظيم ا ماعيل بن حيدر بن جنيد صفوى 909 هجرى قمرى which claimed power based on lineal family. This verse also has been found in a seal by Ismā'īl that indicated claiming the power based on love for 'Alī.

بود مهر على و آل او چون مرا در بر
غلام شاه مردان است اسماعيل بن حيدر

Because love for Ali and his family is in me
Ismā'īl Ibn Ḥaydar is the slave of the kings of men

[23] The fourteen infallibles are the prophet Muḥammad, Fāṭemeh (his daughter), and the twelve Imams from Imam 'Alī to Imam Mahdi. The latter is believed will appear to cleanse the world from corruption.

[24] Isma'ili, *Sikkeh hā wa Muhr hā-yi Dawreh-yi Ṣafavī*, 2006.

The declarations of power on *ṭughrā*s[25] are similar to those found on the seals.
The *ṭughrā*, the symbol of kingship, was engraved on official orders. At first, the
ṭughrā was designed beautifully with carved lines displaying the names and titles of
the kings. From the time of Shah 'Abbās onwards, they developed more complicated
shapes and longer sentences. Some *ṭughrā*s had twelve sections, each dedicated to the
name of one Imam. The most famous sentences on *ṭughrā*s were, "the royal order is
blessed,"[26] "the world followed the royal order,"[27] and "the royal order was dignified
by executions".[28] In general, the changes of titles and benedictions on the coins, royal
seals, and *ṭughrā*s demonstrate that implementation of Shi'i notions into the political
framework of the Safavids experienced constant changes until Shah 'Abbās. Gradually
by Shah 'Abbās period, the forms of titles and statements became stable and continued
on to the periods of his successors.

---

[25] Ṭughrā is a calligraphic monogram, seal or signature of Sultan that was affixed to all official
documents and correspondence. It was also stamped on the coins.

[26] فرمان همايون شد

[27] حکم جهان مطاع شد

[28] فرمان همايون شرف نفاد يافت

Table 2. The Benedictions of Safavid Coins

Kings	Expressions on obverse
Shah Ismāʻīl	The sovereign, the complete, the guide, the vicegerent, Shah, al-Ḥusaynī, al-Ṣafavī
Shah Ṭahmāsb	The sovereign, Shah, the servant of Imam Mahdī, the servant of Imam ʻAlī
Shah Ismāʻīl II	His name, Shah
Shah Muḥammad Khudabandeh	The servant of Imam Mahdī, Shah
Shah ʻAbbās I	The servant of the king of sovereignty, the dog of ʻAli
Shah Ṣafī	Ṣāhib-qirān
Shah ʻAbbās II	Ṣāhib-qirān
Shah Sulaymān	Ṣāhib-qirān
Shah Sultan Ḥusayn	The servant of the king of sovereignty

III. Ceremonies of Royal Investiture

Days of coronation were important historical events for rulers. By transferring power from one ruler to another within the same Muslim dynasty or the change of power from one dynasty to a new Muslim dynasty, the celebration for new kings coming to the throne and the ceremony of coronation were important days to be commemorated and discussed. In chronicles and travelogues of the time the days of enthronements were partially mentioned by historians who attempted to shed light on the different aspects of such an important event.

The role of religious scholars in those days was especially in the center of attention. There exist narratives in which the religious scholars were asked to give an oration for the new king's inauguration. Muḥaqqiq Karakī (d. 1533), famous as Muhaqqiq al-S̲ānī and who supported Shah Ismāʻīl and Shah Ṭahmāsb (b. 1514 – d. 1576)   in making Shiʻism the state religion, had a son by the name of Shaykh ʻAbdul ʻĀli who spread the "rug of sovereignty"[29] for the ascension of Shah Ismāʻīl II

---

[29]Although this term is used to refer to the actual ceremony of royal investiture, there was a rug given to the new king in the ceremony which was famous as "rug of sovereignty." *Sajjādeh-yi*

and Muḥammad Khudābandeh.[30] In the 17th century, when Isfahan became the permanent capital of the Safavid rulers and Shi'ism was the state religion, the inauguration of a new monarch was entrusted to the hands of the *Shaykh al-Islām* of the capital. Mīr Dāmād (d. 1631) conducted the coronation for Shah Ṣafī. The event was recorded by Khawjigī Iṣfahānī in *Khulāṣat al-Siyar*. He wrote that the day "contained the blessing time"; therefore, it was a perfect day for the king who "deserved the throne and crown" to be announced as the king. Khawjigī Iṣfahānī made sure to use the adjectives "completeness" and "comprehensiveness" for Mīr Dāmād in order to show when such a religious scholar legitimizes a king, the king is definitely God's representative on earth:[31]

آن روز که حامل نور سعادت بود به سیادت پناه حقایق و معارف آگاه، جامع المعقول و المنقول، حاوی الفروع و الاصول، کاشف رموز الباطن و الظاهر، صاحب الصلاح و السداد، خاتم المجتهدین امیر محمد

---

irshād with the early Safavids became one of the regalia used in coronations. In Shah Ismā'īl II's coronation, this rug was referred to as the *qālicheh-yi salṭanat* (rug of sovereignty). As Arjomand mentioned, this idea was completely forgotten by the time of Sulaymān. During the reign of Ṣafī II, it was described as the *qālicheh-yi irshād* in one source and as the *qālicheh-yi 'adālat* (rug of justice) in another source. According to Arjomand, "This ceremonial juxtaposition of the norms of *irshād* and justice, deriving respectively from the Sufi and the patrimonial ethos, illustrates the transition from the former to the latter norm, which aimed at legitimating Safavid rule in the eyes of the sedentary majority, and which was in fact completed by that time." See Sa'id Amir Arjomand, *The Shadow of God and the Hidden Imam: Religion, Political Order, and Societal Change in Shi'ite Iran From the Beginning to 1890* (Chicago: University of Chicago Press, 1984), 180.

[30] Āfūshteh narrated a story in which Shah Ismā'īl asked him to attend the inauguration and open up the rug for him, symbolically confirming his kingship and reminding him that his father was a true supporter of the king. Āfūshteh wrote that Sheikh 'Abdul 'Ali rejected this request, stating that his father was not a *farrāsh* to anyone, so the king should not expect him to be one. See Kazim Musavi Bujnurdi, Hasan Riza'i Baghbidi., Mahmud Ja'fari-Dehaghi, Sadiq Sajjadi, *Tārīkh-i Jāmi'-i Īrān* (Iran: Markaz-i Dā'irat al-Ma'ārif-i Buzurg-i Islāmī, Markaz-i Pizhūhish hā-yi Īrānī va Islāmī, 2014, Said Amir Arjomand, also, in a discussion of Safavid sovereignty and its similarity with the royal Persian Sasanid kings, provided an account on the coronation of the Sultan Sulaymān and the following kings. See Sa'id Amir Arjomand, *The Shadow of God and the Hidden Imam: Religion, Political Order, and Societal Change in Shi'ite Iran From the Beginning to 1890* (Chicago: University of Chicago Press, 1984), Rasul Ja'fariyan, in his khabaronline weblog (http://www.khabaronline.ir/detail/567603/weblog/jafarian), presented the coronations and the narratives of these incidents from different historical sources.

[31] For reading about this event, read Muḥammad Ma'ṣūm ibn Khwajigī Iṣfahānī, *Khulāṣat al-Siyar: Tārīkh-i Rūzgār-i Shāh Ṣafī Ṣafavī* (Tehran: 'Ilmī, 1989).

باقر داماد سلمه الله تعالی و حفظ وجوده عن الآفات إلی یوم التناد حاضر ساخته به جهت مثنی ساختن
امر جلوس در آن ساعت سعادت مأنوس بعد از شرایط دعا و فاتحه خوانی یکبار دیگر آن زیبنده ی تاج
و تخت را در عمارت مذکور بر اورنگ سلطنت و مسند دولت تمکن داده

> On that day, which contained the lights of fortune, under the
> supervision of the shelter of truth and awareness of knowledge,
> the uniter of rational and narrated sciences, the comprehender of
> the principles (*usūl*) and ancillaries (*furū'*) of the law, the
> revealer of exterior and inner secrets, the owner of right and
> truth, the seal of mujtahids, Amir Muḥammad Bāqir Dāmād,
> may God keep him safe from all illnesses to the day of judgment,
> was called to enthrone the king for the second time on a good
> omen. After praying and reading *Fātiḥeh*, one more time he who
> is befitting of the throne and crown sat in that mansion on the
> throne of kingship and the buttress of the state.[32]

Vāleh Qazvīnī did not indicate the name of any scholar who read the oration for
Shah 'Abbās II. However, he wrote that the "people of earth" read the oration for him
as his kingship was already confirmed by "the preachers of the nine heavens", i,e the
sun, moon and the stars.

چون خطبای منبر نه پایه افلاک در آن لیلة القدر شادمانی خطبه جلوس همایون را به مسامع آسمانیان
رسانیده بودند. زمینیان نیز خطبه بلیغه ی تفویض سلطنت ربع مسکون را در آن روز فیروز شنیده
گوشوار شادمانی نمودند

> Because the preachers of nine-heaven on the happy night of
> decree had delivered the enthronement oration of the royal
> ascension to the ears of the celestials, the people of earth also
> heard the well-written enthronement oration through which the
> kingship of the inhabited quarter was given to him on that day
> of good fortune and they wear it like earrings.[33]

Khuṭbeh (enthronement oration), an address delivered by a *khatīb* (orator) as
part of a religious service, could be a place for legitimizing the kingship.[34] Elements in

---

[32] Ibid, 38.

[33] Muḥammad Yūsuf Vāleh Iṣfahānī, *Īrān dar Zamān-i Shāh Ṣafī va Shāh 'Abbās-i Duvvum
Ḥadīqah-yi Shishum va Haftum az Rawżeh-yi Shishum-i Khuld-i Barīn*, ed. Muhammad Riza Nasiri,
(Tehran: Anjuman-i Ās̲ār va Mafākhir-i Farhangī, 2001), 371.

[34] The oration fulfills a religious mandate associated with specific occasions such as the
weekly congregational Friday service, the two 'Īd holidays, and the day of 'Arafāt during the *hajj*.
Orations could also be delivered by popular preachers. on other occasions, such as a marriage contract
ceremony or during an eclipse Orations usually were given in mosques but given the expansion of the
Islamic domain and the appearance of imperial caliphal administration, the mosque became less of an
instrument for managing the polity. Instead, it became used for solely religious practices. However, the

the enthronement orations speak of the loyalty between the religious scholars and the kings in managing the affairs of the state and religion.[35] As religion was meant to guide life in general, religious charisma could bestow legitimacy on non-religious activities. The *'ulama* could legitimize non-religious activities, including kingship. Through a speech or a written official letter, it was usually a religious scholar who confirmed the sovereignty of a king. The religious scholars depicted the Safavid king as the spiritual leader of the Muslim community and whose Persianate blood and Shi'i lineage made them a source of power in this world. During these coronations, usually the position of king was displayed as divine, decided by God on the day of creation.

The oration of the last Safavid king, Shah Sultan Ḥusayn, demonstrates that the main attempt of the orator was to establish a tie between the concept of kingship and imamatship for Shah Sulṭān Ḥusayn. In this oration, the notions of Persianate kingship

---

oration, which dealt with political, military, and other state affairs, in earlier days was pronounced by the sovereign himself or his governors and generals but now could be delivered by religious scholarsMubarak Hadia. "Khuṭbah". Oxford Islamic Studies Online, http://www.oxfordislamicstudies.com/article/opr/t236/e0461

[35] The relationship between religious scholars and the Safavid monarchs is a long and documented relationship for both sides. The Safavid monarchs realized that 'Amilīs (a Shi'i family that Shah Ismā'īl provided an opportunity in Iran to spread Shi'ism and educate the people of Shi'i instructions) scholarship was highly regarded among the Shi'ite intellectuals. Patronizing the 'Amilīs provided legitimacy and imperial sovereignty. On the other hand, the Safavids could provide the 'Amilīs with the power and prestige they needed. The 'Amilīs gained significant power during the Safavid rule and achieved important positions in religious and civic institutions such as *shaykh al-Islam*, the highest religious position, and *pīsh namāz*, the prayer leaders for the royal court and the great city mosques. The new empire needed clerics like 'Amilis who could bestow upon them the legitimacy they needed to distinguish themselves from the caliphate kingship. Performing Friday prayers was the best example of a practice that could deepen the theological differences between the community of Shi'is and Sunnis. The 'Amilis opened new vistas in the interpretive capacity of religious law, which was important for the empire as they offered theologically acceptable rationalizations for the ideological shift the Safavids sought to create. Rula Abisaab, in *Converting Persia: Shi'a Islam and the Safavid Empire* (London: I. B. Tauris, 2015), explains how and why the Arab *'ulamā* were brought from Ottoman Syria to Iran. She explains how these émigré scholars changed the face of religion in Iran and furnished source of legitimacy for the Safavid monarchs. For more information, also see Andrew Newman, *Safavid Iran: Rebirth of a Persian Empire*, (I.B. Tauris, 2012).

(titles that also were used to refer to Shah Ismā'īl) mixed with Shi'i ideas of kingship (references to Shi'i doctrine as well as the expressions of servitude towards the Shi'i Imams, those which were similar to the expressions that were dominant during the Shah 'Abbās I's reign) in order to declare power for this particular king.

Shah Ṣafī II had two inaugurations.[36] Mīrzā 'Alī Riżā read his first enthronement oration, which started in praise of God and continued with praise for the Prophet and the other twelve imams. The main body of the enthronement oration indicated that kingship is a gift from God that is given to the Safavid kings. The Safavid kings, as described in the text, were from the *"nijād"* (offspring) of imams elected by God for kingship. He finished the oration by wishing a long life for the king and his throne. Information on the second ceremony is very sparse, but it was known that Muḥammad Bāqir Sabzivārī (d. 1679) was the scholar who confirmed Shah Ṣafī II 's kingship.[37]

Shah Sultan Ḥusayn asked Muḥammad Bāqir Majlisī (b. 1627 – d. 1699), the renowned and very powerful Iranian Shi'i scholar, to read a sermon for his appointment. This enthronement oration was given in 'Abbāsī Congregational mosque. It started with the creation of Adam and the necessity of having a spiritual leader since then. Majlisī, by starting the oration with a discussion of the prophets' responsibility in guiding the people, opened up the path toward comparing the prophets and imams with the Safavid king. He argued that the prophets, who

---

[36] For more reading on his inauguration, read John Chardin, *Safarnāmeh-yi Shārdan: Matn-i kāmil*, trans Iqbal Yaghma'i (Tehran: Tūs, 1993). Vol. 4, 1591-1599. Also see Arjomand, *The Shadow of God and the Hidden Imam,* 178-80.

[37] For more information, see Ja'fariyan, Rasul, http://www.khabaronline.ir/detail/567603/weblog/jafarian, Murdād: 1395.

organized matters of *dīn* (religion) and *dunyā* (world), came to this world to guide the

people who were lost in the deserts of *ḥayrat* (skepticism) and *żalālat* (deviation).

Then, he connected the necessity of guidance with the concept of kingship and

introduced Safavid kingship, the righteous form of kingship in the absence of Imam

Mahdī.

... بعد از غروب خورشید سپهر نبوت در افق عالم بقا و احتجاب اقمار فلک امامت در نقاب غیبت و

سحاب اختفا قادر بی‌منت و خالق بی‌ضنت از مزید لطف و مرحمت بر بقایای این امت مقالید فرمانروایی

و مفاتیح کشورگشایی را در کف کفایت و قبضه‌ی درایت سلاطین عدالت شعار و خواقین فلک اقتدار

سپرده که عامه‌ی رعایا و کافه‌ی برایا در ظل ظلیل ایشان در مهاد امنیت و استراحت بیاسایند و از جور

و عدوان ارباب ظلم و طغیان نجات یابند ...

> ... After that, the sun of the sky of prophecy disappeared in the
> world of eternity; and after hiding the moons of Imamate under
> the mask of absence and the clouds of secrecy; the unfailing
> competitor, and the generous creator, because of its kindness
> and generosity had toward this nation, he put the keys of rule
> and conquest in adequate hands and the knowing grasp of kings
> with tact; the kings whose slogan is justice and the kings whose
> power is similar to eternity. His purpose provided for the entire
> regular and selected people a shadow under which they rest in
> peace and security; and to save them from the oppression and
> enmity of the lords of revolt...[38]

Then, the kings were introduced by their justice, power, and mercy. Their

appointment to rule was the choice of God, who seeks blessing for its people. God is

the merciful, and this principle is evident from God's choice of a king who is kind, just,

and caring:

... اراده‌ی کریم لایزال...تشریف سلطنت و جهانبانی بر قامت استقامت شهریاری پوشد که نصب العین

خاطر خورشید ناظرش بسط بساط رأفت و عدالت و خفض جناح مرحمت و مکرمت بر کافه امت بوده

باشد ...

> ...The undying will of God...put the dress of sultanate and
> world-guarding on the enduring body of an *amīr* who, the target
> of his eyes and his sun-like wisdom is perpetuating kindness,
> just and covering all people under the wings of mercy and
> compassion...[39]

---

[38] Majlisī M. *Khuṭbeh-yi Julūs-i Shāh Sulṭān Ḥusayn bar Takht-i Salṭanat*, Majlis Library, IR 10-26866, http://dlib.ical.ir/faces/search/bibliographic/biblioFullView.jspx?_afPfm=-lj69h0hwa.

[39] Ibid.

Majlisī continued his speech by indicating that the people under the just kingship of the Safavids lived in comfort and ease for many years. He indicated the people enjoyed unlimited favors from the Safavid kingship, and that under their rule, people were saved from the darkness of infidelity and wonder. Majlisī saw it as the people's duty to respect the Safavid kings and appreciate their efforts. He described Safavid kings as suns of the elevated skies and moons of guidance.

... بر ذمت همت کافه شیعیان و عامه‌ی مؤمنان که ضمیر حقایق تصویر ایشان به نور ایمان منور گردیده

شکر نعمت هر یک از افراد انجاد این سلسله عالیه که شموس فلک رفعت و جلالت و اقمار بروج

هدایت و ولایت اند متحتم و لازم است ...

> ...It is the responsibility of all Shi'ites and the believers whose soul is lightened by the brightness of faith to appreciate the blessing of prosperity the bravest people of this family, who are the suns of high and glorious skies and the moons of guidance and leadership...[40]

Unlike the patterns on coins which avoided using the royal titles to refer to the kings from Shah 'Abbās's time, Majlīsī did not hesitate to make connection between the Safavid kings and pre-Islamic kings of Persia. Majlīsī applied the names of historical Persian kings to refer to the current Safavid king to claim the associated sacredness that existed in the position of kingship for the Safavid kings. He also mentioned the link between the Safavid kings and the family of Muḥammad and 'Alid lineage to argue for the Shah Sultan Ḥusayn's legitimacy:

... مالک ملک و واهب سلطنت ... خلعت شهریاری بر قامت با رفعت نونهالی پوشانیده ... أعنی شهریار

عادل باذل گردون بارگاه ملایک سپاه جمشید حشمت فریدون شوکت سکندر شأن دارا دربان گل

گلدسته گلستان مصطفوی نوباوه‌ی بوستان مرتضوی شجره‌ی نبوت و رسالت غصن دوحه‌ی

امامت و ولایت ... رافع لوای دین و دولت اساس ملک و ملت قطب فلک اقتدار مرکز آسمان عدالت

و وقار مجری مراسم ملت و دین و مروج مذاهب ائمه طاهرین ... "

> The owner of kingship and the giver of sultanate ... dressed up the robe of kingship to a seedling tree with sublimity ... I mean the just generous king whose court is the heaven, his army is from the angels, his retinue is similar to Jamshīd, his

---

[40] Majlisī M. *Khuṭbeh-yi Julūs-i Shāh Sulṭān Ḥusayn bar Takht-i Salṭanat,* Majlis Library, IR 10-26866, http://dlib.ical.ir/faces/search/bibliographic/biblioFullView.jspx?_afPfm=-lj69h0hwa.

> glory is similar to Firīdūn and his dignity is comparable to
> Alexander. Darius is his doorkeeper. He is the best flower of
> the muṣṭafavī garden, and the new fruit of murtaẓavī garden.
> He is the tree of prophecy and the new branch of the tree of
> the Imamate and *vilāyat* ... The upholder of flag of religion
> and governance, the basis of kingship and nation, the pole of
> sky of power, the center of the sky of justice and dignity, the
> executive of religion traditions and propagator of religious
> Imams.[41]

The names of historical Persian kings came along with Shi'i expressions for legitimizing purposes. Expressions of servitude also are present.

> ... سلطان دین پرور و خاقان معدلت گستر جم نشان فریدون فر سلیمان مکان خورشید افسر
> نبوی حسب مرتضوی نسب جعفری مذهب موسوی ادب زیبنده تاج وتخت کیانی وارث مرتبه
> سلیمانی ... خسرو جم قدر فلک اقتدار داور دین پرور والاتبار برگزیده کردگار آسمان و زمین
> قهرمان مطلق العنان ما و طین غلام باخلاص امیرالمومنین ملاذ اعظم السلاطین معاذ اکارم
> الخواقین حامی حوزة الدین حارس شریعت سید المرسلین مروج طریقة الائمه الطاهرین ...

> ...The Sultan who nurtures religion, The Khaqan who
> distributes justice, and whose seal is similar to Jam and his
> glory to Firīdūn. His place is similar to Sulaymān whose
> crown is the sun. His dignity is prophetic, and he is
> descendant from Murtaẓā [prophet Muḥammad]. His religion
> is of the Imam Ja'far and his manner is of Moses. He
> deserved the throne and crown of Kianids. He inherited the
> high-valued position of Solomon.... The king whose glory is
> Jam-like, his power is heavenly, he is the judge who nurtures
> the religion, appointed by the creator of the heavens and the
> earth. He is the true hero and the controller of the water and
> earth, the true servant of amīr al-Mu'minīn [Ali], the shelter
> of the greatest Sultans, the shelter of the best Khaqans, the
> supporter of the religion's realm, the guardian of the
> prophet's laws and the traditions of the purest Imams...[42]

In general, tracing the notions of legitimacy in the texts remaining from royal coronations establishes that Shi'i legitimacy was an inseparable theme for claiming power in public. Given power by Shah 'Abbās, the religious scholars found important common ground among the masses; therefore, religious language came to affect the political language of time. Phrases that depicted the kings as the leaders of the religion

---

[41] Ibid.

[42] Jung, Majlis Library IR10-20876, 3455/1,
http://dlib.ical.ir/faces/search/bibliographic/biblioFullView.jspx?_afPfm=wb83b8wvh

and the people became dominant, and Shi'i lineage came to play an important role in

legitimizing the kings. These phrases presented the king as a pious Muslim leader in

charge of affairs of the state. Shah Sultan Ḥusayn, the last Safavid king represented

the culmination of all of the previously practiced sources of legitimacy outlined above.

Majlisī, by discussing the king's special features such as justice, war abilities, and

God-given wisdom, and by emphasizing the kings' similarity with ancient Persian

kings as well as the Shi'i lineage of the Safavid family, legitimized the role of

kingship in the absence of a just Imam. By discussing state and religion as two

important elements for the role of a king, Majlisī encouraged the people to submit to

the authority of the Shah and his instructions, in same way they would submit to the

religious and political instructions of an Imam if such a person were available.

IV. Inscriptions[43]

The inscriptions of mosques, domes, and schools are among the materials that

support our understanding of the public image of the Safavid kings. There are

numerous inscriptions especially from Isfahan's buildings, but their structure and

content offer slight transitions from one king to another. Studying the patterns of these

*katībeh*s (inscriptions) illustrates the intrusion of the religious role of the kings into the

realm of kingship in the absence of an Imam from the middle years of the Safavid

dynasty. The last Safavid inscriptions collected the ideas and phrases from earlier

inscriptions, which emphasized material power of the kingship to serve the religio-

political framework of the Safavids. The content of these inscriptions, similar to the

---

[43] By inscription I mean the writings inscribed on the exterior and interior walls of different places including mosques, schools, and domes. For some pictures of the inscriptions, see end of the chapter.

coins, illustrate the control of a sovereign as the representative of God on earth over religion and state in order to guide the masses.

The inscriptions of Hārūn Vilāyat's mosque is among the earliest inscriptions remaining from Shah Ismāʿīl I. The inscription of this mosque depicted Shah Ismāʿīl as the warrior who deserves to be the caliph. Although the religious aspect of his kingship is implied, the inscription emphasizes the king's right to kingship because of his power and strength in the path of God:

.... فى أيام خلافة والى لواء الولاية فى الآفاق مالك سرير الخلافة بالاستحقاق الغازى المجاهد فى سبيل الله بقاطع البرهان ناصر المؤمنين ابى المظفر السلطان شاه اسماعيل بهادرخان....

> …in the days of the guardian of the banner of guardianship in
> the horizon, the entitled owner of the throne of Caliphate, the
> *mujāhid* conqueror in the cause of Allah with a decisive proof,
> the patron of the believers, the father of the triumphant, Sultan
> Shah Ismāʿīl Bahādur Khān…[44]

The inscription of ʿAlī mosque, however, gives a spiritual quality to the king by asserting that the number of kings' names in the *abjad* system is equal to the times the name of the twelve Imams that have been repeated in Quran. The relationship between the names of prophet, imams, or the Sufis with numbers that are considered as sacred (usually twelve for the twelve Shiʿi imams or 313, the number of Imam Mahdī's supporters upon his return), proves the truth of the kings' claims:

... هذا مسجد ... أسسه فى زمان من بيده مقاليد الزمان السلطان بن السلطان بن السلطان الذي إسمه جميل بعدد الائمة عليهم السلم فى التنزيل ابى المظفر سلطان شاه إسمعيل ...

> …this mosque…was established in the days of whom the keys
> of the time are in his hand, al-Sultan the son of al-Sultan the
> son of al-Sultan whose numerical of his name is equal to the
> times that the name of the twelve Imams, the peace of God upon

---

[44] Lutf Allah Hunarfar, *Ganjīneh-yi Ās̱ār-i Tārīkhī-i Iṣfahān: Ās̱ār-i Bāstānī Va Alvāḥ Va Katība hā-yi Tārīkhī dar Ustān-i Iṣfahān* (Isfahan: Kitābfurūshī-i Saqafī, 1965.), 361.

them, has repeated in Quran, the father of triumph, al-Sultan Shah Ismāʻīl...[45]

Unlike the majority of available Safavid sources, in which the link between the Safavid king and the family of Prophet Muḥammad is important, this *katībeh* does not evoke this tie. However, during the rule of Shah Ṭahmāsb, this theme started to be engraved on *katībeh*s. For example, the title *ḥusaynī* is added to the Shah's name in the inscriptions of Quṭbiyyeh's mosque:

[46] .. فى أيام دولة السلطان الأعظم و الخاقان الأكرم ظل الله على أهل الأيمان ابوالمظفر السلطان شاه طهماسب الحسينى بهادرخان ...

...in the days of the rule of the greatest sovereign and the most honorable king, the shadow of God on the people of faith, the father of triumph, al-Sultan, Shah Ṭahmāsb al-Ḥusaynī, Bahādur Khān[47]

The idea of a just, generous, forgiving king is repeated on the Darb-i Jūbāreh's mosque. Expressions such as "the [one] seated over the throne of justice" came along with titles such as *khāqān*, which are demonstrative of both aspects of a king, his personhood, and his royal features. References to the family of prophet also exist.[48] While loyalty to ʻAlī is evident, the expression of *muqaddama al-jaysh li-ṣāḥib al-zamān* (the vanguard of Imam Mahdi's army)[49] demonstrates the king's desire to be known as a Shiʻi king and to involve his reign with the idea of return.

The expression of *muravvij-i maẕhab-i aʻimmeh-yi eṣnā ʻashar* (the propagator of the right religion of the Twelver Shiʻism) started to be engraved in Shah ʻAbbās I's

---

[45] Ibid, 372.

[46] The first few words were not legible.

[47] Hunarfar, *Ganjīneh-yi Āsār-i Tārīkhī-i Iṣfahān*, 380.

[48] Ibid, 387.

[49] Ibid, 388.

period. Indications of Shi'i and Sufi genealogy also became dominant from his time.

Expressions such as *al-mūsavī* and *al-Safavī* refer to the Safavids' genealogy (see Table

14). Unlike the coins of his time, Shah 'Abbās, was portrayed with royal titles and

benedictions similar to other kings. While his glory is compared to *Jam* and his army

is said to be from the angels, titles such as *akram* (the most honorable), *akbar* (the

greatest), and *'adal* (the most just) are also applied to highlight his appropriateness for

kingship based on his personal characteristics. Inscriptions from Maqṣūd Beyg's

mosque, which was engraved in 1603, blended the notions of the king's personal

characteristics and his material power:

...در زمان دولت پادشاه جمجاه ملائک سپاه گردون بارگاه مروج مذهب ائمة اثنی عشر صلوات الله عليهم

من الملک الأکرم الأکبر الأعدل السلطان الأعظم و الخاقان الأکرم أبی المظفرشاه عباس الموسوي

الصفوي الحسيني...

> ...In the days of the rule of Jam-glorious king whose army is
> the angels, the heavens are his palace. He is the propagator
> of Twelver Shi'i faith, peace of god upon them from the most
> honorable king, the greater, the just king, the father of
> triumph, Shah 'Abbās al-Mūsavī al-Ṣafavī al-Ḥusaynī...[50]

The inscriptions on gates and walls of the buildings in Meydān-i Naqsh-i Jahān are

indicative of Shah 'Abbās I' desire to project the image of a king serving the religion

(see Figure 15). His Shi'i genealogy and his public religious actions emphasized by

various cultural products of his time validate this point. Shaykh Luṭf Allāh's inscription,

for example, introduces him as the reviver of the traditions of his ancestors and applies

all the titles for kings. At the same time, it emphasizes his role as the disseminator of

the religion of Imams.

أمر بإنشاء هذا المسجد المبارک السلطان الأعظم و الخاقان الأکرم محيئ مراسم آبائه الطاهرين مروج

مذهب الائمة المعصومين أبوالمظفر عباس الحسيني الموسوي الصفوي بهادرخان خلد الله تعالی ملکه و

---

[50] Hunarfar, *Ganjīneh-yi Āsār-i Tārīkhī-i Iṣfahān*, 468.

أجرى في بحار التأييد فلكه بمحمد و آله الطيبين الطاهرين المعصومين صلوات الله و سلامه عليه و عليهم ...

> Ordered to construct this blessed mosque the great sovereign and
> the honorable king, the reviver of the traditions of his pious
> fathers, the disseminator of the innocents Imams, the father of
> the triumphant, 'Abbās al-Ḥusaynī al-Ṣafavī al-Mūsavī Bahādur
> Khān, may Allah, exalted He, eternize his reign and sail his ship
> in the oceans of (divine) support by the virtue of Muḥammad and
> his noble, pure and infallible family, the peace of God on him
> and them...[51]

The attribution of *masjid-i* Shāh also invokes notions of genealogy. This attribution did not apply the words such as *al-Sulṭān* and *Shāh*. Instead, the king was presented as the humblest servant of the religion.[52]

أمر ببنا هذا المسجد الجامع من خالص ماله أشرف خواقين الأرض نسباً و أكرمهم حسباً أعظمعهم رفعة و شأناً و اقواهم حجة و برهاناً و أشملهم عدلاً و إحساناً تراب العتبة المقدسة النوبية و قمامة الساحة المطهرة العلوية أبوالمظفر عباس الحسيني الموسوي الصفوي ...

> Ordered to construct this congregational mosque from his
> personal wealth, the noblest kings of the earth racially and the
> most honorable one personally, the greatest of all positionally,
> and the strongest in justifying, his justice and kindness is the
> most inclusive one, the dust of the sacred threshold of the
> prophet, and the rubbish of 'Alī's pure square, the father of
> triumph, 'Abbās al-Ḥusaynī al-Mūsavī al-Ṣafavī...[53]

One of the less common expressions for Shah 'Abbās I is *mawlā mulūk-i al-'arab wa al-'ajam* (the leader of the Arab and Persian kings), which indicated the king's intention to show his authority. This expression was used in the inscriptions of the Sufrehchī and Jārchī mosques, both built in Isfahan during the reign of Shah 'Abbās I.

The inscription on the dome of the Shāh mosque, which begins with praising God who created the earth, the heavens, the Sun, and the Moon, may be one of the latest

---

[51] Ibid, 402.

[52] The same patterns used on the *katībeh*s of Masjid Ḥakīm and 'Āli Qāpū in Qazvin (see Figure 13.)

[53] Hunarfar, *Ganjīneh-yi Āṣār-i Tārīkhī-i Iṣfahān*, 429.

inscriptions in the name of Shah 'Abbās I. The inscription continues with expressions of servitude and love for the Prophet Muḥammad and his family. Furthermore, it announces a commitment to Imam 'Alī and his legacies, and it is a space for re-claiming *bay'at* (pledge of allegiance) with him. It sends wishes of peace to those who believed Imam 'Alī was the prophet's successor and vizier.

As seen with coins, the expression "the guard dog of Ali's threshold" was part of the political language of the king, while the propagation of the Twelver Shi'ism was a popular theme as well. Servitude for Imam 'Alī and expressions of humility in serving Shi'ism were not only minted on coins, but they were also indicated on some mosques, for example the Bābā Rukn al-Dīn mosque:

"بتأييد الله الواحد الباقي قد أرتفع عمارة هذه البقعة الملكوتية في أيام دولة كلب سدة على إبن ابي طالب و سلامه عليه عباس الحسيني بهادر خان ... "

> "with the support of the one everlasting God, I built on this divine building during the reign of the dog of the 'Alī Ibn Abī Ṭalib's threshold, his peace upon 'Abbās al-Ḥusayni Bahādur Khān...[54]

Neither of the two following inscriptions that remained from Shah Ṣafī's time included any notions of the king's interest in being publicly known as serving the religion. Indeed, in contrast to his father, who was relatively well known for his desire to be considered as the leader of religion and state, as well as a pious Muslim king, the charity of Darb-i Ṭūqchī's mosque does not include any religious terms, but includes the names of Persian kings who were famous for their power and glorious nature:

... در زمان دولت خاقان جمشید رای سکندر صولت و سلطان فریدون فر دارا حشمت ابوالمظفر معزالدوله و عز نصره سلطان شاه صفی الحسینی الموسوی الصفوی بهادرخان ...

> ... During the reign of the Jamshīd-wisdom Khāqān, Alexander-authority, Firīdūn-*farr*, Darius-retinue, the father of the triumphant, and glorifying polity, God may glorify his

---

[54] Hunarfar, *Ganjīneh-yi Āsār-i Tārīkhī-i Iṣfahān*, 459.

triumph, the Sultan, Shah Ṣafī al-Ḥusaynī, al-Mūsavī, al-Ṣafavī, Bahādūr Khān...[55]

Some of the inscriptions that remain about Shah 'Abbās II referred to him as the *muravvij-i maẕhab-i ḥaqq-i a 'immeh-yi eṣnā 'asharī* (the propagator of the right religion of the Twelver Imams), but the other titles mostly depicted him as a sovereign power. *Al-khāqān al-afkham* (the greatest sovereign), *mālik riqāb al-umam* (the owner of people's neck), *mawlā mulūk al-'Arab wa al-'Ajam* (the king of Arabs and Persians), and *qahrimān al-mā' wa al-ṭīn* (the hero of waters and lands) are among the titles that remind his audience of the king's earthly power. For example, the inscriptions of *madraseh-yi* Mīrzā Taqī offers the following statement:

قد وفق ببناء هذا المدرسة فى زمن دولة السلطان الأعظم و الخاقان الأكرم مولى ملوك العرب و
العجم قهرمان الماء و الطين مروج مذهب الأئمة المعصومين عليهم السلام السلطان بن السلطان
بن السلطان و الخاقان بن الخاقان بن الخاقان السطان شاه عباس الثاني الصفوي الموسوي
بهادرخان...

> ...was succeeded in building this school in the days of the reign of the greatest sovereign, and the most honorable king, the supporter of all Arab and Persian kings, the hero of waters and lands, the propagator of the religion of infallible Imams, peace upon them, al-Sultan the son of al-Sultan the son of al-Sultan, the khaqan the son of the khaqan the son of the khaqan, al-Sultan Shah 'Abbās II al-Ṣafavī al-Mūsavī Bahādur Khān...[56]

The Safavid kings benefited from the titles that are equal to the word *Shah* in Persian. Although this kind of typesetting was available on coins before his time, it became dominant in the inscriptions during the rule of Shah 'Abbās II. Titles that emphasized his war skills also added royal features to public perceptions of him. For example, this is the inscription of Kūchak-i Jūrchīr mosque in Isfahan:

---

[55] Ibid, 542.

[56] Ibid, 610.

فى أيام خلافة السلطان الأكرم الأعظم الأعدل الأشجع قهرمان الماء و الطين مولا ملوك العرب و العجم أبوالغازى أبوالنصر أبوالفتح أبوالمظفر شاه عباس بهادرخان ...

> ...in the days of the guardian of al-Sultan the most
> honorable, the greatest, the best just king, the bravest, the
> hero of the oceans and lands, the leader of all Arab and
> non-Arab kings, the father of warriors, the father of
> triumph, the father of victory, the father of triumph, Shah
> ʿAbbās Bahādur Khān...[57]

The inscriptions of Shah Sulaymān's buildings emphatically mix the religious role of the king with titles that portray his material power. In the inscriptions of Khalvat Nishīn mosque, the king is compared with Solomon and Alexander the Great. The expression *ẓil-allāh* (the shadow of God) is also used for legitimizing purposes.[i] One of the last inscriptions of Sulaymān's time demonstrates this coexistence between religion and state in depictions of the king. This inscription dated 1685, the last year of the king's rule, is for *madreseh-yi* Kārgarān:

لقد وفق الله تعالى فى ظل حماية أشرف السلاطين رافع الوية الشرع المبين مشيد أساس العلم و اليقين فرع الشجرة الطيبة الأحمدية غصن الدوحة العلية العلوية الخاقان بن الخاقان بن الخاقان السلطان سليمان الحسيني الموسوي الصفوي ...

> It was built by support of God and under the shadow of the noblest
> kings' support, the custodian of the flag of the brightest legacies,
> the establisher of the knowledge and faith's foundation, he is the
> branch of the pure tree of the prophet's family, the highest branch
> in a plane, the khaqan the son of the khaqan the son of the khaqan,
> al-Sultan Sulaymān al-Ḥusaynī al-Mūsavī al-Ṣafavī...[58]

The inscriptions of Shah Sultan Ḥusayn's time did not change in comparison to Shah Sulaymān's. However, they present a complete version of what can be understood as the basic ideology of a Shiʿi sovereign system. The religious aspects of Shah Sultan Ḥusayn's kingship were emphasized by the application of the terms of servitude (similar

---

[57] Ibid, 621.

[58] Ibid, 652.

to Shah 'Abbās I's time) and titles of Persian kings (similar to Shah Ismā'īl). Indeed, the declaration of power through inscriptions in Shah Sultan Ḥusayn's time is the culmination of all the patterns through which legitimacy was previously sought by the other Safavid kings. For example, the words on 'Alī Qāpū's gate, which were engraved after the palace's construction, depict Shah Sultan Ḥusayn as the head of religion and the state, an idea that remained until modern times:

(يا الله) ... شهنشاه دين (يا محمد) داور دين پرور ايران زمين (يا على مدد) كلب درگاه على فخرشهان (يا لله) حامى دين نبى... (يا محمد) آنكه از آب رحمت و خاك بهشت (يا على مدد) دست قدرت طينت گردون سرشت (يا الله) پايه ايوان قدرش بى حجاب (يا محمد) باشد آنجايى كه سر زد آفتاب (يا على مدد) منتظم باشد از آن گردون مآب (يا الله) ... شاه دين شاه زمان سلطان حسين (يا الله) بن سليمان ابن سليمان بارگاه

   (O Allah)…The king of the religion (O Muḥammad) the judge and the religion nurturer of Irān Zamīn (O 'Alī help) the dog of the threshold of 'Alī who is the honor of all king (O 'Alī help), the supporter of the prophet's religion… (O Muḥammad) who from the water of mercy and the clay of heaven (O 'Alī help), the powerful hand of the faith (O Allah), the column of his Iwān is with no veil (O Muḥammad) the place where sun raises (O 'Alī help) is under the king whose attitude is the faith, (O Allah)…the Shah of the religion, the Shah of the time, Sultan Ḥusayn (O Allah), Ibn Sulaymān, whose palace is similar to Sulaymān. [59]

Table 3. Inscriptions[60]

Kings	Expressions
Shah Ismā'īl	The guardian of the banner of guardianship, entitled owner of the throne of Caliphate, the conqueror, the patron of the believers, al-Sultan

---

[59] Ibid, 423.

[60] The most dominant ideology came first for emphasis.

Shah Ṭahmāsb	The greatest sovereign, the most honorable king, the shadow of God on the people of faith, the father of triumph, al-Sultan, al-Ḥusaynī, the greatest sovereign
Shah ʻAbbās I	The propagator of the right religion of the Twelve Imams, the most honorable, the greater, the more just, the dust of the sacred threshold of the prophet, the rubbish of the ʻAlī's pure square, the dog of the ʻAlī Ibn Abī Ṭalib's threshold al-Ḥusaynī al-Ṣafavī al-Mūsavī
Shah Ṣāfī	Jamshīd-wisdom Khāqān, Iskandar-authority, Firīdūn-*farr*, Drius retinue, the father of the triumphant, the Sultan, al-Ḥusaynī, al-Mūsavī, al-Ṣafavī
Shah ʻAbbās II	The propagator of the right religion of the Twelve Imams, the greatest sovereign, the owner of people's neck, the king of Arabs and Persians, the hero of lands and water, the father of warriors, the father of triumph, the father of victory, the father of triumph
Shah Sulaymān	The custodian of the flag of the brightest legacies, the establisher of the knowledge and faith's foundation, the branch of the pure tree of the prophet's family, the greatest sovereign, al-Ḥusaynī al-Mūsavī al-Ṣafavī
Shah Sultan Ḥusayn	The king of the religion, the religion nurturer of Persian empire, the dog of the threshold of ʻAlī, the supporter of the prophet's religion, the powerful hand of the faith, the shah of the religion, the shah of the time

V. Conclusion

Examining the verbal representations of power in different cultural products of the Safavid reign demonstrates that the formation of Iran's Shiʻi political system was not as strong until the reign of Shah ʻAbbās I' time. The titles and benedictions found on the first four Safavid kings' coins were similar to those of Sunni kings, although the reverse of Safavid coins used the names of Shiʻi Imams. During Shah ʻAbbās's time, these public titles displayed the religious devotion of the king and his servitude towards the Shiʻi Imams. While claiming the Safavid king as the head of Sufi order was an important element of Safavid ideology from the beginning, the last two Safavid kings do not invoke the Sufi characteristics of their Sufi ancestors. The last two Safavid kings were mostly presented as similar to the Persian kings of pre-Islamic times but both of them as defenders of Shiʻism.

The examination of patterns of legitimacy in public life over time demonstrates that the religio-political ideology of the Safavids was constantly changing from the beginning of the reign and changes continued until the fall of the last Safavid king. The main elements of the Safavid ideology—being similar to the pre-Islamic Persian kings, possessing the spiritual characteristics of the Sufi saints, and ruling as the shadow of God on earth—were not simultaneously emphasized throughout Safavid history. The shifting emphasis throughout the different periods of Safavid rule urges us to consider circumstances in which these patterns changed and how the changes were precipitated and perceived by the different communities of that period.

Figures of Coins

Figure 1 (Shah Ismā'īl I)

ID Number: 5000-06-00741
Coined: Astarābād
Obv: السلطان العادل الهادى الوالى ابولمظفر شاه اسمعيل بهادر خان خلدالله ملكه و سلطنه
Rev: Central cartouche with the Shi'i Shahādat and the names of twelve Imams on the margins

ID Number: 5000-06-00853

Obv: السلطان العادل الكامل الهادى الوالى ابوالمظفر سلطان اسمعيل بهادر خان الصفوى الحسينى خلدالله ملكه

Rev: As above

Figure 2 (Shah Ṭahmāsb)

ID Number: 5000-06-00857

Obv: Central cartouche: ضرب سبزوار

Margin: الكامل الهادى الوالى ابوالمظفر شاه طهماسب السلطان العادل

Rev: As above

Figure 3 (Shah Ismā'īl II)

ID number: 5000-06-0742

Obv: اسمعیل شاه ضرب دارالموحدین قزوین

Rev: زمشرق تا به مغرب گر امام است / علی و آل او ما را تمام است

Figure 4 (Shah Muḥammad Khudābandeh)

ID number: 5001-06-01803

Obv: السلطان العادل محمد خدابنده

Rev: ضرب بار فروش ده

Figure 5 (Shah Muḥammad Khudābandeh)

ID number: 5000-06-0727
Rev: Shahādat

Figure 6 (Shah 'Abbās I's coins)

ID number: 5000-06-00714
Obv: Central cartouche: ضرب دورق
Margin: بنده شاه ولایت عباس
Rev: Central cartouche: Shahādat

Figure 7 (Shah Ṣafī I)

ID Number: 5000-06-00785
Obv: هست از جان غلام شاه صفی
Rev: Shahādat

This special coin was found in a personal collection in Isfahan during my visit in 2016. On the central cartouche of the coin it is زد از توفیق حق عباس ثانی بگیتی سکه صاحبقرانی and on the margin the اردبیل is inscribed.

Figure 9 (Shah 'Abbās II)

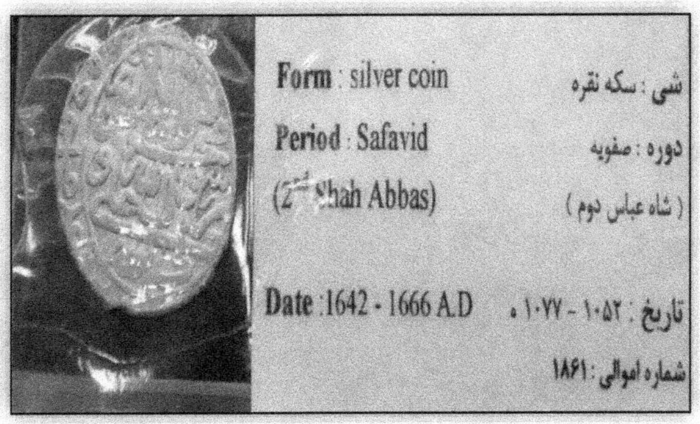

This picture was taken during my visit to Qazvin's national museum in the summer of 2016. The world of Shahādat is in center and the name of twelve imams are in the margin. On the reverse the word of Shahādat is available.

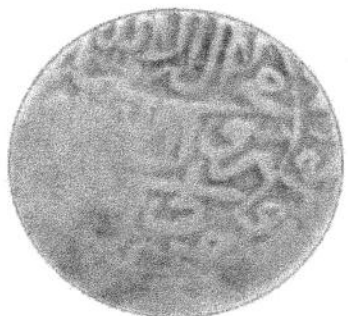

This special coin was found in a personal collection in Isfahan during my visit in 2016. The coin is from Irawān. On the Reverse the words of Shahādat are visible.

Figure 11 (Shah Sultan Ḥusayn)

ID number:5000-06-00856
Obv: ضرب نخجوان بنده شاه ولايت حسين
Rev: the word of Shahādat

Figure 12 (Shah Sultan Ḥusayn)

A very unique coin was displayed at the Malek Museum in the summer of 2016. This is one of the very first coins on which the lion and sun as the emblem of Persian empire appears. It is copper and minted in Isfahan in 1703.

Figures of Inscriptions

Figure 13 (Ālī Qāpū in Qazvin)

Figure 16 (Left miḥrāb of Congregational mosque in Isfahan)

CHAPTER THREE:
IDEOLOGY AND LEGITIMACY IN SAFAVID QAṢĪDEHS

I. Introduction

This chapter focuses on the trajectory of poetic representations of Safavid
ideology in the *qaṣīdeh* form to demonstrate how poets perceived Shiʻism and
kingship in affiliation to Safavid kings from the rise of the Safavid dynasty through its
fall. This chapter also investigates which Safavid ideologies the poets responded to the
most. I argue that in panegyric *qaṣīdeh*, the Safavid poets refrained from combining
depictions of the king with Shiʻi doctrines. In the *qaṣīdeh*, the Safavid king was often
presented as a pious Sufi and a talented warrior in possession of *farr*, that traditionally
associated with pre-Islamic Persian kings. Images of kings in panegyric *qaṣīdehs* fall
into the binary metaphors of just/suppressing and strong/weak, which not necessarily
locate the king in a Shiʻi religious sphere. In panegyric *qaṣīdeh*s, the kings' ethics and
their similarity with pre-Islamic Persian kings legitimized their kingship. The kings
are presented as the possessors of a unique power, similar to the Sufi saints' power
famous as *Karāmat*, through which the natural process of subjects or the relationship
between people and animals in the world could change.

This representation depicted the Safavid kings as Sufi saints and traditional
Persian kings of pre-Islamic times as was presented in *Shāhnāmeh*. This divine nature
allowed them to be perceived as sinless Imams and, therefore, righteous individuals

worthy of filling the position of king in the absence of a just leader. My study

demonstrates that the poets did not fully respond to the Shi'i ideology of the Safavid

kings in *qaṣīdeh* form. Whether they were writing to entertain the king circle's or to

present their work at the court stage for more formal ceremonies, the poets did not

include Shi'i images and terms in their work. My study demonstrates that the kings

who reigned during the end of the 16th century were mainly presented as Sufi *shaykh*s

whose saintly nature was embodied in Persian *farr* and in other notions related to pre-

Islamic forms of kingship. The kings were presented in possession of special and

unique power that could have special impact on the world process and the living

people. This power is similar to the *karāmāt* of the Sufis through which they presented

miraculous acts similar to the prophets.[1]

This chapter is written in four parts. Part II attempts to shed light on the

structure of panegyric *qaṣīdeh* and on images that depicted the kings during the

Safavid period. Part III investigates the panegyrics of different court poets throughout

Safavid history to demonstrate the trajectory of images that represent kingship and

Shi'ism. The chapter ends with Part IV as the conclusion.

II. Sunni and Traditional *Qaṣīdeh*: Structural Change for a New Purpose?

I analyze Safavid panegyric *qaṣīdeh* written for kings in accordance with the

findings of Sholeh Quinn to pinpoint which ideologies were active in portraying the

Shi'i Safavid king. In this chapter, I focus on the *qaṣīdeh*s of seven poets from the

nine Safavid courts. I did not include Ṣā'ib Tabrīzī (b. 1592 – d. 1676) here because

his poetic representation of the Safavid kingship does not match that of the other poets

---

[1] To read about *karāmāt* see the Introduction, 23.

of the Safavid period. The poets I study in this chapter are: Vaḥshī Bāfqī (d. 1583),

Muḥtasham Kāshānī (d. 1588), Shānī Takallū (d. 1614), Salīm Tihrānī (d. 1647),

Faṣīḥī Hiravī (d. 1639), Ṭarzī Afshārī (d. 1679), and Muḥsin Taʿsīr Tabrīzī (d. 1717).

See Table 4 below for information regarding the number of poems each poet dedicated

to each king.

Table 4: Poetry Sources

Poets	Safavid rulers
Vaḥshī (d.1583)	Shah Ṭahmāsb (2)
Muḥtasham (d. 1588)	Shah Ṭahmāsb (3)
	Shah Ismāʿīl II (1)
	Muḥammad Khudābandeh (3)
Shānī (d.1614)	Shah ʿAbbās I (3)
Faṣīḥī (d. 1639)	Shah ʿAbbās I (1)
	Shah Ṣafī (1)
Salīm (d.1647)	Shah ʿAbbās I (1)
	Shah Ṣafī (1)
Ṭarzī Afshār (d.1679)	Shah ʿAbbās II (2)
Muḥsin Taʿsīr Tabrīzī (d.1717)	Shah Sulaymān (3)

While the three traditional sections of panegyric *qaṣīdehs* are typically very distinct, in Safavid *qaṣīdehs*, the sections are less distinct and could blend together. Sperl demarcated the structure of the Arabic Abbasid panegyric to strophe and anti-strophe,[2] suggesting that topics of the strophe (i.e. descriptions of love in *nasīb*[3] or portraying nature in *raḥīl*[4])[5] are linked to those of the antistrophe (i.e. patron's merits or images of war and peace).[6] According to Sperl, the relationship between strophe and antistrophe is usually one of either contrast or congruence between the beloved and the ruler.[7] The Safavid *qaṣīdeh*, however, does not necessarily present a binary of the beloved/patron or the discourses about these two subjects (e.g. a romantic space versus court) in the strophe and antistrophe. Furthermore, the description of nature and court, whether in congruence or conflict with each other could appear in *nasīb* and then could continue in the body of a *qaṣīdeh*. In this case, both nature and the court

---

[2] Stephen Sperl, *Mannerism in Arabic Poetry: a Structural Analysis of Selected Texts:3rd Century AH/9th century AD-5th Century AH/11th Century AD*, (Cambridge; New York: Cambridge University Press. 1989), 25. See also Stephen Sperl, Christopher Shackle, *Qasida Poetry in Islamic Asia and Africa*, vol. 20, (Leiden ; New York: E.J. Brill, 1996).

[3] In *nasīb* or *tashbīb* the poet usually laments a lost love, asks his travelling companions to stop, and weeps over the traces of ruined encampments.

[4] In *raḥīl*, the poet usually reports the hardships met on his journey from the encampments of the beloved—who left him—to the ruler.

[5] Usually these two are indistinguishable in Persian *qaṣīdeh*s. The strophe in Persian *qaṣīdeh*s is comprised of the introductory lines that appear before the main body of *qaṣīdeh*, i.e. *madīḥ*.

[6] Sperl, *Mannerism in Arabic Poetry*, 1989. Sperl's division of Abbasid *qaṣīdeh*s is compatible with the tripartite classical definition of *qaṣīdeh* by Ibn Qutaybeh. The strophe and its themes are in *nasīb* or *tashbīb*, while the themes of antistrophe represent the patron in the *raḥīl/madīḥ* (praise) section. *Madīḥ* is the section praising the patron.

[7] Jocelyn Sharlet also pays special attention to the themes of the introduction and body of a *qaṣīdeh*. She argues that the themes of space and time speak of intimacy and distance between the patron and protégé. She also argues that how a poet describes and addresses a king is not only a matter of style, but it is also related to the power relationship. For more on this issue, see Jocelyn Sharlet, *Patronage and Poetry in the Islamic World: Social Mobility and Status in the Medieval Middle East and Central Asia*, (London: I.B Tauris, 2011).

represent the king and his power synecdochally as spaces under the king's governance.
Both nature and the court respond to the king's other-worldly influence on the cosmos.
In these cases, the borders of the *qaṣīdeh* sections typically disappear and the poet, by
mixing the images of nature, court, and the king, offers his praise. While Sperl argued
that the themes of *nasīb* appear in the second section, known as *raḥīl*,[8] the Safavid
qaṣīdeh demonstrates that description of court or nature could be a shared theme
between *nasīb* and *madīḥ*. The elements of nature repeatedly reappear in *madīḥ* to
argue that the king is not disconnected from the world he is ruling. Finally, the *qaṣīdeh*
ends with *sharīṭeh*, or benediction. In the benediction, the poet usually asks for the
patron's everlasting kingship or eternal life.[9]

The *nasīb*s relating to nature, love, and ethical issues during the Safavid period
took different forms in panegyrics. Muḥtasham and Vaḥshī's poems are usually set in
the court sphere and follow the traditional written form of *qaṣīdeh*. Muḥtasham's
description of the king is different in his works. Once, he started his panegyric with a
description of his beloved so that his following description of the king's merits would
outweigh that of the beloved.[10] In another example, he delved into praise of a
prosperous king who, after being severely ill, sat back on the throne. In his two poems
for Shah Ṭahmāsb, Vaḥshī started his panegyric with direct praise of the king,
describing him as a very traditional king whose power is rooted in his strength,

---

[8] Julie Meisami, "Ghaznavid Panegyrics: Some Political Implications," *Iran*, Vol. 28 (1990),
31-44.

[9] Sirus Shamisa, *Anvā' Adabī*, (Tehran, Mītrā, 1370/1991), 269.

[10] Muḥtasham, *Dīvān-i Muḥtasham-i Kāshānī*, ed. Ali Akbar Behdarvand, (Tehran:Nigāh,
2000), 299-302.

military power, and divine right to rule through the will of God.[11] The poets of Shah ʿAbbās I's time paid more attention to the description of nature in *nasīb*. They usually started their poems with descriptions of nature and, in the body, praised a warrior king whose ethics positioned him for direct comparison with Sufis. In the late Safavid period, this imagery shifted towards kings' similarity with pre-Islamic Persian kings. In general, compared to the traditional panegyrics, the *qaṣīdeh* structure during the Safavid period did not experience extreme change. The few changes that occurred throughout different courts are not dominant enough to constitute stylistic features of the period.

III. Safavid *Qaṣīdeh* and Treating Kings

A. Shah Ismāʿīl and his Claim to Power

Moin remarked "Although Iran is thought to have been converted to Shiʿism by royal edict under the Safavids beginning in the 16th century, this process was gradual—even desultory—and took more than a century to gather momentum."[12] During his reign, Shah Ismāʿil was occupied with establishing a new religion, seeking ways for distributing Shiʿi legacies, and educating the masses with Shiʿi rules. Ismāʿil's messianic claims played an important role in forming his sacred authority. Most of the information about his "saintly" nature and claim of political authority comes from his own poems.[13] His poems, which were written in Turkish and in *ghazal*

---

[11] See Kamāl al-Dīn Vaḥshī Bāfqī, *Dīvān-i Vaḥshī Bāfqī*. ed. Husayn Nakhaʿi, (Tehran: Mu'assiseh-yi Intishārāt-i Amīr Kabīr, 1977), 187-191. (Cited hereafter in text and footnotes as Vaḥshī)

[12] Azfar Moin, (2010). *Islam and the Millennium: Sacred Kingship and Popular Imagination in Early Modern India and Iran*. Available from ProQuest Dissertations & Theses Global. (763441641), 7.

[13] See Vladimir Minorsky, *The Poetry of Shāh Ismāʿīl I*, (London, 1942), 1026a. Building his poetry on love for Imam Ali and union with him, Ismāʿīl's poetry benefited from dominant beliefs

form, fused the dual meaning of the title *Shah* that was prominent in political and religious cultures throughout the central and eastern regions of Islamdom.[14] In this way, the Persian designation for monarch became an appellation for spiritual guide. In his poems, scholars have seen the identity of a messianic figure mixing with the identity of the king himself. Expressions such as "seal of prophets" and "God's light"[15] indicate Ismā'il's intention to claim the political authority of the Muslim world as a sacred man and a holy savior. Claims of divination, magic, and prophecy that were performed publicly in different stages of Shah Ismā'il's reign helped the social process by which the "sacred" charisma of Safavid kings was produced and institutionalized. He also presented himself as the reincarnation of Islamic figures as well as of those from pre-Islamic Iran much celebrated in *Shāhnāmeh*.[16] Furthermore, if not promoting himself as the eschatological Mahdī, internal evidence within the poetry suggests that Shah Ismā'īl intended to present himself as the Mahdī's representative. It is under this representation that Shah Ismā'il was believed by his Qizilbāsh supporters to be sacred by virtue of being born in a Sufi family. This idea allowed him to gain and keep the respect and trust of his devotees throughout most of his reign. An Italian traveler indicated that Shah Ismā'il's followers adored him as a

---

about the will of God in assigning someone to reign, the spirituality of Imam Ali's personality, and pre-Islamic Persian kings and respected Persian warriors creating the image of a sacred and legitimate king. He played the role of the Mahdi, or messiah, interceding with God on behalf of the common believers.

[14] Babayan, *Mystics, Monarchs and Messiah,* 296.

[15] Ibid.

[16] Minorsky, *The Poetry of Shāh Ismā'īl I,* 1026a.

prophet and that the rug he sat upon when celebrating Mehregan,[17] having been

touched by the sacred Ismāʿīl, was torn into pieces to be used by his followers.

European travelers also wrote about how Ismāʿīl's followers considered him to be

divine. Because of his special power and devotees, and especially because of his

spiritual genealogy, they regularly compared him with Alexander the Great or with

Xerxes and Darius, showing him the same respect that they had for pre-Islamic kings

of Persian Empire.[18]

Nevertheless, Gallagher, in her 2018 article on poetry of Shah Ismāʿīl, argues

against automatically considering apocalyptic themes as political or eschatological in

the literal sense. According to her study, the apocalyptic themes that consist of images

referring to Imam Mahdī as well as other prophets such as Khiżr, Alexander the Great,

and Moses demonstrate literary depth that "explains not only the survival of the corpus

but how it may have been perceived among subsequent generations."[19] Shah Ismāʿīl's

poetry and his construction of images with an apocalyptic perspective was praised by

Azeri scholars.[20] Due to this acclaimed literary value of his poems, Gallagher

mentioning Said Amir Arjomand's point of view on distinguishing the "apocalyptic

---

[17] Mehregan is a Persian and Zoroastrian festival celebrated to honor Mitra, the goddess of love and friendship.

[18] This was mentioned in Theodore Spandounes, *La Vita di Sach Ismael et Tamas Re di Persia Chiamati Soffi,* in Sansovino, *Historia Universale dell'Origine et Imperio de Turchi,* 98-100. For more information about perceiving Shah Ismāʿīl with European notions of kingship read, Brummett Palmira, "The Myth of Shah Ismāʿīl Safavi: Political Rhetoric and Divine Kingship. *"Medieval Christian Perceptions of Islam: a* Book of Essays, ed. John Victor Tolan, (New York: Garland Pub., 1996).

[19] Gallagher, 378.

[20] Gallagher, 378. In this work Ghallagher is citing from Memdedov, "Le plus ancient manuscrit du dīvān de Shah Ismail Khatayi." Turcica 6 (1972): 8-23.

worldview" from "political messianism."[21] According to Arjomand "the latter is often expressed through the language of the former," so the concepts are easily conflated. Although both Arjomand and Gallagher invite the readers of Shah Ismāʿīl's poetry to perceive the poet and the political propagandist as two distinct concepts and to perceive apocalyptic expressions as metaphoric concepts rather than literal insights into the king's public life, panegyrics for kings were means of political propaganda and continue to be sources that, through literary interpretation, help the understanding of concepts related to kingship. Therefore, literary reinterpretation of these sources, which are obviously engaged with religious and political circumstances of their time, portray the ideas of kingship in the context of religious and political tumult.

B. Shah Ṭahmāsb: Warrior, Pious, and Persian

Babayan argues that Shah Ṭahmāsb avoided being associated with the exaggerated claims of his father. She interpreted Shah Ṭahmāsb's interest in fishing (rather than wild-boar hunting) and his pious and isolated lifestyle (in contrast to the festivities and glorious lifestyle of his father's court)[22] as steps taken to disassociate himself from his father's unbearable situation after the battle of Chāldirān in 1514.[23] After this battle, Ismāʿīl lost respect from his supporters and never recovered from that loss. Shah Ṭahmāsb and his ministers centered their attention on transforming the

---

[21] Ibid, 375.

[22] Kathryn Babayan, *The Safavids in Iranian History* (1501–1722), in *Oxford Handbook of Iranian History*. Edited by Touraj Daryaee (Oxford: Oxford University Press, 2012), 294.

[23] A battle occurred between the Ottomans and the Safavids at 1514 in which Sultan Selim I experienced a decisive victory. For more information on time and place and the reasons of the battle see Tony, Bunting, *Battle of Chāldirān,* in Encyclopedia Britannica, (February8, 2018), https://wwww.britannica/event/Battle-of-Chaldiran

basis of the Safavid concept of sovereignty from messianic claims to claims based on justice and the defense of *dīn-i ilāhī* (Divine law), which changed the structure of his army and the nature of his supporters. This change mainly took place during the 1530s. During this period, Shah Ṭahmāsb's propaganda was no longer framed by the Qizilbāsh but was controlled by Shiʻi theologians who tried to empower themselves against their Sunni rivals in the Ottoman Empire.[24]

The 1530s, as Babayan has argued, represented an important period in history in respect to Shah Ṭahmāsb's dynastic self-view. Under the influence of *mujtahid*s such as al-Karakī (d. 1533), the religious and cultural activities of the dynasty moved toward a deprecation of popular Sufism and suppression of Sunnism. The pressure that the religious scholars applied on Sufis and Sunnis was a means of establishing doctrinal Shiʻism. No other religious discourse beyond Shiʻism was allowed. The goal was to sideline any ideology that could undermine the new state religion. Shah Ṭahmāsb's 1532 public proclamation of repentance, which was followed by decrees banning of alcohol and other irreligious behaviors, supported the religious scholars in forming doctrinal Shiʻism against the "heretical" practices of Sufis and Sunnis. The activities of taverns, drug dens, wine cellars, and brothels, among other places of "corrupt" activities, were banned and the reign of Shah Ṭahmāsb entered a new phase that, unlike during the reign of his father, had no place for the messianic claims.[25] Al-

---

[24] See Colin Mitchell, *The Practice of Politics in Safavid Iran: Power, Religion and Rhetoric.* (London: I.B. Tauris, 2012).

[25] Shah Ṭahmāsb, *Tazkireh-yi Shah Ṭahmāsb beh Ghalam-i Khudash,* (Chāpkhāneh-yi Kāvyānī: 1343/1963), 30-31. For reading the letters and orders of the ban, see ʻAbd al-Ḥusayn Navāʼī, *Shāh Tahmāsb Ṣafavī: Majmūʻeh-yi Asnād va Mukātibāt-i Tārīkhī Hamrāh bā Yāddāshthā-yi Tafṣīlī.* (Tehran: 1971), 42-45.

Karakī's treatises, which were widely circulated in 16th century Iran and had followers among the Shi'i nobles and *sayyid*s of cities such as Qum, Mashhad, and Astarabad as well as among the Shi'i clerics across the Arab world, were aimed at the denunciation of other forms of religious practices, particularly those of Sunnis and Sufis. Adding in *mūsavī* lineage, which appeared in Ṭahmāsb's memoirs and has been discussed at length by Babayan, was among the other steps taken by Shi'i jurists during this period to legitimize Ṭahmāsb's right to kingship.

While 1532 is known as an important date for the Safavid ideological narrative due to the growing power of sedentary *'ulamā* who had *uṣūlī* doctrines, which were shaped by the declaration of al-Karākī as deputy of the Imam and granting him authority of all religious affairs, the *qaṣīdeh*s written during this period did not reflect this important aspect of Shah Ṭahmāsb's kingship.[26] The content of *qaṣīdeh*s written for Shah Ṭahmāsb does not refer to this transition from popular Shi'ism to doctrinal Shi'ism. While appropriate steps were taken to rearrange the Safavid genealogy "to concretize the Safavid claim to Imam Mūsā Kāzim,"[27] poets such as Muḥtasham and Vaḥshī declined to include this lineage. Moreover, there is no indication of Sunni-Shi'i encounters in the poems that could showcase the importance of these themes for the kings' self-image. Vaḥshī did refer to the king's decree banning corrupt activities, but these factual references are absent from the *qaṣīdeh*s in general.[28]

---

[26] Mitchell, *The Practice of Politics in Safavid Iran*, 69.

[27] Ibid.

[28] To repulse and repel any sins
He prohibits like a judge,
That from his fear, the bride of the flute's song,
Will hide behind the curtains (Vaḥshī, p. 187)

These two poets employed the pre-Islamic notions of imperium to describe

Shah Ṭahmāsb profoundly. Muḥtasham connects the concept of *farr* to Shah

Ṭahmāsb's reign and compared the king with heroic Persian kings such as Darius and

Firīdūn in terms of possessing *farr*. In addition, he refers to the king as *ṣāḥib-qirān*, a

legitimizing epithet denoting power, which Timur and his descendants were known for

by. In Vaḥshī's portrait of the king, too, the king was depicted with a *chatr* (parasol)

and a falcon, which are both symbols of Persianate kingship in the history of Iran.[29]

Farr and *ṣāḥib-qirān* do not appear in expressions of praise in Vaḥshī's poems.

The representation of Shi'ism is limited to few examples in Muḥtasham's

works, however the representation of Shi'ism is in Muḥtasham's works is more

evident in comparison to his contemporary poets and his precedents In those

examples, the king is depicted as serving Shi'ism and distributing its legacies but, still,

presenting Shi'ism as a motif for the Safavid *qaṣīdehs* is not a frequent theme. Even

the inclusion of lineage such as *mūsavī* or *ḥusaynī*, which could be implemented by

------

از پی دفع و رفع هر منهی

قاضی نهیش آنچنان باشد

که ز بیمش عروس نغمه نی

در پس پرده ها نهان باشد

To read the full *qaṣīdeh* see Vaḥshī's *Dīvān*.

Another example:
[He is] a sun, the shadow of whose parasol (i.e the king)
covers the king of the east (i.e the sun) (Vaḥshī, p.187)

آفتابی که سایه ی چترش

بر سر شاه خاوران باشد

including an adjective alongside other titles and expressions of political legitimization, does not occur in these poems.

In a *qaṣīdeh* that was written after the king's recovery from a very difficult illness, Muḥtasham compared the king to the Prophet Muḥammad. Muḥtasham started his poem with celestial references to the king. The Shah was represented as the moon, which *vilāyat* (sovereignty) brought back to the stage of power. He was the *najm* (star) in the sky of kingship. The king was compared to *shahbāz* (a bird of prey larger than a hawk or falcon that, in Persian myths, was a god who helped the Iranians and guided the royal *farr* to the land of Iran).[30] After these two metaphors, both rooted in symbols of Persianate monarchy in pre-Islamic period, reference to *nakhl* (palm) reminds readers of Imam Ḥusayn and the battle of Karbala. However, in the *qaṣīdeh* form, this is an infrequent and unusual image:

ماهی که یک دو مرحله آمد فرو ز اوج

بازش نشانده است ولایت بر آسمان

نجم سپهر سلطنت آن رجعتی که داشت

با استقامت ابدی یافت اقتران

شهباز اوج ابهت از باد تفرقه

دل جمع کرد و شد متمکن بر آشیان

نخل بزرگ سایه بستان سروری

رو در بهار کرد و برون آمد از خزان

A moon which was one or two days past its apogee
Was placed by Sovereignty atop the heavens once again[31]

---

[30] For reading more on the falcon and its relationship with *farr*, see Abolala Soudavar, *The Aura of Kings: Legitimacy and Divine Sanction in Iranian Kingship*, (Costa Mesa, Calif: Mazda Publishers, 2003). Touraj Daryaee, "Religio-Political Propaganda," *Cambridge History of Iran*, III (1):325; IX:43.

[31] The ambiguity in *bāz* provides another interpretation for the line. *Bāz*, meaning falcon, as the symbol of Persianate kingship, can be the subject of the second line. Therefore, the line can be interpreted this way: His falcon, sat his sovereignty on the sky. In this case apogee, sky, and falcon make a collection of similar concepts that claim power based on the Persianate forms of kingship.

The star of the sky of kingship returned
And made conjunction with everlasting permanence

The falcon of the peak of splendor, amidst scattering winds
Pulls himself together and settles into the nest

The towering palm that shades the garden of lordship
faces the spring and leaves the fall behind (Muḥtasham, 302)

The lines continue with descriptions of the king's military power until the idea

of Twelver Shi'ism appears. However, the Shi'i images do not fit with the other

images of praise. While the first two lines and the last two lines of the following

verses portray the king's palace, the two lines of Twelver Shi'ism interrupt the

cohesiveness of the king's image and the power that was consolidated in his palace:

از بهر زیب دادن اورنگ خسروی

شد بارگه نشین ملک پادشه نشان

طهماسب پادشاه که پیش درش به پاست

صد پاسبان همه ملک و پادشاه و خان

شاهنشهی که گشت ازو پای کاینات

در شاه راه مذهب اثنی عشر روان

فرمان دهی که رونق دین محمدی

داد آن چنان که بود رضای خدا در آن

زنجیر عدل بسته چنان که اعتماد پاس

دارد شبان به گرگ ستم پیشه عوان

در جنب کاخ رفعتش افتاده بس قصیر

ارکان قصر قیصر و ایوان اردوان

To glorify the kingly throne
The king, who sit other kings on throne, himself sat upon the throne

Standing before the gates of Ṭahmāsb Shah,
Were a thousand guardians, all nobles, kings, and rulers

A king of kings who, because of him the world moved
along the path of the Twelver Shi'ism

A commander who gave splendor to the Muḥammadan religion
in such a way that God's satisfaction was affirmed

He tied the chain of justice and in such a way
that the shepherd trusted the wicked wolf in guarding [the sheeps]

Beside his palace of loftiness fall short
The pillars of the palaces of Chosroes and the verandah of Ardavān (Muḥtasham, 302)

One of the most important elements of Shah Ismāʿīl's claim was his declaration of "being Mahdī" or messiah. With respect to Shah Ṭahmāsb's initial goal to move away from the unorthodox statements of his father, the idea of "ruling until the return of Mahdī" became dominant. Rather than the head of state and religion, the king became known as the servant of religion, whose leadership supported Mahdī for his return. The image of a religious servant is the most relevant image to Shiʿi discourses of the time and one that Muḥtasham brought into his poetry. In a context where "sacred" and "divine kingship" were the characteristics of the Timurid-Safavid-Mughal emperors, Shah Ṭahmāsb was depicted not as a "reviver," but as the ruler whose breath could inject a new soul into the world. He lives long and secures the world to turn over the power to Imam Mahdi upon his return. This image not only argues a sort of sacred power for the king in his long life, but also it implies that the king is a qualified ruler who can fulfill the position of an Imam:

داده است ذوالجلال به شخص جلالتش
تشریف عمر سرمدی و عز جاودان

هر یک نفس ز عمر ابد اقتران وی
روح جدید می‌دمد اندر تن جهان

امن و امان عالم کون و فساد راست
آن خسرو زمین و زمان تا ابد ضمان

خواهد نهاد غاشیه مدت حیات
آن شهسوار بر کتف آخرالزمان

The majestic God (lit. owner of eminence) on the body (of the king) bestowed his grandeur
The robe of honor of perpetual life and eternal dignity

A breath of his life which is joined by eternity
will blow a new soul into the body of the world

He is the security and peace of the material and heavenly worlds
The eternal king of realms and time for as long as time allows

He (the king) will place the cloak of long life,
That warrior-king, over the shoulder of the end of time (Muḥtasham, 303)

Muḥtasham asks for the continuity of Ṭahmāsb's reign until the return of Imam Mahdī because, in his opinion, Ṭahmāsb could reinforce the religion:

یا رب به صفدری که اگر اتصال شرق

خواهد به غرب واسطه برخیزد از میان

کز بهر استقامت دین ساز متصل

این سلطنت به سلطنت صاحب‌الزمان

Oh God! In the name of that breaker of ranks (in wars) that if he wishes the east,
And West to be conjoined, what lies between them would vanish

For reinforcing the religion,
join this kingdom to the kingdom of Ṣāḥib zamān (i.e., the twelfth Imam) (Muḥtasham, 305)

In general, in the four *qaṣīdeh*s that Muḥtasham wrote for Shah Ṭahmāsb and in Vaḥshī's *qaṣīdeh*s for him, the Shah's image is different from that of his father. In terms of military prowess, Ṭahmāsb is very similar to the patrons in most of the early Arabic 'Abbasid *qaṣīdeh*s. The structure of both Muḥtasham and Vaḥshī's *qaṣīdehs* are very similar to the structure of traditional 'Abbāsid *qaṣīdehs*. The king is a lion and defeats all his enemies. Playing on the archetypal image of the ancient Near Eastern king, the king is depicted a bringer of life and as a bringer of death. His power changes destiny, and destiny saves him from any harm. His generosity is presented through traditional metaphors such as a cloud, a sea, and a mine. Among Ṭahmāsb's most important virtues is his justice towards all creatures, human and non-human alike. He has the pre-Islamic and Timurid attributes of kingship, and he was often portrayed similarly to Persian kings and the heroes of the *Shāhnāmeh*.

C. Shah Ismā'īl II and His Brother: Becoming Shi'i Kings

The reign of Shah Ismā'īl II, as attested by references of contemporary court chronicles, is characterized by tensions between Sunni proclivities and Shi'i religio-political discourses. Twelver Shi'ism still had the sociopolitical power to secure its position at the central or provincial level; however, the reappearance of Abu Muslim traditions, the uprisings among Nuqtavīs in Kashan, and Ismā'īlī traditions in Andian demonstrated that there was a challenge to the dominant Safavid discourse at the time of uncertainty the king faced.[32] The action of Shah Ṭahmāsb's daughter, Parī Khān Khātūn (b. 1548– d. 1578)—appointing Mirzā Makhdūm (d. 1587)[33] as the head of religious scholars—demonstrates that there was a tolerance of Sunnism at the heart of Iran's political system. During this period, the ritual of cursing the first three caliphs was put to an end and, as mentioned in Chapter Two, the phrase of *shahādat* was removed from the reverse side of coins.[34] These actions raised questions about the Shah's religious beliefs. Some Qizilbāsh generals, with the support of Shi'i clerics, rejected Ismā'īl's flirtation with Sunnism. Shah Ismā'īl died of an opium overdose in

---

[32] Andrew Newman, *Safavid Iran: Rebirth of a Persian Empire*, (London: I.B. Tauris, 2012), 45-46. To read about the Nuqtavīs and their rebellion against the Safavids read Kathryn Babayan, "The Safavid Synthesis: From Qizilbash Islam to Imamite Shi ism", *Iranian Studies*, 27(1–4) (1994), 135–61. In "The Waning of the Qizilbash: The Spiritual and the Temporal in 17th Century Iran,", unpublished PhD dissertation, Princeton University, June 1993, Babayan discussed the rebellions against the Safavids, as well as the anti-Sufi polemic specially during the reign of Shah 'Abbās II. (see 297-298). In "Sufism and Anti-Sufism: The Authorship of The Hadiqat al-Shī'a", Newman through analyzing the anti-Sufi porotion of Ḥadīqat examined the detail descriptions of the beliefs and practices of twenty-one sects offered in this book and attempted to shed light on a series of writing on the relationship of Safavid kings and the Sufis. See Andrew Newman, "Sufism and Anti-Sufism in Safavid Iran: The Authorship of the "Hadiqat al-Shī'a", Iran, Vol. 37 (1999), 95-108, Published by: British Institute of Persian Studies, URL: http://www.jstor.org/stable/4299996.

[33] A Sunni scholar of Shah Ṭahmāsb and Ismā'īl II's time.

[34] See Chapter Two, 75.

1577, and following his death, his brother, Muḥammad Khudābandeh, took the throne.[35]

Muḥtasham's *qaṣīdeh* for Shah Ismāʿīl II deals with the worldly power of the king, and it starts to give ground to appearance of Shiʿi terms and expressions. The king was referred to as *ṣāhib-qirān* and he was compared to Darius, the ancient Persian king. However, the term *farr* was not used to refer to him. He was mostly mentioned as *khusraw* (the general Persian term for king) and his military prowess was colored by Persian heroism:[36]

وانکه گر رخش تسلط گرم تازد بر زمین
گاو و ماهی را به یک دم نرم سازد استخوان

The one if runs his *rakhsh* of domination on earth
he powders the bones from Taurus to Pisces (Muḥtasham, 308)

In the only panegyric that Muḥtasham dedicated to Ismāʿīl II, the king's Sunni tendencies, if there were any, were not revealed. The king's divinity was described with the metaphor of light. After depicting the world in submission to the rule of Ismāʿīl II through use of worldly symbols of power such as *khuṭbeh* (enthronement oration), *kūs* (drum), and coins, the poet describes the king as a rising sun. His *ẓuhūr* (epiphany) and magnificence are described with the idea of light:

آفتابی کز طلوعش بعد چندین انتظار
آمدند از خرمی در رقص ذرات جهان

کامکاری کز ظهورش شد به یکبار آشکار

---

[35] Ibid, 46.

[36] For example:

The one if runs his *rakhsh* of domination on earth
he powders the bones from Taurus to Pisces (Muḥtasham, 308)

وانکه گر رخش تسلط گرم تازد بر زمین
گاو و ماهی را به یک دم نرم سازد استخوان

صورت عیسی که بود از دیدهٔ مردم نهان

آسمان شان و شوکت آفتاب شرق و غرب
پاسبان ملک و ملت پادشاه انس و جان

The sun whose rising, after endless longing,
Caused every atom in the world to dance in celebration

The victorious king whose appearance immediately revealed
The face of happiness, which had been concealed from the eyes of the people

The sky of honor and glory, the sun of the east and the west
The guardian of the kingdom and the religion, the king of men and daemons (Muḥtasham, 308)

Between these lines and the next six lines which I include here, the poet compares the king with the sun and refers to the king's *jalveh* (splendor), making references to Imam Zamān (i.e the 12th Imam) and Dajjāl, who is believed to have claimed to be the Imam Zamān by the return of him. The poet compares the king's accession to return of Imam Mahdī in the near future:

گرچه آن رخشنده خورشید جهان آرا نگشت
مدتی پرتوفکن بر ساحت این خاکدان

کرد آخر جلوهای کاعدای دجال اتفاق
بر بسیط خاک پاشیدند از هم ذرهسان

بعد ازین غیبت ظهور عالم آرائی چنین
هست مرآت ظهور و غیبت صاحب زمان

Although that shining world-beautifying sun has not returned
shining on this desolate earth for a while,

Finally, he displayed his magnificence thus that, his *Dajjāl*-like enemies[37]
dispersed from the earth like dust

After such an absence the return of such a world-beautifier
is the mirror of the absence and presence of *ṣāhib zamān* (Muḥtasham, 309)

Unlike the *qaṣīdeh*s written for Ṭahmāsb and Ismāʻīl I, which did not benefit from the dominant terms and expressions that were available in public domain, the

---

[37] Dajjāl is an evil figure in Islamic eschatology who claims to be Imām Mahdī, the 12th Shiʻi Imām, before the Day of Resurrection.

two *qaṣīdehs* in praise of Muḥammad Khudābandeh show interest in bringing those terms into the poetic discourses. Many of the terms, expressions, and benedictions that he applied were not previously seen in the panegyrics of other kings, and they are in congruence with the patterns of legitimacy used in public places such as mosques and coins:

یارب از عز الهی قرنها دارد نگاه
جای شاهان جهان سلطان محمد پادشاه

صاحب عادل دل دین پرور دارا سپاه
مالک دریا کف فرمان ده عالم پناه

حامی شرع معلی ملجاء دین نبی
مالک دهر و همایون رتبت و دیهیم گاه

I wish O God from your divine glory, for many centuries, watch over
Sultan Muḥammad, in the place of other worldly kings

The ruler with a just heart, he is the nurturer of the religion and his army resembles that of Darius
the potent one, generous as the sea, command-giver, and world-shelterer

He is the supporter of the elevated religion, he is the refuge of prophet's religion
He is the owner of world, he is with an imperial rank and throne is his sitting place (Muḥtasham, 310)

Dīn-parvar (nurturer of religion), *ḥāmī-yi shar'-i mu'allā* (shelter of the elevated religion), and *malja'-i dīn-i nabī* (refuge of the prophet's religion) are among the most important expressions that appear in this *qaṣīdeh* and they highlight the king's role in fortifying the religion. Unlike the other *qaṣīdeh*s that could not integrate the ideas of a worldly king and a religious or pious king together, in the opening lines of this *qaṣīdeh*, Muḥtasham applied the titles and benediction of Shi'i discourse with titles that emphasize the king's military prowess, which is colored by Persian heroism. In one hemistich, the poet combined images of the king's physical features (military prowess) and personality (justice) with political claims of Persianate notions of kingship (comparing the king military power with Darius's) as well as the religious role of the king.

As discussed earlier, both Sufi and Shi'i genealogy were important for the Safavid kings and their claim to authority. The earlier *qaṣīdeh*s, such as those that Muḥtasham wrote for Shah Ṭahmāsb and Ismā'īl II, did not mention the Sufi or Shi'i lineage of kings; this idea became crucial from Muḥammad Khudābandeh's time. Expressions such as *nahāl-i būstān-i aḥmadī* (a sapling of Prophet Muḥammad's garden) and *khulāṣeh-yi nasab-i ḥaydarī* (the exemplar of Ali's lineage) are among the common expressions that were applied to demonstrate the Shi'i background of Muḥammad Khudābandeh:

نهال نورس بستان احمدی که به گردش
هنوز جز دم روح القدس نگشته هوایی

خلاصه نسب پاک حیدری که شنیده
نسب ز عمر ابد نسبتش نوید بقائی

A new sapling of Prophet Muḥammad's garden around which,
has not yet blown anything, but the Holy Spirit

The exemplar of 'Alī's lineage who heard
the lineage from his eternal age the news of eternity (Muḥtasham, 320)

In terms of titles and benedictions for addressing the kings, the *qaṣīdeh*s written for these two brothers, Ismā'īl II and Muḥammad Khudābandeh, are the closest to the legitimizing expressions in the other political propaganda media such as inscriptions and coins, which I studied in Chapter Two.

D. Shah 'Abbās I: a Sufi or a King?

As mentioned in Chapters One and Two, after moving his capital to Isfahan, Shah 'Abbās fashioned himself as a pious king isolated from political power—a king for whom being known as the servant of the religion was more important than being known as having political authority. At first, Shah 'Abbās established his kingship on the foundation of his father's legacies. Shah 'Abbās kept his father's Qizilbāsh affiliation and was open to different sources of religious practices, even heterodox practices such as those propagated by the Nuqṭavīs.[38] However, he extended his religious and political boundaries gradually, which helped him to gain more power. His societal transformation from being a heterodox king to be an orthodox one was organized through various forms of power representation, from the court histories to architecture. Architecture, chronicles, paintings, and other visual cultural materials of his time represented him as a king whose power was rooted in his religious beliefs and his care for his subjects.[39]

The visual materials of his time represented him as both a Sufi and a religious king who brought peace and security to the community.[40] Whether it was through vast renovations of Sufi sanctuaries and investments in the reconstruction of commercial trade routes or through the endowment of his belongings and building of mosques and educational institutions that supported his religious aspirations, Shah 'Abbās was understood as a king serving the Shi'i Imams and the Shi'i people. However, the

---

[38] To read about the relationship between Shah 'Abbās and the Nuqṭavīs, read *Mystics, Monarchs and Messiah: Cultural Landscape of Early Modern Iran*. (Cambridge, Mass: Harvard University Press, 2003). This relationship was defined on tolerance and acceptance of heterodox notions of Islam; however, the king later denounced his intimacy with them and suppressed this group of Sufis vehemently.

[39] Kishwar Rizvi, "Architecture and the Representations of Kingship during the Reign of the Safavid Shah 'Abbās ," in Mitchell Lynette, C.P Melville. *Every Inch of a King: Comparative Studies on Kings and Kingship in the Ancient and Medieval Worlds*, (Brill:2013), 371- 97. See also Sussan Babaie "The Sacred Sites of Kingship," in Sussan Babaie and Talinn Grigor. *Persian Kingship and Architecture: Strategies of Power in Iran from the Achaemenids to the Pahlavis*, (London: I.B. Tauris, 2015), 175 – 218.

[40] Ibid.

literature of his time, particularly the *qaṣīdehs* that were dedicated to him, did not represent this dynamic.

Shah 'Abbās's relationship with poets in general was ambiguous. The *tazkirehs* mention names of Shah 'Abbās I's poets more than other periods; however, more emigration of poets also occurred during this period compared to earlier periods. Beyond Shānī Takallū, who was much praised by the Shah, the other poets did not gain such fame and wealth at his court. For example, Faṣīḥī Hiravī, who served the king for a short period of time, did not gain much success in the king's service.[41] In praise of Shah 'Abbās and in *qaṣīdeh* form, there is not much left from Faghfūr Lāhījī[42] and Masīḥ S̱ānī,[43] the two famous poets of his court. Mīrzā Malak Mashriqī (d. 1642) was also among the other important poets of 'Abbās's time who the author of *Tazkireh-yi Meykhāneh* mentioned as an eloquent *qaṣīdeh* writer; however, his *dīvān* is not available.[44] Ḥakīm Shafā'ī (b. 1588) was also among the poet-doctors of Shah 'Abbās's reign. He received awards from the king for his poetry but never managed to become part of the king's circle.[45]

---

[41] 'Abd al-Nabī Fakhr al-Zamānī Qazvīnī, *Tazkireh-yi Meykhāneh.* ed. Ahmad Gulchin Ma'ani (Tehran: Shirkat-i Nisbī-i Ḥāj Muḥammad Ḥusayn Iqbāl va Shurakā'), 576.

[42] Sayyid Muḥammad Ḥusayn ibn Aḥmad Lāhījī. His father worked at the court of Aḥmad Khān the ruler of Gilan in 16th century. He traveled to Azerbaijan and Georgia from Lahijan. He was good in Arabic, chess, math, and music. (Dehkhoda)

[43] In the biographies, the *sāqīnāmeh* and two or three pieces have been narrated from Masīḥ. The two cases that are narrated in *Meykhāneh* demonstrate that the poet did not perceive the king as God or God's appointee on earth; however, by following his order, one can understand God and reach him. Look at Qazvīnī, *Tazkireh-yi Meykhāneh*, 497 and 513.

[44] Qazvīnī, *Tazkireh-yi Meykhāneh*, 589.

[45] Ibid, 525.

Shānī was the most famous court poet of Shah 'Abbās's time. He did not

become a popular poet until after he wrote a *qaṣīdeh* in praise of Imam 'Alī, which

greatly pleased the Shah. He received gold equal to his body's weight in return for the

poem.[46] Most of Shānī's works are in praise of Shi'i Imams, especially Imam Ḥusayn,

Riżā and Mahdī. He also wrote panegyrics in praise of some of the courtiers of the

time. Although Shah 'Abbās was interested in public demonstration of servitude

towards Shi'ism, Shānī did not praise him with such elements. More than emphasizing

the religious aspects of the king, Shānī attempted to portray him as a sacred person

with Sufi traits. Although, the king's military prowess was still central to his poetry,

the images do not show similarity with the kings or the heroes of pre-Islamic times.

Shānī pointed to the king's good fortune by referring to the king's falcon-like power in

order to demonstrate him as a sacred king.[47] Unlike the earlier poems of our study, he

did not repeatedly apply the vocabulary of "king" and "kingship" to refer to Shah

---

[46] This event has been narrated by Iskandar Beyg Munshī in *Tārīkh-i 'Ālam Ārāy-i 'Abbāsī*. It
has been said that Shānī, in a *maṣnavī* which was written for the Shah, praised him with the following
line:

If the enemy serves the wine or the friend
Both do it for the beauty of the beloved

The king enjoyed his skill and nobility and gave him gold equal to the weight of his own body.
See Iskandar Beyg Munshī, *Tārīkh-i 'Ālam Ārāy-i 'Abbāsī*, Tehran: 1955, 516. Zabih Allah Safa
mentioned that this event was in 1596 (during the ninth year of 'Abbās reign) and not in 1592. In 1592
Shānī presented a *qaṣīdeh* in praise of Imām 'Alī when the Uzbek and Russians were meeting with the
king. (Zabih Allah Safa, *Tārīkh-i Adabīyāt dar Īrān*, (Tehran: Intishārāt-i Firdawsī, 1984), Vol 5/2, 945.
Naṣrābādī also confirmed this anecdote.

[47] Your falcon of power and magnificence
imagined the phoenix of the faith, on the day of hunting like as dove

شاهین اقتدار تو عنفای چرخ را

روز شکار صید کبوتر گرفته است

Shānī Takallū, *Dīvān-i Shānī Takallū (953-1023 Hijrī)*, ed. Banu Musaffa (Tehran: Anjuman-i
Āsār va Mafākhir-i Farhangī, 2011), 55, line 26. (cited hereafter in the text and footnotes as Shānī).

'Abbās. Shah has not been known responsible for dissemination of religion, but his sword and power were compared to Imam 'Alī's:

ترکیب ذوالفقار تو را مرد کارزار

در پیش چشم مرگ مصور گرفته است

your Ẕulfiqār,[48] form is what the man of war
materializes before the eyes of death (Shānī, 55)

Claiming lineage of Sufi *shaykhs* was a practice that goes back to *Ṣafvat al-Ṣafā* and imitated by later Safavid histories such as *Futūḥāt Shahī* and *Ḥabīb al-Siyar*. These two sources introduced Imam Mūsā al-Kāẕim as the ancestor of the early Safavid leaders. In *Tārīkh 'Abbāsī*, Ibrāhīm Yazdī traced Shah 'Abbās's family lineage on both sides back to Imam 'Alī Ibn Abī Ṭālib through Imam Ḥusayn and Zayn al-'Ābidīn.[49] Yet, the lineage was not an important issue for Shānī and his depiction of the king.

In general, in Shānī's poem of Shah 'Abbās I, the Shah was not depicted in service of Shi'ism; however, his sacred personality was emphasized through images that claim the most similarity between him and the Sufi *shaykh*s. For example, in a *tarkīb-band* that supposedly was written after moving the capital to Isfahan, the king was compared to Khiżr and a *murshid-i kāmil*, who could save the poet by inviting him to Isfahan. Isfahan is painted as the life-giving lake:

دارم طمع که سوی صفاهان بری مرا

از کشور بدن به سوی جان بری مرا

خضر رهم شوی بشکوه سکندری

یعنی به سوی چشمه حیوان بری مرا

---

[48] The name of Imam 'Alī's sword.

[49] Sholeh Quinn, *Historical Writing During the Reign of Shah 'Abbas: Ideology, Imitation, and Legitimacy in Safavid Chronicles*, (Salt Lake City: University of Utah Press. 2000).

I am longing for you to take me to Isfahan
To take me from the land of the body to the spirit

You will become the Khiżr of my road with your Alexandrine glory
That is, you will take me to the water of life (Shānī, 102)

Salīm Tihrānī also depicted the king as an approachable, sympathetic, and generous king.[50] Salīm's *qaṣīdeh* starts with a *tashbīb* about morality and ethics including the fear of God, self-respect, and avoiding debauchery. In these lines, the poet uses a language similar to that of the Iraqi style, which is generally known for being applied in *ghazal* form and depicting love scenes to advise the audience against falling for the beauty of this world or becoming captive to material life. As the symbol of desire, a nightingale speaks of the dangers associated with love. *Gulistān* (garden) refers to the material world and *maqsūd* (aim, beloved), *'āfiyat* (peace and health), *chaman* (grass, a metaphor for the world), *shabistān* (bed-chamber), and *ṭurreh* (locks) come together to represent the themes of love, salvation, and piety in this *qaṣīdeh*:

کی توانی برد سوی منزل مقصود راه
توشه تن تا نسازی پاره دل همچو ماه

از خطر در سیرگاه این چمن غافل مباش
چهچه بلبل ندانی چیست یعنی چاه چاه

خوش نشین این گلستان باش همچو نخل موم
ریشه خود را مکن زنجیر پا همچو گیاه

در شبستان جهانت گر سر آسودگی است
از سر خود دور کن جان را چو شمع صبحگاه

عافیت خواهی چو عنقا پارسایی پیشه کن
طره خوبان بود آزادگان را دام راه

How can you reach the abode of your goal (beloved)
if like the moon you do not feed your body from the soul

---

[50] Muḥammad Qulī Salīm Tihrānī, *Dīvān-i Kāmil-i Salīm Tihrānī*, ed. Muḥammad Qahriman (Tehran: Nigāh 1385/2006), 359. (Cited hereafter in the text and footnotes as Salīm.)

Do not be careless about the dangers existing in this green world
You hear a nightingale sing without understanding it cries a well! a well![51]

Enjoy the beauty of this garden like a palm of wax[52]
Do not be like a plant with your roots chained to the earth

if you look for tranquility in the bed-chamber of the world
Let life to not be in your head and be like a morning candle[53]

If you want health, be pious like a phoenix[54]
The locks of beauties are traps for noble men (Salīm, 359)

Before turning the poem into its panegyric form, the poet continues with a description of his miseries. He explains that he is drawn into sorrow. He boasts about his poetic skills and compares them with the beauty of flowers. He discusses his *himmat* (high-mindedness) that prevents him from asking for others' help by presenting his poems. The dominant Sufi vocabulary and themes of satisfaction and isolation from worldly matters make this *qaṣīdeh* different from the other court poems that either begin with direct praise of the king or depict the court lifestyle:

در میان خلق از اسباب تعلق چاره نیست
ترک سر کردن بود آسانتر از ترک کلاه

چون توانم شد خلاص از تنگنای غم که نیست
راه بیرون رفتن از هیچ سو چون آب چاه

بر نمی آید ز دستم این که همچون دیگران
شعر را سازم پی وجه معیشت خضر راه

دست همت در فضای دهر نتوانم گشود
تنگ تر از آستین باشد مرا این دستگاه

When living amongst people, dependence cannot be avoided
To give up your head is easier than to take off your hat

---

[51] The poet made a relation between the word *chah chah* (the sound of a singing bird) and *chāh* (a well) to describe the dangers behind the beauty of the world.

[52] The palm of wax was a fake tree that were made for decorative purposes (Dehkhoda).

[53] Not thinking about material issues lit your thoughts (head), similar to ta candle which its love for a moth burns it.

[54] The relationship between the phoenix and piety comes from the idea of this bird's way of living which is in isolation.

How can I become free from the ties of sorrow,
There is no way out (I am trapped) like the water of a well

Unlike the others, it is beyond my ability,
to make poetry Khiżr of path (spiritual guide) to reach living[55]

In the world, I cannot extend my full of spiritual energy hand to ask for alms
Tighter than my sleeve is my means of living[56] (Salīm, 360)

The poet is miserable. He complains of not having proper dress and that his lifestyle gives him no option but to ask the king for support. To praise the king's physical features (for example strength and war skills) and personality (for example his morality), Salīm applies a literary language that is not similar to the conventional language of praise. This language highlights the king's Sufi character with emphasizing the king's spiritual and sacred power on the life of his people:

آن نهنگ بحر کین خواهی که مرغ روح خصم
می کند در آب تیغش همچو مرغابی شناه

جوهر شمشیر شاهی، آبروی تاج و تخت
شعله شمع عدالت، شاه دین، عباس شاه

ای غبار درگهت از تاج شاهان باج خواه
یک حباب بحر قدرت نه فلک را بارگاه

گر سلیمان نیستی اما بود از حشمتت
جانورداران تو هر یک سلیمان دستگاه

از ترحم کبک کهساری ز بیم عدل تو
می دهد شهباز را در زیر بال خود پناه

کعبه کوی تو دارد جذبه ای کز شوق آن
همچو اشک از بطن مادر، طفل می افتد به راه

چون کند لطف تو از زندان اسیران را خلاص
می کند فواره نی را از برای آب چاه

---

[55] The poet makes a connection between making a living out of poetry and following Khiżr to reach to the water of life.

[56] *Tang-ī* (tightness) of his sleeve and *tang-dastī* (poverty) come together to mention that the poet is poor, but his elevated mind does not allow him to ask for money.

That whale of the sea of revenge, makes the dove-like soul of his adversary
swim into the water (luster) of his sword like a duck

He is the essence of the kingly sword, he is the honor of crown and throne
He is the flame of the candle of justice, he is the king of the religion, 'Abbās Shah

Oh you who the mere atoms of your court demand tribute from the crown of other kings
the court of nine skies is a bubble of the sea of your magnificence

Although you are not Solomon because of your pomp,
Any of your living subjects look like Solomon in glory

A mountain partridge, being merciful and scared of your justice,
shelters a falcon under its wings

Your abode is the Ka'beh and its attraction is so strong [that],
As quickly as the first cries of the baby detached from its mother's womb begins its journey [towards it]

Your kindness frees the prisoners from jail
like a fountain that draws water from the well through a pipe[57]

The painter of eternity called your battle horse "the best of acts" (i.e. *jihad*);
The executioner of fate said to your sword "my soul is for it!"[58] (Salīm, p. 361)

In the first line, when the poet speaks of the king's revenge, he invokes the enemy's soul of a dove of, a metaphor that, by considering the context in which this metaphor has previously been used to refer to the spiritual Sufi and human beings, does not reflect the hatred between the king and his enemy. In the second line, where the dominant theme is the king's authority over religion and the state, Salīm applies the image of a candle and flame to refer to the king's justice, which does not match the ideas and concepts that are represented in the second line. The concept of travel expressed through the poet's passion for the king's residence positioned the king similarly to the spiritual leader and the beloved. These ranging images are not usually

---

[57] There is a far-fetched metaphor between "fountain" and "straw". The poet looked to imply the fountain similar to a straw, that could take out the water from a jar, will take the water out of a well.

[58] To show obedience to his sovereignty. Both lines praise the military ability of the king

combined with images that mainly represent the king's power and dominance. The king is represented as a Sufi leader, but there is no strong imagery that reinforces the idea of a king leading a Muslim community.[59]

E. Shah Ṣafī and ʻAbbās II

While historians have mostly accepted Chardin's verdict about the failures of ʻAbbās I's successors, there are new perspectives in historical analysis of Shah Ṣafī I and ʻAbbās II's periods. Despite the external challenges after ʻAbbās I's death, the realm experienced far less domestic disorder during Shah Ṣafī I's reign in comparison to earlier rulers. The great vizier of Ṣafī, Sārū Taqī, managed to maintain sufficient support from Persians, Turks, and Tajiks to secure economic growth.[60] The resulting prosperity from foreign relationships caused an increase in revenue and, furthermore, the court could resume court-sponsored activities and projects. The peace treaty of Zuhab in 1639 ended Safavid-Ottoman conflicts. The resulting peace helped to lessen Iran's military concerns as the borders had become stable both in the west and the east. The Safavid relations with maritime companies improved and the empire's revenue increased due to the high price of silk.[61]

---

[59] Ṭalib Āmuli has a *qaṣīdeh* which, in terms of representing the king and in terms of structure, is similar to the Salīm's *qaṣīdeh*. He starts with description of nature and demonstrates his poetic skills, and then he continues with the king's praise. The king also is portrayed with Sufi characteristics rather than the characteristics of conventional king in panegyric *qaṣīdeh*s. To read the poem in praise of Shah ʻAbbās I, see Ṭālib Āmulī, *Kulliyāt-i Ashʻār-i Malik al-Shuʻarāʼ Ṭālib Āmulī*, ed. Shahab Tahiri, (Tehran: Kitābkhānek-yi Sanāʼī, 1980), 17.

[60] To further reading on the life and work of Mīrzā Sārū Taqī read Rudi Matthee, *Persian in Crisis: Safavid Decline and the Fall of Isfahan* (London: I.B. Tauris: Iran Heritage Foundation.2012), 40-42.

[61] See Rudi Matthee, *The Politics of Trade: Silk for Silver, 1600-1730*, (Cambridge, U.K: New York: Cambridge University Press, 1999). 120-145. To read on the context of Zuhab treaty, see Matthee, *Persian in Crisis,* 119-121, 250-252. Also see Joao Teles a Cunha, PORTUGAL i.

The support for court projects continued during the reign of 'Abbās II. Despite the external challenges in the transition period after Ṣafī's death, there are signs of a healthy and dynamic economy and culture. The self-confidence of the king and the power of the court is reflected in the court chronicles. Lengthy narratives of Safavid genealogy connected the Safavid house to the seventh Imam through great architectural mosques and palaces of the period and prove that the court was prosperous enough to support court culture.[62] By building on the relationship between 'Abbās I and religious scholars, both kings supported their higher philosophical writings on orthodox Shi'ism, which usually targeted unorthodox practices of other religious groups, especially Sufism, which was popular at that time. The most important poets of this period were Faṣīḥī, Salīm, Ṭarzī, and Ṣā'ib. In this chapter, I limit my analysis to Faṣīḥī and Salīm's poems. I examine Ṣā'ib's works in Chapter Four because he approaches the Shi'i Safavid kings differently. Most of the poems written for these two kings represent a king whose spiritual power overweighs his material power. Faṣīḥī and Salīm were not supported by the central court, however Ṭarzī Afshārī was very welcome by Shah 'Abbās II.[63]

RELATIONS WITH PERSIA IN THE EARLY MODERN AGE (1500-1750), originally published July 2009, http://www.iranicaonline.org/articles/portugal-i.

[62] Newman, *Safavid Iran*, 73-93. To read more in detail about the time of Shah 'Abbās II, see Matthee, *Persia in Crisis*, 42-53. In these pages Rudi Matthee investigated the role of Shah 'Abbās II's viziers, Khalīfeh Sulṭān (1645 – 1654) and Muḥammad Beyg (1654 – 1661).

[63] In biographies that remained from Ṭarzī, it is mentioned that he loved traveling and he was constantly on the move. However, as Shāh 'Abbās II enjoyed his companionship, he forced him to marry in Isfahan and stay there. For reading a short biography on his life and work, see Reza, Anzabinejad, "Ṭarzī Afshār: Shā'irī Yigāneh" *Nāmeh-yi Farhangistān*, murdād 1379/2001, *dawreh* 4, no.3, 96-103.

In Salīm's work for Ṣāfī I, the king is not identified as Shiʻi. The poet praises the king as a perfect warrior whose main features are generosity and justice. Salīm's *qaṣīdeh*, like Faṣīḥī's, represents the king as a non-Shiʻi ruler.[64] The poetry of Ṭarzī Afshār is no different in this regard. Ṭarzī wrote panegyrics for Shah ʻAbbās II in which the king was praised for his military power but Shiʻi legitimacy has no place in his poetry.[65]

Faṣīḥī's *qaṣīdeh*, similar to Salīm's *qaṣīdeh* in praise of Shah Ṣafī I, did not make a direct affiliation between Shah Ṣafī and the house of the Prophet. He started his praise for the king with the king's political authority, which soon transformed to the king's generosity and his other personal characteristics. The poet did not center his praise on the political authority of the king; instead, he mentioned the king's personal traits such as magnanimity and hot temper.

ز پرده پرده ساز جهان نوا برخاست
که فر شاه صفی تخت و تاج را آراست

دهان سکه چو نامش گرفت پر ز زر شد
زبان خطبه ثنایش سرود کامرواست

به نیم موجه دلش آز را کریم کند
سپهر الحق دریا دلی چنین می خواست

مرض ز ملک طبیعت گریخت از بیمش
همین عقیم به دورش سپهر حادثه زاست

بهار خلقش عطری فشاند بر عالم
که هر کجا خس و خاریست همچو گل بوباست

شکفت در جگر لاله نیز غنچه داغ
اگر سیاه دل نشکفد گل سوداست

---

[64] Salīm Tehrānī, *Divān-i Kāmil-i Salīm*, 390-391.

[65] Look at *qaṣīdeh*s in praise of Shāh ʻAbbās II in Muḥammad Ṭarzī Afshār, *Dīvān-i Ṭarzī Afshār*, ed. Fatemeh Mudarrisi and Vahid Riza'i Hamzeh Kandi (Tehran : Farhangistān-i Zabān va Adab-i Fārsī: Nashr-i Ās_ār, 2014).

چو اوست قبله شاهان زبان ثنایش گفت

به راستی که زبانم به کام قبله نماست

ستم به عهدش همچون دفینه در خاک است

جهان به دستش همچون سفینه بر دریاست

From every single frets of the world's instrument raised a melody
Because Ṣafī's *farr* beautified the throne and the crown

The mouth of coin became gold as it mentioned his name,
The praising tongue of his oration is a prosperous song

[the king by] showing half of his generosity makes a jealous heart generous
The sphere definitely needed such a person, with a heart like an ocean

In fear of him (the king), illness fled from the kingdom of nature
The calamity birthing is barren around him

The spring of his good nature spreads perfumes throughout the world
(for this reason) the thorns smell like flowers

In the heart of the tulip, the black brand [of love] blossomed
But the black-hearted, like clay, does not bloom

Because he is the *qibleh* (aim) of other kings the tongue praised him,
The tongue in my mouth shows the direction of *qibleh*

Oppression in his age is buried beneath the ground,
The world in his hand is like a ship on the sea[66]

Faṣīḥī's language in praising the king makes his *qaṣīdeh* similar to the *ghazal*s

of his time. This language, which was mostly dominant in the *ghazal* form, especially

the *ghazal*s of the Indian/Isfahani style, gives a caring sympathetic sense to the king's

portrait, which is not the image of an awe-inspiring king but rather of a king whose

presence drives out illness and brings prosperity. This language continues when the

poet describes the sorrow following Shah ʿAbbās I's death. The sacred and spiritual

characteristic of the king demonstrated itself in the influence that the king had over the

world:

---

[66] Faṣīḥī Hiravī, *Dīvān-i Faṣīḥī Hiravī*. ed. Ibrahim Qeysari, Muhammad Dehqani (Tehran: Amīr Kabīr, 2004), 207. (lines 1-6 and 8) (cited hereafter in text and footnotes as Faṣīḥī)

شها چو جد تو آن شاه آسمان خرگاه

به عزم سیر بهشت از سر جهان برخاست

جهان چو مردم چشم بتان سیه پوشید

سپهر چون مژه صفهای فتنه می آراست

به نیم لحظه تو گفتی که آفتاب منیر

خمیرمایه ی شام و شب غم و یلداست

ز باد حادثه بنشست آسمان به زمین

ز موج اشک زمین همچو آسمان برخاست

Oh king! When your forefather, the king whose tent was like a sky
Left the world aiming to visit the heavens,

The world wore black, like the pupils of the beautiful young idols
While the sphere, like [their] eyelashes, adorned the lines of tumult

As if in a second the brightest sun
Became molded [like dough] into night, the night of grief and of Yaldā[67]

From the blow of this incident the sky fell to the ground
Waves of tears lifted the ground to the sky (Faṣīḥī, 207, lines 15-18)

The poet compares the advent of Shah Ṣafī to a new sun for the world bringing justice with it:

که ناگه از افق غیب صبح دولت تو

طلوع کرد و جهان را به عدل و داد آراست

When suddenly the brightness of your kingship from the horizon of the world of the unseen
Arose and beautified the world with justice and fairness (Faṣīḥī, 208, line 21)

No expressions of 'Alid sentiments or Mahdism have a place in this work. The king Faṣīḥī represented is not a Shi'i king. The king is divine, and the world responds to his spiritual character, but this spirituality does not relate to his role as a Shi'i leader of the empire.

---

[67] The longest and darkest night of the year, the winter solstice celebration, which traditionally is celebrated by Iranians.

F. Shah Sulaymān: A Pre-Islamic King with Sufi Charisma

Muḥsīn Ta'sīr Tabrīzī (b. 1650) represented Shah Sulaymān with the dominant images of political authority and military power. This representation seems to be related to the country's dominant socio-economic circumstances. Although the transition of power from Shah 'Abbās II to Shah Sulaymān was smooth and peaceful, with only minor uprisings at the borders, the domestic socio-economic crises generated problems for the new king that undermined the king's political power. Poor harvest, plague, famine, and an earthquake created critical conditions in Isfahan and, in turn, for the Shah during the late 17th century.[68]

The political authority and military power of the king still is the dominant theme of the *qaṣīdeh* in this period. Muḥsīn's panegyric begins with direct praise of the king. A drum announces Sulaymān's kingship. Then, the poet compares the king with ancient Persian kings including Darius, Firīdūn, and Jamshīd in magnanimity and the king is said to possess both *farr* and magnificence. His will rules over the faith and his justice defeats suppression:[69]

---

[68] Newman, *Safavid Iran*, 93-103.

[69] Muḥsin Ta'sīr Tabrīzī, *Dīvān-i Muḥsīn Ta'sīr Tabrīzī*, ed. Amin Pasha Ijlali. (Tehran: Markaz-i Nashr-i Dānishgāhī, 1994), 89. (Cited hereafter in the text and footnotes as Ta'sīr). For more examples:

Sulaymān, whose divine glory is like that of Jamshīd's, the just king
In dignity and respect he is Firīdūn, in knowledge he is Alexandria (Ta'sīr, 93)

سلیمان جمشید فر شاه عادل
به حشمت فریدون به دانش سکندر

The kind-hearted king, with the magnificence of Jamshīd
Who from fear of him, the sun's heart is also shaking (Ta'sīr, 95)

بحمدالله که زد در ملک ایران کوس سلطانی

خدیو دادگستر مظهر الطاف ربانی

سلیمان شاه بن عباس شه دارای دریا دل

فریدون فر جمشید احتشام اسکندر ثانی

شهنشاهی که در پیش رکاب نصرتش هر دم

به پای سر دوان بینی سران انسی و جانی

اساس سلطنت بر پایه ای بگذاشت اقبالش

که همچون بیت معمورش نیابد دست ویرانی

Thank God that in the Persian empire he beat the drum of kingship
The king, the distributor of justice, the manifestation of God's kindness

Sulaymān Shah the son of ‘Abbās Shah, a king as ocean-hearted as Darius
with the divine glory of Firīdūn, and Jamshīd's pomp, [he is] the second Alexandria

The king of kings, towards whom rush constantly o serve of the king, every moment
[you] will see the best of human beings and *jinn's* running [towards him] with their heads for feet

His auspiciousness was the pillar that formed the foundation of his kingdom
Like a prosperous house,[70] the hand of destruction shall never reach it (Ta‘sīr, 89-90)

By considering the power of religious clerics in this period and the legitimacy they gave to this community, it is not surprising to see that Muḥsīn Ta‘sīr Tabrīzī, like most of the poets during the post-‘Abbās I period, for legitimizing purposes did not mix Twelver Shi‘i authority with the king's political features. Several times, the poet mentions that God directs special attention toward the king, but this idea still is related to the concept of "the king as the shadow of God" and is separate from the Shi‘i discourse. In the opening lines of the second part of the panegyric, which I quoted above, the poet addresses the king and praises him with images that emphasize the king's political authority:

خسرو روشن روان جمشید گردون احتشام

آنکه از بیمش دل خورشید لرزان آمده است

[70] The prosperous house is the *Ka‘beh. Bayt-i ma'mūr* in Quran refers to *Ka‘beh* (52:4). Bayt-i ma'mūr in narrations is believed to exist in the fourth or seventh sky where the angels reside to pray to God.

شها خالی نگردد از تو دوران جهانبانی

فلک گردد به گردت همچو زنار سلیمانی

ز حکمت قیصر و فغفور و خاقان سر نمی پیچد

که منشور از شهان داری به مهر بنده فرمانی

به رنگ شاه بیت بسته در قید نولایت

هزاران خسرو والاگهر بندی و زندانی

ز مهر و مه فلک هم از تو چشم تربیت دارد

ز فطرت تا مربی شد ترا الطاف ربانی

Oh king! may you never be absent from the era of kingship.
The sphere is around you like the sacred belt[71] of Sulaymān

Caesar and Faghfūr and Khaqan will never disobey your order
Because the royal signet, by other kings, was bestowed upon you with a seal commanding obedience

Similar to the paramount verse (lit. the king of lines),[72] in the chain of your obedience
There are thousands of noble kings shackled and imprisoned

Amongst sun and the moon, the sphere expects you to guide him well
Because the God's grace was your guide (Ta'sīr, 90)

While Sufi lineage was an important element of the Safavid kingship, Muḥsin Ta'sīr Tabrīzī did not bring this idea into his poems of praise. He also did not mention the role of the king in promoting the religion until the final lines. Although the poet mentions that the king's ancestors were *pādishāh* (king), *sayyid*, *sultan*, and *khaqan* (Ta'sīr, 95), there are no specific references to any Imams showing the relationship between the Safavid kings and Shi'i Imams. The source of spirituality is not the king's relation to the House of the Prophet or being from a Sufi family. Rather, his personality gives the king the Sufi legitimacy he required. These characteristics follow the features of political authority that were mentioned at the beginning of the *qaṣīdeh*.

---

[71] Zunnār is any rope. The poet probably did not have the religious meaning of Zunnār in mind, because it refers to Solomon. In Christianity, Zunnār is a rope that Christians put on their clothes around the waist. Zunnār distinguished Christians from Muslims (Dehkhoda).

[72] The "king verse" of a poem is the verse that is distinguished from the other lines because of its imagery.

As I mentioned, the king was first praised for his political authority over the kings of other empires and subsequently with the notion of "justice" as the main element of kingship. The poet then returns to comparing Sulaymān with Kīyūmars, only to further state that Sulaymān was the supporter of religion and the people. Not only did the 'Alid sentiments have no place in his panegyric: there is also no mention of Imām Mahdī's return or waiting for that day:

جهان از فیض عدلت هم مرنج و هم مرنجان شد
نرنجی از کسی بیهوده و کس را نرنجانی

دلت آینه آسا کاشف اسرار لازمی
ضمیرت بحر مانا واقف اسرار پنهانی

پی منع بدی هر جا که از بأست نشان باشد
ز نام خویش بدنامی کشد لعل بدخشانی

کیومرث ار چه بانی بود شغل پادشاهی را
اگر می دید درگاهت شدی مشغول دربانی

سخن در پرده کس در عهد احسانت نمی گوید
ز بس برداشت از عالم عطایت عیب عریانی

اگر در حال پیدا بود ضعفی دین و ملت را
قوی از بال و کوپال تو شد پشت مسلمانی

The world benefitting from your justice is not bothered [by anyone] and does not irritate
You will not be irritated by anyone with no reason and you will not irritate anyone

Your heart is a mirror revealing unknown secrets
Your nature is an ocean understanding hidden secrets

To repel wrongdoing, when your anger shows its face,
The ruby of Badakhshan becomes infamous because of its name[73]

Although Kīumars was the founder of the profession of kingship,
If he would see your court, he would become your gate-keeper

No one talks behind the veil during the reign of your compassion
Because your generosity removed from the world the problem of nakedness[74]

---

[73] The line in Persian applied the word *bad* (Bad) to further employ it in *badnāmī* (disrepute) and Badakhshan (the province near Afghanistan which in literature is famous for its garment).

[74] The line indicates because the king was generous in giving to the poor, revealing poverty and needs was not a problem.

If there was a weakness in the religion and the faith,
From your support (lit 'lion's mane') the Muslims' back became strong (Ta'sīr, 92)

In praising the king with his physical features and his personality, the poetic language of Muḥsin shows difference from when he praises the king's political power. When the poet describes the king's physical features, he applies a language similar to the dominant language of *ghazal*s. In this situation, the king is praised similarly to the traditional beloved of *qaṣīdeh*s of earlier Persian poetry:

لبت آنجا که از شیرین کلامی قند می ریزد
نماید طره های حورو رضوانش مگس رانی

ز عارض شاهد رایت اگر برقع براندازد
زداید زنگ ظلمت از دل شبهای ظلمانی

When your lips bring sugar speaking sweetly
The locks of angels and the guardians of heaven swat the flies

if the beauty witness of your face lifts veil from your cheeks
The dark rust will be driven away from the heart of dark nights (Ta'sīr, 92)

In the final lines where the poet wishes good for the king's followers and death for his enemies, his choice of vocabulary makes his work similar to *ghazal*s of the Safavid period or even the earlier times:

نماید تا بناگوش بتان در دعوی دلها
یدبیضایی از اعجاز و مشکین طره ثعبانی

محبان ترا دیدم ز نور وادی ایمن
چراغ بخت روشن باد چون موسی عمرانی

معاند با تو چون در معرض کین و نفاق آید
غریق نیل بدبختی اسیر تیه حیرانی

As long as the cheeks of beautiful idols appear to hearts
as the miraculous radiant hand of Moses [beneath] fragrant black locks like snakes,

I saw your lovers in the brightness of the holy Sinai valley
May The lights of their fortune be as bright as Moses of 'Imrān

Your adversary, if he disagrees with you and becomes your enemy
[I wish will be] drowned in a deep Nile of miseries and captured in a desert of wandering (Ta'sīr, 93)

In general, Muḥsīn Ta'sīr Tabrīzī represented Shah Sulaymān by comparing him with the Persian kings of pre-Islamic times. He described the king with the title *pādishah-i dīn va dunyā* (the king of the religion and the world). The 'Alid sentiments and any notions of popular Sufism are also dismissed despite the fact that they were the dominant discourses of the time.[75]

IV. Conclusion

In this chapter, I study the works of seven Persian poets from the nine Safavid courts that span from the reign of Shah Ṭahmāsb to the end of Shah Sulaymān's reign. By investigating the panegyrics of these poems, I sketch the trajectory of the monarchs' images. I demonstrate that the poets of Shah Ṭahmāsb's reign presented Shi'ism in relation to the idea of return with ambiguous references to the battle of Karbala and represented the king's role as distributing the doctrines of Shi'ism. However, in the poems of the next courts, this image lost its position to images that represented the Safavid kings as Sufi *shaykh*s with personality traits of the pre-Islamic kings of the Persian Empire (see Tables 5 and 6).

Furthermore, this chapter explores the literary representation of Safavid monarchs in panegyrics of the Safavid period to shed light on the idea of rulership in the absence of an Imam. In Shi'i doctrine, the right to leadership over the Muslim community can only belong to an innocent Imam (i.e. the Twelfth Imam, or Imam Mahdī). My analysis demonstrates that, by combining the personality of a spiritual

---

[75] The king whom Mullā Muḥammad Vā'iẓ Qazvīnī described visibly represented the characteristics of pre-Islamic period kings as well. See Muḥammad Rafī' Vā'iẓ Qazvīnī, *Dīvān-i Mullā Muḥammad Rafī' Vā'iẓ Qazvīnī*, ed. Hasan Sadat Nasiri (Tehran: Akbar 'ilmī, 1980), 485.

power and a temporal king, the Safavid poets presented the Safavid kings similarly to *awlīyā Allāh* (the friends of God) to legitimize their kingship. This occurred through emphasizing pre-Islamic notions of kingship in the Persian Empire and the characteristics of Sufi *shaykh*s in affiliation with the Safavid monarchs. Analysis of Tables 5 and 6, which present patterns of Shi'i images and of Persian notions of kingship in panegyrics, demonstrates that by the time of Shah Sulaymān, the poets' attempt in praising the Safavid kings colored the ideal image of king with ideas related to Persian culture in ruling. This is in congruence with the titles and benedictions of state sponsored materials during the reign of Shah Sultan Ḥusayn (see Tables 2 and 3). Additionally, while the benedictions of coins from Shah Ṣafī's time attempt to associate the Safavid king with Tīmūr, Timurid legitimacy is absent from the poems of his time and those that followed. Instead, emphasizing on special influence of the kings over the world and the people that presented itself in a language that usually belonged to the world of *ghazal* writing with Sufi themes, argued for sacred aspects of the Safavid rulers in kingship and allowed them to be known as the representatives of Imām Mahdī until his return.

As mentioned earlier, the reign of Shah 'Abbās I is marked with religious devotion and public display of servitude towards the Shi'i Imams, especially after the relocation of the capital to Isfahan. In other materials such as the benedictions of coins and inscriptions (see Tables 2 and 3), expressions such as "the guard dog of the threshold of *vilāyat*" and "the guard dog of the 'Alī's threshold" are indicative of the king's religious ideology in kingship. However, these expressions do not appear in the poetry of his time and the next kings. Instead, the panegyric poems became lyrical and similar to the *ghazals* of the Safavid period. This change is also evident in representations of the king. The kings from Shah 'Abbās I's period are mostly praised for their pious personality and for features such as justice and wisdom rather than their military prowess and strength. This representation depicted the Safavid kings as similar to the sinless Imams and, therefore, righteous individuals worthy of filling the position of king in the absence of a just leader.

Table 5 (Patterns of Shi'i Images in Panegyrics)[76]

Kings	Shi'i Notions				
	Lineage	Servitude	Distribution of Twelver Shi'ism	Mahdism	Karbala
Shah Ismā'īl	-	-	-	-	-
Shah Ṭahmāsb	N/A	N/A	*	*	N/A
Shah Ismā'īl II	N/A	N/A	*	*	N/A
Shah Muḥammd Khudābandeh	*	N/A	*	N/A	N/A
Shah 'Abbās I	N/A	N/A	N/A	N/A	N/A
Shah Ṣafī I	N/A	N/A	N/A	N/A	N/A
Shah 'Abbās II	N/A	N/A	N/A	N/A	N/A
Shah Sulaymān	*	N/A	N/A	N/A	N/A
Shah Sultan Ḥusayn	-	-	-	-	-

Table 6 (Patterns of Persian Notions of Kingship in Panegyrics)

Kings	Persian Notions of Kingship				
	Titles	Comparisons	Symbols		
			Farr	Light	Falcon/Parasol
Shah Ismā'īl	-	-	-		
Shah Ṭahmāsb	*	*	*	*	N/A
Shah Ismā'īl II	*	N/A	N/A	*	N/A
Shah Muḥammad Khudābandeh	*	N/A	N/A	N/A	N/A
Shah 'Abbās	*	N/A	N/A	N/A	*
Shah Ṣafī	*	N/A	*	N/A	N/A
Shah 'Abbās II	*	N/A	N/A	N/A	N/A
Shah Sulaymān	*	*	*	N/A	N/A
Shah Sultan Ḥusayn	-	-	-	-	-

---

[76] In tables (-) indicates no poet was found to be discussed. (*) demonstrates the images of a particular pattern of legitimacy was found, and N/A is for what could not be found from that particular pattern of legitimacy

CHAPTER FOUR:
ṢĀ'IB TABRĪZĪ AS A PERSIAN COURT POET

I. Introduction

Ṣā'ib (d. 1676) is justly regarded as one of the most outstanding poets of the

17th century. He was a source of inspiration for his contemporaries and the poets of

later years, especially in *ghazal* writing.[1] His *ghazal*s brought him much fame and

respect. They portray different aspects of human life from the individual to the social.

Ṣā'ib makes use of the elements of nature and the world of Sufism to present his ideas

about human beings and the world.[2] While in the *ghazal* form he pays particular

attention to the inner feelings of human beings, in the *qaṣīdeh* form he expresses

interest to the world of religion and politics to show his allegiance to the Safavid

court.[3] In the *qaṣīdeh* form, he does not show an interest in reflecting upon morality,

---

[1] Paul Losensky, *Welcoming Fighani: Imitation and Poetic Individuality in the Safavid-Mughal Ghazal*, (Costa Mesa, Calif: Mazda Publishers, 1998). Ṣā'ib's life and style, as well as his influence over the other poets, have been the subject of numerous scholarly writings. These writings include comparative analyses between Ṣā'ib's style of writing and that of other poets as well as examinations of Ṣā'ib's use of specific literary devices. For comparison between Ṣā'ib and other poets that specifically discusses the role of Sufism on Ṣā'ib's literature, see the comparison between Ṣā'ib and Ḥāfiẓ, Banu Karimi, "dar Hāshīyeh-yi Sabk-i Ṣāib", *The Faculty of Persian Language and Literature*, (Fall and Winter 1356/1975), no 1 and 2, pp 114-129. On the similarity between Ṣā'ib's works and Ḥāfiẓ see Muahmmad Amin Riyahi, "Ṣā'ib Tabrīzī: Shā'ir-i Zamāneh-yi Khīsh", *Yaghmā*, (Farwardin 1355/1976), no 331, 2-12.

[2] On Sufism, see Nargis Usku'i, "Ṣā'ib Tabrīzī va Maktab-i Jamāl dar Shi'r-i Fārsī", *Kayhān-i Farhangī*, (Day and Bahman, 1384/2005), no. 231-232. In this article, Uskui tries to introduce Ṣā'ib as a Sufi by reviewing the motifs of Sufi literature in his works. Ahmad Guli "'Irfān-garāyī-yi Ṣā'ib", *Pajūhishnāmeh-yi Adab-i Ghanāī*, (Fall and winter, 1383/2004), no.3, pp 97- 116 attempted to examine Ṣā'ib's approach towards Sufi themes through categorizing them in his *dīvān*.

[3] Numerous works discuss the use of specific literary devices in poems also. Scholars have placed the most attention towards the function of *tamsīl* in Ṣā'ib's works. *Tamsīl* (exemplum orable) is the dominant feature of the Indian/Isfahani style and Ṣā'ib is famous in applying it in his *ghazal*s. Using *tamsīl* allowed the poet to create images which enter the world of Sufism as well. On the function of

162

nature, or love if they do not buttress the idea of a Safavid king as a Shiʻi-Sufi-Persian king.[4] Ṣāʻib's *qaṣīdeh*s are highly concerned with the religio-political circumstances of the Safavid period and with promoting the Safavid ideology. For manifesting the Safavid power, Ṣāʻib's *qaṣīdeh*s integrate the characteristics of Shiʻi Imams and Sufis in addition to the titles, symbols, and notions of the pre-Islamic form of kingship in Persian Empire to praise the Safavid kings and to legitimize them. By doing so, Ṣāʻib establishes Shah Ṣafī I (b. 1611 – d. 1642), and his primary patron, Shah ʻAbbās II (b. 1632 – d. 1666) as the promoters of Shiʻi thoughts and legacies and as a *murshid-i kāmil* (the perfect guide), as well as the shadow of God on Earth. Ṣāʻib, writing in *qaṣīdeh* form, is fully committed to the Safavid ideology in public, and, in this regard, he is unique among the many poets who wrote for the Safavid kings. His poetry works similar to the other means of legitimation in public such as the inscriptions of mosques or the charities of the charitable trusts.

---

tamsīl in Ṣāʻib's pomes see Muhammad Hakim Azar, "Bahs dar Tashbīh, Tamsīl va Kārkard-i ān dar Ghazal-i Ṣāʻib Ṭabrīzī," *Funūn-i Adabī*, Summer 1395/2016, no. 15, pp 117-136. This is an example of many works written on Ṣāʻib's literary devices. The most important aspect of these writings is that the scholars chose Ṣāʻib's *ghazal*s and not the many forms in which he wrote. For reading more about Ṣāʻib, his biography or style of writing see Abulqasim Radfar, "Kitāb Shināsī-yi Ṣāʻib: Buzurg Shāʻir-i Sabk-i Iṣfahānī,", (Bija), (Fall and Winter, 1370/1991 and Spring 1371/1992), no 5, 6, 7, pp.81-108.

[4] "Persianate form of kingship" in my dissertation refers to Sasanid ideas of kingship and its origins within other cultures, which referred to the kings of the Persian Empire. Ascribing *farr* to the Safavid kings, and the appearance of falcons as the symbol of Sasanid kingship, are among the most dominant symbols used to refer to the Safavid kings. Also, titles such as *shāh-i shāhān*, as well as *pādishāh-i pādishahān* (the king of kings) and its variations, represent the idea of Persianate kingship within the Safavid context. The litany of names of pre-Islamic kings of Iran is another way to color legitimacy sought by the Safavid kings who held Persianate ideas of pre-Islamic times. Usually, the pre-Islamic kings of Persia become a source of comparison for the Safavid kings in regard to their form of kingship or for having specific features such as justice, wit, or bravery. Firīdūn, Alexander, Darius, Kāvūs, and Jamshīd are some examples. The Persian heroes of *Shāhnāmeh* and the objects or animals close to them—for instance, Rustam, his horse (*Rakhsh),* and Isfandīyār—were among the other images in poems that I examine as elements connecting the Safavid kings and their sacred form of kingship to the Persian forms of kingship from the pre-Islamic period.

In this chapter, I demonstrate that the images of legitimacy given in Ṣā'ib's panegyrics match the public claims of power during the Safavid periods (see Table 2 and 3.)[5] Drawing any specific conclusion as to why Ṣā'ib strikes such a contrast with the other Safavid poets in his own poetic language, style of writing, and approach to represent the kingship is a challenging task. Newman argues that Ṣā'ib's panegyrics reflected "the complex, multi-constitutional nature of the broader Safavid project" and that they were broad enough so that "each of the realm's individual constituent elements, rural and urban, elite and non-elite, Muslim and non-Muslim, indigenous or foreign, perceived itself to have a vested interest in the present, and future, thereof."[6] Newman considers Ṣā'ib's additional references to the Shah's role as a Sufi leader, a promoter of the faith, a *sayyid* and a defender of the realm to be a "point[ing] up to…[the] inclusive nature and broad appeal" of Safavid legitimacy.[7] In the lack of enough evidence to support Newman's argument, the only certain fact is that Ṣā'ib's

---

[5] Mazahir Musaffa discusses the issue of literature of praise and its literary value specially during the 16th and 17th century. He argued that writing panegyrics for a reward is not against the literary value of a text. He further criticizes those who look at the literary production of India during this period negatively. According to Musaffa this approach is the influence of "colonialism" and the "enmity of west with east and the religion and lineage." He provides examples of good panegyrics that—only because of being a panegyric—were left out without examination. Musaffa pays special attention towards Anvarī whose *qaṣīdeh*s were perceived as worthless. He considers ignoring Anwari's panegyric poems to be "tearing out pages from the national identity" of the Iranians. Although in this article Musaffa does not provide any example of the Safavid poetry to further support his argument about the literary beauty of the Safavid panegyrics and in some parts, he emotionally gets involved with his argument, the basis of his argument is very solid. He presents the idea that a poem is not its literary value, but that it should be examined also through its religio-political ideas it presents, although its representation is against the dominant discourse of the time. According to him even a poem that is very bad linguistically still needs attention, because it not only gives a lesson to the new generation about what good or bad poetic language is, but also has its own lessons when approached from the historical perspective. See Mazahir Musaffa "Ṣā'ib dar Seh Bakhsh", *The Faculty of Persian Language and Literature University of Tehran*, (Spring and Fall 1356/1978), no. 97, 98. pp. 202-221.

[6] Andrew Newman, *Safavid Iran: Rebirth of a Persian Empire*, (I.B. Tauris, 2012), 117.

[7] Ibid.

poems were recited in non-court stages and for a broader public, as their political

discourse and patterns of legitimacy were similar to the patterns of other cultural

materials that broadly propagated the Safavid ideology.

Ṣā'ib and to some extent Muḥtasham's references to Shi'i doctrines along with

concept of kingship could be related to the access that the merchant families had to the

means of education including religious education on Shi'ism. Ṣā'ib's family belonged

to the mercantile elite. His father, Mīrzā 'Abd-al-Raḥīm, was a successful merchant

and his uncle was a talented calligrapher. His family members were all educated in

Tabriz and moved to Isfahan by the time of Shah 'Abbās I. Ṣā'ib's family's wealth

assured his financial independence and this wealth and security in his profession

paved the way to the Safavid court.[8] Muḥtasham was also from a mercantile family.

Muḥtasham's father, Khwajeh Mīr Aḥmad (d. 1554), was active in the textile industry

and the poet seems to have pursued the same occupation until a business setback led

him to choose poetry as a full-time job.[9] Muḥtasham also pays attention to the

different aspects of Safavid ideology including Shi'i doctrines; however, Muḥtasham's

poems do not have the same quality and emphasis as Ṣā'ib's in representing Safavid

ideology. Unlike for Ṣā'ib, the literary representation of the monarch patron did not

influence the structure of Muḥtasham's poems.

---

[8] Paul Losensky. "ṢĀ'EB TABRIZI," *Encyclopædia Iranica*, online edition, 2003, available at http://www.iranicaonline.org/articles/saeb-tabrizi (accessed on 20 September 2016).

[9] To read more about Muḥtasham's life see Paul Losensky, "MOḤTAŠAM KĀŠĀNI," *Encyclopædia Iranica*, online edition, 2014, available at http://www.iranicaonline.org/articles/mohtasham-kashani (accessed on 20 September 2016).

In contrast to most of the medieval Persian poets who were dependent on Muslim courts and were therefore obligated to praise the kingship and the king, Ṣāʿib did not have such obligations. According to his biography, Ṣāʿib employed his own resident calligrapher, Ārif Tabrīzī, to transcribe copies of his *divān*,[10] which means he had financial support for his own career. In general, he was not constrained to the court for documenting and circulating his poems to the same extent as the other poets. Collectively, scholars agree that Ṣāʿib was independent from the court. Even when ʿAbbās II appointed Ṣāʿib to the position of poet laureate, the poet did not take up residence in the palace.[11]

However, Ṣāʿib explicitly demonstrated that court patronage was important to him. In the early years of his life when he could not find his desirable position at the Safavid court, he left Iran for India and the Mughal courts in search for a better future for his literary career.[12] He lived in India, first in Kabul and then in the Deccan, for seven years (1625 – 1632). During this period, Ṣāʿib enjoyed his close relationship with Ẓafar Khān until 1628 when the poet was called to the imperial court to pledge allegiance to Shah Jahān (b. 1627 – d. 1658).[13] He accompanied Ẓafar Khān in some of his military campaigns and wrote panegyrics to dedicate to this Mughal ruler. He left the court of Ẓafar Khān when his father traveled to India to ask for his return to Isfahan. Upon his return, Ṣāʿib joined the court of Shah Ṣafī I and later became Shah ʿAbbās II's

---

[10] Losensky, "ṢĀʾEB TABRIZI," *Encyclopædia Iranica*.

[11] Ibid.

[12] Zabih Allah Safa, *Tārīkh-i Adabīyāt dar Īrān.* (Tehran: Intishārāt-i Firdawsī, 1984), Vol 5/2, 1271-1284.

[13] Losensky, "ṢĀʾEB TABRIZI", 2003.

poet laureate. His attempt to retain his relationship with the court is demonstrated through his harsh criticism against the ruler of Qandahar when Shah ʻAbbās II occupied the city in 1649. In a series of qaṣīdehs, the poet celebrated Shah ʻAbbās II's superior position in the world of light and righteousness, characterizing the Indian army as people in the world of darkness and infidelity.[14]

In short, Ṣāʼib, for most of his life, was in communication with nobles of the Safavid courts. His literary representation of the Safavid ideology is influenced by his lifestyle and his courtly relationships. The three dimensions of the Safavid ideology are coherently connected to the poems' other themes. The similarity between Safavid kings and the pre-Islamic Persian kings integrate with the images which give Sufi and Shiʻi legitimacy to the Safavid kings. This well-balanced image promotes the Safavid king as the shadow of God on Earth, the head of Sufi order, and the promotor of Shiʻi legacies. In each instance, these ideas are integrated and compressed in a line or a hemistich, and each line is related to the next several lines. The portrait of the kings mostly revolves around the idea of light, which is a common motif between the three pillars of Safavid legitimacy.

In Part II of this chapter, through analyzing Ṣāʼib's panegyrics for the Safavid kings, I demonstrate how the concept of light creates a sacred image for a king who possesses all the legitimizing aspects of a righteous king. Light, a symbol of perfection, describes the prophets. In his commentary on the Quran, Fakhr al-Dīn Al-Rāzī (d. 1210 CE) describes the perfect souls of prophets emanating their light on the

---

[14] Sharma notes the significance of the fight over Qandahar for the Safavids, and specially Saʻib. See *Mughal Arcadia*, 2017, 188.

souls of deficient people. This illumination can purify the souls of deficient people, moving them from darkness into light and from corporality into spirituality. Al-Rāzī endorses that people's religious belief can be strengthened through divine inspiration and that religious knowledge can bestowed on believers' souls through inspiration. Divine knowledge is also represented by light while lack of knowledge is likened to darkness. Rashīd al-Dīn also describes Oljaitu (d. 1316 CE), the eighth Ilkhanid ruler, with divine knowledge through divine inspiration. With such a claim, Rashīd al-Dīn mentions that Oljaitu occupies both the rank of rulers and the rank of sainthood.[15] Ṣā'ib's panegyrics, unlike the earlier poets of the Safavid courts, are coherent due to the poet's choice of vocabulary with *radīf*s (repeating rhyming words), which are connected with the idea of light and illumination. Through contradictions of light versus darkness and Muslims versus infields, Ṣā'ib further develops the king's characters into a sacred entity.

In Part III, I demonstrate that metaphors of illumination and light in relation to the Safavid kings spread throughout each of Ṣā'ib's poems. In this regard, it seems that Ṣā'ib was inspired by Rashīd al-Dīn's discussion of the characteristics of kings in comparison to prophets. According to Rashīd al-Dīn, a king, who has perfect knowledge and reason and whose interior is lit by the light of sacred meanings, possesses an extremely high rank, especially if he is a Muslim. Ṣā'ib praises his patrons by ascribing them with divine knowledge. He further praises them by saying

---

[15] See Jonathan Brack. "Mediating Sacred Kingship: Conversion and Sovereignty in Mongol Iran." PhD diss., University of Michigan, 2016, Al-Rāzī, Fakhr al-Dīn Muḥammad Ibn ʿUmar. Al-Tafsīr al-kabīr. Cairo, 1938. 32 vols, 16 (Cairo, 1938), 116-117.

that they are the Lords of the Conjunction and in possession of *farr*. This position is the highest stage within a hierarchical system of sacral kingship.[16]

In Part IV, I study the poems that Ṣā'ib wrote for the celebration of Shah 'Abbās II's victory over Indians in Qandahar. Built upon the idea of light versus darkness (with the latter as the symbol of the infidelity and ignorance of the king's enemies), I demonstrate that Ṣā'ib claimed that the Safavid king's religious and political power was due to God's special attention toward his patron. Ṣā'ib frequently wrote panegyric *qaṣīdeh*s for specific occasions such as the king's arrival to a city, the construction of a building, and, as mentioned, the king's victory.[17]

The three aspects of Safavid ideology are not disengaged in Ṣā'ib's poetry from one another, because the light, as the metaphor for that which is splendid and holy, is present in every verse and connects the images of legitimacy. Further, Ṣā'ib frequently applies terms and expressions that refer to the king as the disseminator of Twelver Shi'ism. These expressions, along with images that demonstrate the kings' lineage and spiritual power (similar to the Sufi leaders), describe the Safavid patrons as sacred kings.

---

[16] Ibid, 230.

[17] Sharma discussed the significance of this victory for the Safavid side in *Mughal Arcadia*. The victory in this battle helped the Safavids to stay in the game of power played by the Ottomans. As discussed by Sharma, Ṣā'ib is not the only poet who wrote about this victory (Sharma, *Mughal Arcadia*, 188-191)The battle was an important event for the Safavids and this victory also inspired other poets, most famously Muḥammad Ṭāhir Vaḥīd secretary-poet-chronicler under Safavid monarchs. In his *'Abbāsnāmeh*, Vaḥīd described the events of Qandahar. His description provides information about the war and the encounter of the two armies. The poet wrote about the personal strength of the king, compared him with pre-Islamic Persian kings. However, the motif of light is not dominant in this piece of poem. Only a few times the poet described the Indians with color black; however, this metaphor does not play a significant role in this poem. To read Vaḥīd's lines on the battle see *'Abbāsnāmeh*, ed. Ibrahim Dehgan, (Arak), 1961, 98-117.

II. Structure: What Does Ṣā'ib Do Differently?

Unlike his earlier peers, Ṣā'ib wrote longer *tashbīb*s before delving into praise of the king.[18] Like the other themes in his qaṣīdehs, these tashbībs attempt to legitimize the kingship from both religious and political standpoints. The *tashbīb*s in Ṣā'ib's panegyrics usually depict nature as calm and full of happiness. His *tashbīb*s represent the world in growth and prosperity. They usually present spring or the end of winter, when the world finds a fresh soul after the seasonal death of its body. Nature is described in terms of its beauty, its light, and its fragrances. This combination of beauty and illumination was a response to the new king coming to the throne. Celestial references play an important role in the overall structure of Ṣā'ib's poetry. Ṣā'ib pays special attention to the stars and their movements, which not only brings the idea of light into the poem but further reinforces the idea of the destined kingship of the Safavids. The illuminated world under the Safavid ruler is usually presented through portraying a cluster of shining objects (mostly the stars) and ideas such as *ṣāḥib-qirān* (the lord of conjunction), *sa'd* (with good omen), *sa'ādat* (fortune), *nūr* (light), and the Sun.

This interest in utilizing the themes of nature and light for praise especially demonstrates itself in Ṣā'ib's choice of *radīf*.[19] From a total of twenty-seven *qaṣīdeh*s by Ṣā'ib in praise of the kings and their affiliated palaces and monuments, four *qaṣīdeh*s possess *radīf* words which signify whiteness in color or bright objects. These

---

[18] Introductory lines of the *qaṣīdeh* form which typically is description of nature or presents love theme.

[19] *Radīf* is a repeated rhyming phrase that may appear at the end of each line. *Radīf* is specific to Persian poems. To read about its function and its influence on the general structure of poetry see Muhammad Riza Shafi'i Kadkani, *Musīqī-yi Shi'r*, (Tehran: Āgāh, 1994).

*radīf*s are *shukūfeh* (blooms), *āyineh* (mirror), *āftāb* (the Sun), *mahtāb* (moonlight). The *qaṣīdeh*s with no *radīf* often invoke elements of nature from the sky and stars to the seasons, rivers, and trees. These *radīf*s and rhymes at the end of each line reaffirm the images of light, beauty, and the prosperity of the Safavids' reign.

Ṣā'ib employs these *radīf*s in a unique way. For example, in a *qaṣīdeh* written for Shah 'Abbās II, *āftāb* (sun) is a *radīf* that plays a double role. While the Sun has been used as an element of nature to describe the coming of the new year and the beauty of the world after a cold winter in the *tashbīb*, the Sun can be considered to be representing the Shah in most of the lines. The Shah, similar to the Sun, came to the throne to give a new order to the world's affairs:[20]

روی در برج شرف آورد دیگر آفتاب
کرد ازین تحویل عالم را مسخر آفتاب

کشور ایجاد را از ماه تا ماهی گرفت
بر حمل از حوت شد تا سایه گستر آفتاب

می توان دانست دارد فکر عالمگیری
زین که می بخشد به لشکر با سپر زر آفتاب

می کند مانند ذوالقرنین از نور دو صبح
قاف تا قاف آفرینش را مسخر آفتاب

برق می سوزد به آسانی حجاب ابر را
وحشت از ظلمت ندارد چون سکندر آفتاب

The Sun moved towards exaltation in Aries again
And conquered the world with this movement

It took over the entire realm of existence, from the moon high above to the fish below the sea
As soon as it extended shadows from Pisces towards Aries

---

[20] The *qaṣīdeh* with *mahtāb* (moonlight) as its *radīf* is similar to this piece in terms of structure and applying *mahtāb* to refer to both the moonlight and the king. See Muḥammad 'Alī, Ṣā'ib Tabrīzī, *Divān-i Ṣā'ib*, ed. Muḥammad Qahirman, (Tabriz: Intishārāt-i Mu'assiseh-yi Tārīkh va Farhang-i Īrān, 1977), vol 6, 3574- 3575. (Hereafter cited in text and footnotes as Ṣā'ib).

One can see that it is thinking of world dominance
As it bestows gold[en rays] upon the warriors and their shields

Like the "Two-Horned" Alexander the Great, by the light of two sunrises
It conquers the whole universe, from one [side of] Mount Qāf [21] to the other

Lightning burns the veil of the clouds effortlessly
Like Alexander, the Sun is not frightened by the darkness (Ṣā'ib, 3586)

The Sun came into the house of Aries (*burj-i ḥamal*), which in the Persian calendar marks the new year. On this date, the equinox represents the balance that the king offers to the world after taking the throne. The Sun's movement into the house of Aries has been presented as an act of conquering the world. The metaphor of shining and giving light generously to the people has been used to refer to the king's generosity toward his army. The king is known as "the Sun," who gives his army enough security to conquer the world with him. The last line refers to the king's courage in war as it presents the Sun as the killer of darkness:

دایم از خط شعاعی مد احسانش رساست
زین سبب بر اختران گردیده سرور آفتاب

دولتش زان گشت روزافزون که فیضش می رسد
در بهاران بیش از ایام دیگر آفتاب

چهره اش زان است نورانی که نگذارد به شب
از دل بیدار پهلو را به بستر آفتاب

گر چه در زیر نگین اوست سرتاسر زمین
برندارد از سجود بندگی سر آفتاب

سجده می آرند پیشش گر چه ذرات جهان
می کند دریوزه همت ز هر در آفتاب

کرد تسخیر جهان در جلوه ای، گویا گرفت
همت از صاحبقران هفت کشور آفتاب

The rays of his benevolence constantly touch every corner
It is for this reason that the Sun has become the lord of all the stars

---

[21] It is an enormous mountain which is believed to be extended around the world.

The Sun found its ever-increasing glory by virtue of the fact that its generosity
Is more abundant during the spring than any other time[22]

Its face is radiant since at nights
Its vigilant heart does not let its back to touch the bed

Although the entire globe is under its command,
The Sun is in everlasting prostration before him

Although every atom in the universe is in prostration before it,
The Sun still wanders around seeking benefaction (spiritual ambition)

It dominated the world in one appearance, as if it received
its spiritual ambition from the *ṣāḥib-qirān* of the seven climes (Ṣāʿib, 3586-87)

Going to the section praising the king, the poet still uses the Sun to describe the king's attributes, especially the features that portray him as a spiritual and religious leader. Both the Sun and the king are bright, and both are generous. The Sun's generosity makes all stars to look smaller with no light. This claim is intended to show the king's superiority over other rulers. The everlasting nature of the Sun has also been used to refer to the king's constant effort in praying. The Sun is bright and shining because it never sleeps, and it is thus similar to the king, who does not sleep because he prays continuously.

In the antistrophe, the poet takes another stance in comparing the Sun with the king. The king and the Sun no longer resemble each other, because the king is "the shadow of God" and it is impossible for the shadow and the sun to be equal:

نسبت خورشید با آن روی نورانی خطاست
چون به ظل حق تواند شد برابر آفتاب؟

تیغ او را گر به خاطر بگذراند، می شود
چون مه از انگشت پیغمبر دو پیکر آفتاب

شبنمی بی رخصت از گلزار نتواند ربود
در زمان دولت آن دادگستر آفتاب

کرد در زر خاک را دست زر افشانش نهان

---

[22] The Sun also refers to the Safavid kingship. It glorifies, and its glory increases daily.

ساخت پنهان در ضمیر خاک اگر زر آفتاب

شد تمام از فیض عالمگیر او هر ناقصی
ماه نو را کرد گر بدر منور آفتاب

It is mistaken to draw comparison between the Sun and that radiant countenance
How can the Sun stand equal to the shadow of God?

By merely thinking of his blade,
The Sun will split in two, as did the moon by the fingertip of the Prophet

The Sun shall not be able to steal a drop of dew from the flowers without permission
In the time of his justice-spreading rule

His gold-spreading hands buried the earth in gold,
While the Sun merely concealed gold under the ground

All incomplete beings became complete under his universal blessing
While the Sun merely caused the new moon to grow into a full moon (Ṣā'ib, 3587)

Ṣā'ib ends this *qaṣīdeh* by referring to the authority of the king in the absence

of *Imam Zamān* (the twelfth Imam), who is also represented in the metaphor of the Sun:

تا به آب قدرت این نه آسیا گردان بود
تا به امر حق شود طالع ز خاور آفتاب

بر مراد این بلند اختر بود گردان سپهر
برنتابد از خط فرمان او سر آفتاب

As long as these nine mills (i.e. the heavenly spheres) keep on turning,
As long as the Sun rises from the east by the command of God

The turning sphere be desirous of this highest star (i.e the king)[23]
And the Sun shall not disobey his commands (Ṣā'ib, 3588)

In the following lines, which constitute the beginning of a *qaṣīdeh* in praise of

Shah 'Abbās II, Ṣā'ib delves into praise by utilizing light and related ideas in four

consecutive lines and in three discourses related to the Safavid ideology. The presence

of morning (*ṣubḥ*) in the king's forehead is a metaphor for light and is a supernatural

event (*karāmat*), which was considered to be exclusive to the friends of God. By this

description, Shah 'Abbās II is identified as one of the God's friends (*awlīyā*). This

---

[23] *Buland akhtar* which in here is an adjective replacing the noun (shah) is a trope for fortuity.

idea presents the king as the leader of a Sufi order. In the second line, pure (*pāk*),

noble (*sharīf*), and jewel or lineage (*gawhar*), are all images that remind the reader of

attributes such as "clean" and "bright" that refer to the king's genealogy going back to

Imam Mūsā Kāẓim, the seventh Imam. The idea of light is used in the third line to

refer to the king's military skills by connecting him to Imām 'Alī. In the fourth line,

the Sun refers to the title "the shadow of God on Earth," which is the basis of the third

pillar of Safavic legitimacy and is in line with pre-Islamic notions of Persian kingship:

ای زمان دلگشایت نوبهار روزگار

صبح نوروز از جبین بخت سبزت آشکار

طینت پاک تو از خاک شریف بوتراب

گوهر تیغ تو از صلب متین ذوالفقار

صولت شیر خدا از بازوی اقبال تو

می شود چون نور خورشید از مه نو آشکار

آفتاب سایه پرور را تماشا می کند

هر که می بیند ترا در سایه پروردگار

You are the one whose pleasant reign is like the spring for the earth
The green fortune of your forehead bears the morning of Nawrūz[24]

Your immaculate being is made from the blessed soil of the Father of Soil (Abu-Turāb, i.e. Ali)
The lineage of your blade goes back to the loins of Zulfiqār

The awe of the lion of God ('Alī) becomes visible in your might
Just as the light of the Sun begins to appear in the new moon

It is the shadow-casting Sun that they see
When they look at you under the shadow of God (Ṣā'ib, 3588)[25]

III. Sources of Legitimacy

Ṣā'ib's *qaṣīdeh*s are different from those of the earlier poets of Safavid courts

in particular in regard to approaching patrons. Ṣā'ib's *qaṣīdeh*s mainly seek to

---

[24] The morning of Nawrūz can be the appearance of Nawrūz, the new year for Persian calendar (21st of March) which is associated with light.

[25] This *qaṣīdeh* will be discussed further in the chapter as it is a good example of how Ṣā'ib considered Safavid king religiously responsible for dissemination of Shi'ism.

legitimize the kingship by depicting the king as the promoter of Twelver Shiʿism. Assuming this religious role for the Safavid monarchs distinguishes them from the other Muslim kings in the eyes of Ṣāʿib. I am not arguing that other themes of legitimacy such as generosity or military prowess, which were common in praise of kings, were utilized differently by Ṣāʿib. However, he coherently integrates all these sources together within a very solid structure in which the concept of light is dominant as the symbol of the sacred/holy. His attention toward the use of places in describing the king's influence over nature, which is accompanied by the special *radīf*s, that as mentioned earlier, marks this difference between his panegyrics and those of his peers. His poetic language, direct references to the king as the promoter of Twelver Shiʿism, and portraying the glory of palaces and cities legitimize the Safavid kingship in Ṣāʿib's poems. The king is mostly presented as a divine ruler whose divinity is not only related to his special *farr*, but also to attributes of earlier Persian Sasanid and Safavid kings who were considered legitimate. In the body of *qaṣīdeh*, Ṣāʿib usually moves among different characteristics of a king, mostly from the religious responsibility of the king to his personal traits. These features are connected to each other with the ideas of "light," "elevation," "fortune," and "power" to imply divinity and sacredness for the king.

A. The Concept of Light

Ṣāʿib frequently compares his patrons (Ṣafī and Abbās II) to the Sun and light. The comparison of royalty to the Sun and to the broader symbolism of light as a metaphor for splendor is widespread in Iranian, Mesopotamian, Hellenistic, and later

Roman kingship.[26] In ancient Iranian kingship, the king's charisma was sometimes physically apparent as light to his subjects and it was sometimes associated with the attributes of a crown. The metaphor of light is ubiquitous among Iranian, Mesopotamian, Hellenistic, and Roman representations of kingship and mostly appeared in poetry. While the king's administration of justice or knowledge is like the sun illuminating the world, he is also the shadow of God, which provides shade where peace and security flourish.[27] The concept of light connects the Safavid kings to the House of the Prophet.[28] In Shi'i narrations, it is said that the Prophet was created from

---

[26] Aziz Al-Azmeh, *Muslim Kingship: Power and the Sacred in Muslim, Christian and Pagan Polities.* (London: I.E. Tauris, 1997), 17.

[27] Ibid.

[28] 'Light of Muḥammad' is a symbolic light to the world. In the early hadith material, the Muḥammadan light is referred to as *nūr-i Muḥammad.* The light is said to have reached Muḥammad from his progenitors through the process of procreation. (U Rubin, "Nūr Muḥammadī" in: *Encyclopaedia of Islam*, ed. P. Bearman, Th. Bianquis, C. Bosworth, E. van Donzel.) In hadith and narrations, the light of Muḥammad is a light through which the divine light shines upon the world and humanity finds its path towards truth. In Sufism the light of Muḥammad has existed before the creation of Adam (see Annemarie, Schimmel, *And Muhammad is His Messenger: the Veneration of the Prophet in Islamic Piety*, (Chapel Hill: University of North Carolina Press, 1985.) It is also believed the other prophets were created from Muḥammad's light. Muḥammad Ghazālī defines the perfect guide between God and a human being in whom the light of God has been appeared. In Shi'i traditions, not only Muḥammad, but also 'Alī and his family, including the Imāms, share the same light from God. The light passing through was split in two parts, so that both Muḥammad and 'Alī received equal shares of it (U Rubin, "Nūr Muḥammadī" in *Encyclopaedia of Islam*). Schimmel presented the literature on development of these theories in her underling work, *And Muḥammad is His Messenger,* in which she examines the place of Muḥammad in Muslim piety through the works of Persian, Turkish, Arabic, and Urdu literature. Each chapter of Schimmel's work studies different elements of the Prophet's life and character through Muslim views, all of which draw their examples and discussions from works of literature. Chapter 7 of this work in particular pays attention to the idea of Muḥammad's light in mystical poems. In general, the goal of Muslim's life is to ascend to union with the state of *ḥaqīqat Muḥammadiyya* ("archetypal Muḥammad") as the first principle of creation. As the perfect guide and being created from the light of God, light became a poetic motif for poets to argue for the authenticity of the rulers, their knowledge, noble lineage, and in general their perfect being. Theories concerning Muḥammad's luminous character have been constructed in the works of philosophers, Sufis and theologians such as Muqātil ibn Sulaymān (b. 767), Sahl al-Tustarī (b. 818), and Ḥallāj (b. 858.) For an interpretation of the light of Muḥammad see Muqātil ibn Sulaymān al-Balkhī, *Tafsīr Muqātil ibn Sulaymān*, ed. 'Abd Allāh Maḥmūd Shiḥātah, (al-Qāhira: Mu'assisa al-Ḥalabī, 1969.) al-Ḥusayn ibn Manṣūr Ḥallāj, Rūzbihān ibn Abī al-Naṣr, Baqlī, *Kitāb al-Ṭawāsīn*, ed. Louis Massignon (Bagdad: al-Muṣannā Library, 1970). Muḥammad al-Ghazzālī, *The Niche of Lights (Mishkāt al-anwār)*, David Buchman, (Utah: Brigham Young University Press, 1998), Sahl ibn 'Abd Allāh Tustarī, *Tafsīr al-*

light. His descendants also were believed to possess that light. ‘Allāmeh Majlisī (d. 1660) collected a series of these narrations in *Biḥār al-Anwār*, which explain that the first object created in the world was the light of Prophet Muḥammad. For example, it has been recounted from Jābir, who was narrating the Prophet's words, "the first that God created was my light…"[29] Furthermore, Aḥmad Ibn Ḥanbal narrated the words of the Prophet that "[b]efore creating the world from fourteen hundred years ago, ‘Alī and I were lights in the hands of God…"[30] Ṣafvān also narrated from Imam Ṣādiq that "[w]hen God created the earth and the skies commanded two lights from his own light to go around the sky seventy times… [t]hen he said these two lights will follow my rules, then God created from that light Muḥammad and ‘Alī and the purest from his line and a group of his followers and from that group the light of the eyes."[31] In a similar narration that is ascribed to Jābir, God created fourteen lights from his own light before creating the world. The Prophet mentioned that those fourteen lights emanated from himself, ‘Alī, Fāṭimeh, Ḥasan and Ḥusayn, and the nine successors of Ḥusayn's line.[32]

Ṣā‘ib combines the concept of light with *vilāyat* (sovereignty), a religious term which is associated with the legitimacy of Muslim leadership. It juxtaposes the king

---

*Qur'ān al-‘Aẓīm: Shaykh al-‘Ārifīn al-Imām al-Tustarī.*ed. Mahmud Jirat Allah (al-Qahirah: al-Dār al-Siqāfīyah lil-Nashr, 2002.)

[29] Muḥammad Bāqir ibn Muḥammad Taqī Majlisī, *Biḥār al-Anwār*, (Tehran: Dār al-Kutub, 1956). v. 15, 24.

[30] Ibid.

[31] Ibid, v 25, 21.

[32] Ibid.

with Imams who exclusively were believed to have the exclusive right to Muslim

leadership after Prophet Muḥammad:

از جبهه ی تو نور ولایت بود عیان

زان سان که آفتاب نماید در آینه

Your forehead glows with the radiance of vilāyat
Like the sun reflecting in a mirror (Ṣā'ib, 3556)

Or in a similar context:

چو آفتاب نمایان بود زسینه ی صبح

بر طرف جبهه ی او نور اختر اقبال

Just as the Sun is visible amidst the breast of morning horizon
The glow of the star of good fortune radiates from his forehead (Ṣā'ib, 3562)

In general, Ṣā'ib succinctly invokes the different discourses of Safavid

legitimacy and further ties them together with the concept of light in one or two lines

to give the king the sacred and sovereign image that the Safavid king required to be

accepted as the righteous ruler.

B. Lineage

While Shi'i genealogy of the Safavid kings did not appear in the *qaṣīdeh*s of

other Safavid court poets (see Table 5), Safavid Shi'i genealogy holds a significant

position for Ṣā'ib. He attests that the connection between the family of Safavids and the

Prophet is a privilege for the Safavid kings, giving them the rightful ruler. The following

verse is written for Ṣafī I:

کدام فخر به این می رسد که از شاهان

تو را به شاه نجف می رسد نژاد و تبار

What honor can compete with this honor that but of all kings,
Your lineage goes back to the King of Najaf ('Alī) (Ṣā'ib, 3553)

The right to rule in the absence of Imam Mahdī is not claimed only through the relationship with Imam ʿAlī. Sāʾib also justifies Ṣafī's kingship by foregrounding his similarities with Imam Mahdī. He notes that both the king and Imam Mahdī stand in the twelfth position from the founder of their family. Ṣafī was the twelfth son after Shaykh Ṣafī, the grandfather of Shah Ismāʿīl, and Mahdī was the twelfth Imam after the Prophet. Therefore, the king's justice is similar to that of Imam Mahdī, who is going to rule the world:

تویی دوازدهم از نژاد شیخ صفی

جهان چگونه نگیری به عدل مهدی وار؟

You are the twelfth descendent of Shaykh Safī
Why shouldn't you fill the world with justice like Mahdi? (Ṣāʾib, 3553)

C. Virtues

Images dealing with the king's virtues play an important role in legitimizing the Safavid king as the rightful ruler. Shah Ṣafī has the right to rule, not only because of his genealogy, but also because he possesses virtues that no other kings possess. Sāʾib describes the king with *taqaddus* (sacredness/holiness) along with adjectives such as *rawshan żamīr* (bright-hearted), *darvīsh ṣifat* (dervish-like), and *āyat-i khudā* (God's sign) to combine the characteristics of both Sufis and Imams in the king and to argue for the religio-political authority of the king:

چون تقدس بود غالب بر مزاج اشرفش

داشت دایم خاطرش از عالم خاکی غبار

هیچ رازی بر ضمیر روشنش پنهان نبود

ابجد او بود خط سرنوشت روزگار

باطنش درویش و ظاهر پادشاه وقت بود

داشت پنهان خرقه در زیر لباس روزگار

آب می شد از گناه دیگران آزرم او

آیتی از رحمت حق بود و عفو کردگار

Because his noble temperament inclined towards the holy,
The dust of the earthen world would irritate his soul

No secret was hidden from his pure spirit
His name's numerical value marked the fate of the world[33]

He was a Dervish on the inside and the king of his time on the outside,[34]
Underneath his worldly garment, he had a Sufi cloak

His dignity would feel remorse for the sins of others
He was a sign of the mercy and forgiveness of the creator [35]

Similar to Shah 'Abbās I, who demonstrated to have no interest in political authority as other Muslim rulers, Ṣā'ib portrays his patron with no desire for political power. In part of an elegy that he wrote for Shah Ṣāfī, Sā'ib compares the king with Ibrāhīm Adham.[36] The king, like Adham, could repudiate the power of his kingship:

پادشاهی و جوانی سد راه او نشد

کرد چون ادهم ز ملک عالم فانی کنار

---

[33] Literally abjad "alphabet," a word formed from the first four letters of the Semitic alphabet. In particular, it refers to the use of letters as numbers (*ḥisāb-i abjad*), the numerical values of the letters following the original letter sequence found in the older Semitic alphabets. See G. Krotkoff, "Abjad," *Encyclopædia Iranica*, I/2, pp. 221-222; an updated version is available online at http://www.iranicaonline.org/articles/abjad (accessed on 25 January 2014).

[34] *Bāṭin* means "inner," "inward," and "hidden," etc. It is in contrast to the exterior and what is apparent. Sufis believe every individual has a bāṭin (the inward self) which when is cleansed with the light of one's spiritual guide elevates a person spiritually. In this verse the poet describes the king with spiritual soul as a dervish inwardly, but a king on the outside.

[35] Muḥammad 'Alī Ṣā'ib Tabrīzī, *Dīvān-i Ṣā'ib Tabrīzī: Muṭābiq-i Nuskheh-yi Daw'jildī-i 1072 H.Q, beh khaṭṭ-i Ṣā'ib "az Majmū'eh-yi Shakhṣī"*, ed and preface, Jahangir Mansur, Shiblī Nu'mānī, and Parviz Natil Khanlari. (Tehran: Mu'assiseh-yi Intishārāt-i Nigāh, 2005). V2.1378/1999-1379/2000. (Cited hereafter in the text and footnotes as Ṣā'ib/I to distinguish it from the manuscript edited by Qahriman.

[36] Ibrāhīm Adham (b.718 – d.782) was one of the most prominent Sufi saints who abandoned his throne to become an ascetic. His legend is recounted in Farīd al-Dīn 'Aṭṭār, *Tazkirat al-Awlīyā*, ed. Muhammad Ist'ilami, (Tehran: Zavvār, 1346/1995), 75-96.

در خور اقبال روز افزون خود جایی نیافت

بال بر هم زد برون رفت از جهان بی مدار

Neither kingship nor youth could hinder his (spiritual) progress
Like Adham, he turned away from sovereignty in the ephemeral world

He did not find a position (in this world) worthy of his ever-increasing grandeur
He flapped his wings and left the turbulent world behind (Ṣāʿib/I, 1378)

For Sāʿib, the king was the perfect being and could not achieve more in the material world. Therefore, he moved to the spiritual world of the afterlife.

The king's spiritual character is represented through the use of the abjad system. As a karāmat of the king (like the Sufis), Saʿib points out that the year of the king's death in 1613 (1021 AH) corresponds to the word *ghabn* (loss) in abjad:

رفت سال "غبن" از عالم زهی غبن تمام

سوخت عالم را به داغ غبن آن عالم مدار

The year of "loss" left the world, what a loss!
That pivot of the universe burnt the world with the brand of loss (Ṣāʿib/I, 1378)

Also, his enthronement in 1599 (1007 AH) can be mapped to the phrase *ẕill-i ḥaqq* (the Shadow of God) in the abjad system,[37] and the year of his death can can be mapped to the phrase *āh az ẕill-i ḥaqq* (Alas, the Shadow of God!):

"ظل حق" چون بود سال شاهیش سال رحیل

گشت "آه از ظل حق" تاریخ آن عالی تبار

Since the year of his enthronement was marked by [the phrase] "shadow of God" (in abjad)
The year of the departure of his majesty became "Alas, the shadow of God" (Ṣāʿib/I, 1379)

Furthermore, the poet claims "perfect knowledge" for the king that was granted to him by God's will.[38] Divine knowledge was known as knowledge that

---

[37] See Chapter One, p. 44.

[38] It is a knowledge that could be achieved with no education. This knowledge with no mediation occurs to the heart of *ahl-i qurb* (the people of proximity). To read about the terminology and

could be gained without the need to conventional education. It is achieved by God's

grace and attention towards specific figures, such as prophets and Imams:

هر چه باید با خود آورده است ذات کاملت
بی نیاز از مایه دریاست در شاهوار

Your perfect essence has everything in itself
The royal pearl is not in need of what the sea has to offer (Ṣā'ib/I, 1381)

Furthermore, the poet claims "perfect knowledge" for the king that was

granted to him by God's will.[39] Divine knowledge was known as knowledge that

could be gained without conventional study. It is achieved by God's grace and

attention towards some specific people, such as prophets and Imams:

هر چه باید با خود آورده است ذات کاملش
فارغ از کسب کمالات است چون قدوسیان

دارد از علم لدنی بهره چون اجداد خویش
پیش او طفل نو آموزی است عقل خرده دان

فطرت والای او بی زحمت تعلیم و درس
صاحب تیغ و قلم گردید در اندک زمان

His perfect being has all it needs in itself
Like heavenly creatures, he is not in need of acquiring perfection

Like his forebears, he has access to divine knowledge;
Petty-minded Reason is like a small child in front of him

His elevated nature is above teaching and education
He became the master of the sword and the pen in no time (Ṣā'ib, 3565)

---

its different aspects see Mujtabā Muṭahharī, "'ilm-i Ladunnī," *Rahyāft-i Inqilāb-i Islāmī*, Fall
1386/2007, no 3. 65-87. Also see 'Abd al-'Aẓīm Karīmī, "'ilm-i Nā-āmukhteh", Literature and
Languages, Fall 1391/2012, no.28, 68-95.

[39] It is a knowledge that could be achieved with no education. This knowledge with no
mediation occurs to the heart of *ahl-i qurb* (the people of proximity). To read about the terminology and
its different aspects see Mujtabā Muṭahharī, "'ilm-i Ladunnī," *Rahyāft-i Inqilāb-i Islāmī*, Fall
1386/2007, no 3. 65-87. Also see 'Abd al-'Aẓīm Karīmī, "'ilm-i Nā-āmukhteh", Literature and
Languages, Fall 1391/2012, no.28, 68-95.

D. The King's Role in Distributing Twelver Shi'ism

Unlike the poets whom I investigated in the last chapter, who did not make the connection between the Safavid kings and twelve Shi'i Imams (see Table 5), Ṣā'ib frequently refers to the Safavid kings as the protectors of Twelver Shi'ism. Promoting Shi'ism and following the rule of God and Imams legitimize a king, and Ṣā'ib praises Ṣafī for both:

چارده سال هلالی مذهب اثناعشر

بود از شمشیر گردون صولت او پایدار

با همه فرماندهی فرمان پذیر شرع بود

سرنی پیچید از فرمان حق در هیچ کار

For fourteen years, the Twelver Shia religion
Endured because of his heaven-conquering sword

Though he was the commander, he followed the commands of God's law.
He would never disobey the order of God in any action (Ṣā'ib/I, 1378-79)

Both Ṣafī and 'Abbās II are praised for defending Twelver Shi'ism and promoting its' doctrines in Ṣā'ib's qaṣīdehs. The Twelver Shi'i expressions in Ṣā'ib's panegyrics are either connected to the image of celestial bodies or are used where the poet demonstrates that Shi'ism has become the official religion in India.[40]

In addition to mentioning the king's role in promoting, defending, and establishing Twelver Shi'ism, expressions indicating the king as the leader of religion and *dawlat* (state) or *dunyā* (material world) are applied to demonstrate the king's

---

[40] The *khuṭbeh* of Isnā 'asharīs has been proclaimed,
  Gold has become of perfect standard with the name of the eight plus four (Ṣā'ib, 3568)
  (Translated by Sunil Sharma, *Mughal Arcadia*, 188).

در هند گشت خطبه اثناعشر بلند

شد کامل العیار زر از نام هشت و چار

religious and political responsibility. These expressions are often used in the texts of endowed foundations, mosque inscriptions, and orations of royal investitures,[41] which suggests this poetry had a broader audience. However, Ṣā'ib only uses these expressions to refer to Shah 'Abbās II, and not Shah Ṣafī:[42]

Ṣā'ib wrote these panegyrics in a period when both kings, specially 'Abbās II, tried to promote orthodox notions of Shi'ism in Persian language. Similar to his father, 'Abbās II invited Shi'i clerics associated with higher philosophical inquiry who proved to be committed to the Safavid house to his court to promulgate orthodox notions of Shi'ism against popular Sufism. However, the Safavid kings still did not seek to immediately uproot the popular religious discourses. Shah 'Abbās II espoused a more public interest in Sufism and was openly associated with a number of prominent figures who were linked to those popular discourses.[43] Attacks against popular Sufism became more coherent during and after the 1660s following 'Abbās II's appointment of Muḥammad Mahdī, son of Ḥabībullāh Karakī, to the vizierate.[44]

---

[41] See Chapter Two.

[42] You are the one true leader of religion and the state,
   Though there are countless kings on the face of the Earth (Ṣā'ib/I, 1380)

دین و دولت را تویی فرمانروای راستین

گرچه در روی زمین هستند شاهان بی شمار

Other rulers have worldly possessions only
He, of all rulers, is the king of religion and the earthly world together (Ṣā'ib, 3559)

شهریاران دگر دارند دنیایی و بس

پادشاه دین و دنیا اوست از شاهنشهان

[43] Newman, *Safavid Iran,* 86.

[44] Ibid.

Anti-Sufi polemics gained even more power when Shaykh ‘Alī ‘Amilī, a descendent of Zayn al-Dīn ‘Amilī who was killed by the Ottomans in 1559, highly criticized the Sufi traditions, especially the practice of singing. However, the disagreement with the Sufi traditions did not change the poetics of Ṣā‘ib's panegyrics dedicated to his patrons. In the following lines, Ṣā‘ib develops the idea of a Safavid king as a spiritual leader by applying the title *murshid-i kāmil* or *‘iṣmat* (infallibility) that generally is for Sufi leaders:

تا به لوح آفرینش نقش ایجاد تو بست
بوسه زد بر دست خود کلک قضا بی اختیار

مرشد کامل تویی سجاده ارشاد را
تا شود نور ظهور صاحب الامر آشکار

گرچه بر فرمانروایان جهان فرماندهی
سر نمی پیچی ز فرمان خدا در هیچ کار

دین و دولت را تویی فرمانروای راستین
گر چه در روی زمین هستند شاهان بی شمار

همچو سبابه کز انگشتان شهادت حق اوست
دین حق قایم به توست از خسروان روزگار

از رسوخ اعتقادات آسمان بنیاد شد
چون بروج آسمانی مذهب هشت و چهار

بیضه اسلام از سنگ حوادث ایمن است
عصمت ذات تو تا شد آفرینش را حصار

در حسب ممتازی از فرمانروایان جهان
در نسب داری شرف بر خسروان نامدار

You are the one whose pleasant reign is like the spring for the earth
The green fortune of your forehead bears the signs of the appearance of Nawrūz

Your immaculate being is made from the blessed soil of the Father of soil (Abu-Turāb, i.e. Ali)
The lineage of your blade goes back to the loins of Ẕulfiqār

The ferocity of the lion of God (‘Alī) becomes visible in your might
Just as the light of the sun begins to appear in the new moon

It is the shadow-casting sun that they see
When they look at you under the shadow of God

After it limned your figure on the tablet of creation
The pen of fate kissed its own hand in admiration

You shall be the perfect guide for the rug of sovereignty[45]
Until the day when the reappearance of the Owner of Authority (the twelfth Imam) starts to shine light

Even though you command the commanders of the world
You never disobey God in any of your deeds

You are the true ruler of religion and state
Although there are numerous kings on Earth

Like the index finger, who has the privilege of testimony among all the fingers
The religion of truth relies on you, of all the kings on Earth

By the firmness of its tenets, the religion of eight and four (Twelvers) reached the skies
Like the twelve houses of the Zodiac

The egg of Islam is immune from the stones of time
As long as the innocence of your being protects the whole creation

Your glory makes you unique among the rulers of the world
Your lineage gives you advantage over renowned kings (Ṣā'ib, 3588)

The first line serves to further support the idea of a sacred king, a Sufi-Shi'i-Persian king whose responsibility is safeguarding the religion and the faith of Twelver Shi'ism. These lines are also bound to each other by presenting concepts related to the three aforementioned pillars: the perfect guide, the religion of truth, the religion of eight and four, innocence which is exclusive to Imams and the friends of God, and, finally, references to the king's lineage, which is said to be better than the famous *khusraw*s of the past,[46] claim a better lineage for the Safavid king in comparison to other kings (probably the Ottomans and the Mughals).

Ṣā'ib utilizes the concept of light, which is affiliated with the ideas of Persian kingship, divine law, and sacredness. Other themes, such as life, justice, day, and

---

[45] See Chapter Two, p.80.

[46] *Khusraw* is the Persian word to refer to the king. However, here it is used to refer to the pre-Islamic Persian kings. In general, I could not track the different function of the various words that are used to refer to the king. Usually the words *Sultan, Amir, Khusraw, Shah,* and *Padishah* have been used interchangeably.

spring further help the poet to portray a righteous king. On the other hand, death, suppression, night, and winter in some panegyrics of his, come to support the idea of a sacred king through complementary binary oppositions. The concept of light is an inseparable element of Ṣā'ib's *qaṣīdeh*s. It frequently appears in introductory lines or the main body of the *qaṣīdeh*s and builds the foundation of the poetic presentation of a legitimate ruler.

IV. Factual and Ceremonial Considerations

چه دولت بود یارب اصفهان را در کنار آمد
که از خاور زمین صاحبقران کامکار آمد

به آیینی که در برج شرف خورشید باز آید
به دارالملک خود آن پادشاه تاجدار آمد

What an honor for Isfahan
That the victorious *ṣāḥib-qirān* coming from the east landed there

Like the Sun approaching the heavenly station of honor,
The crowned king came to his capital[47] (Ṣā'ib, 3571)

These two lines are the opening verses of a *qaṣīdeh* that Ṣā'ib wrote for Shah 'Abbas II's successful return from Qandahar. It was in 1648 that Shah 'Abbās II succeeded in forming a strong army numbering 40,000 and took back the city.[48] Ṣā'ib describes this return as the arrival of the Sun to its home in the spring (*burj-i ḥamal*). To portray the glory of this triumph and to present the circumstances as the victory of faith over infidelity, the poet uses the binary opposition of light versus darkness. Light and darkness appear repeatedly in Ṣā'ib's poems to depict the splendor of the Safavid

---

[47] 21th of March when the night and day even out in duration. This is the same day as Persian New Year, famous as Nawrūz.

[48] Rudi Matthee and Mashita Hiroyuki, Ehsan Yarshater, *Kandahar: From The Mongol Invasion Through the Safavid Era,* (Routledge & Kegan Paul, 1985). Archived from the original on 11 September 2014. Retrieved 11 September 2014.

king who represents God's will on Earth as opposed to the Indian enemies whose dark skin, according to the poet, speaks of their infidelity and degraded position. The war between them is the war between light and dark, or between believers and infidels. Ṣā'ib did not hesitate to use the term *jihād-i akbar*[49] (the greater *jihād*) for this encounter of light and dark, a term which is generally used for one's encounter with the degraded self. The king was supported by *bāzū-yi vilāyat* (the arm of sovereignty), and therefore his person brightened the world:

چه اقبال است کز فضل خدا روداد ایران را
که منصور از جهاد اکبر آن عالم مدار آمد

ز ظلمات سواد هند، از اقبال روزافزون
به صد شادابی خضر آن سکندر اقتدار آمد

گواهی می دهد سرسبزی بخت برومندش
که در ظلمت ز آب زندگانی کامکار آمد

ز گرد موکبش شد چشم ها روشن که از مشرق
به نور آفتاب آن سایه پروردگار آمد

هلالش آفتاب و آفتابش عالم آرا شد
چه گویا با چه سامان زین سفر آن شهریار آمد

How auspicious for Iran, that by God's grace,
That pivot of the universe returned from the greater *jihād* victoriously

By virtue of his increasingly favorable omen, back from India's darkness,
He who has the might of Alexander, came back with the vigor of Khiżr very fresh

The virility of his prosperous fortune bears witnesses
To the fact that he returned triumphantly from the fountain of youth in the darkness

Seeing the dust (raised by the hooves of the horses) of his entourage, eyes were blessed
Since from the East, the shadow of God was approaching amidst the sunshine

---

[49] *Jihād-i Akbar* (lit. the greater war) is the one integral struggle. This term is in opposition to Jihād-i Aṣghar (lit. the smaller war), which refers to go to war in the battle field with enemies. For further reading on this concept, see Muḥammad Ḥusayn, Ṭabāṭabā'ī, *Tarjuma-yi Tafsīr-i al-Mīzān.* ed. Muhammad Baqir Musavi Hamadani, (Tehran: Muḥammadī, 1984), vol 14, 582. Also, Fayż Kāshānī, *Rasā'il-i Fayż Kāshānī,* (Tehran:Madrasa-yi Ālī Shahīd Muṭahharī, 1387/2008), vol 1, 16, Ibn Maysam, Baḥrānī, *Sharh-i Nahj al-Balāgha,* trans. Muhammadi Muqaddam and Navai, (Mashhad: Majma' al-Buhus al-Islamiyyah), vol 2, p. 74-75.

His (distant figure, resembling the) new moon, grew to become like the Sun world adoring:
How and in what a manner from this trip the king came! (Ṣā'ib, 3572)

Comparisons between the Safavid king and Imam 'Alī comprise another motif for Ṣā'ib, which he uses to argue for the king's authority over the Indians. Although this is not a unique image and was also dominant in *qaṣīdeh*s composed for Sulṭān Maḥmūd, Ṣā'ib uses this image more than any other Safavid poet to make the connection between the masculinity of the king and Imam 'Alī. His double-edged sword brings the *'arūs* (bride) of India to its marriage:

چنان کز خیبر آمد شاه مردان خرم و خندان
به دولت شاه عباس آنچنان از قندهار آمد

به خاک راه یکسان کرد چندین حصن خیبر را
ز خونریز سپاهان سرخ رو چون ذوالفقار آمد

به آغوشی که از شمشیر کج واکرد اقبالش
به شیرینی عروس ملک هندش در کنار آمد

Just as the king of all men ('Alī) returned jubilantly from Khaybar
King Abbas came from Qandahar with like prosperity

He laid waste to several castles like Khaybar
Having spilled the blood of the blacks, he returned with a red face, like Ẕulfiqār

Rushing towards the embrace that straightened her fortune with a curved sword
The bride, the domain of India, came to his side delightfully (Ṣā'ib, 3572)

This is not the only *qaṣīdeh* Ṣā'ib wrote in celebrating the king's victory over his Indian rivals. In all of these *qaṣīdeh*s, there is a dichotomy between dark and light which is extended to associated meanings such as infidelity/faith, ignorance/knowledge, and winter/spring. The color black stands as a symbol of infidelity and ignorance against the white flag of Shah 'Abbās, whose light nature represents the true belief of him he and his followers. The Indians are compared to ravens and crows whose dead bodies feed the vultures:

چون لوای شاه، روی قلعه داران شد سفید

هندیان گشتند یکسر زردروی و شرمسار

از سیاهی گر چه بالاتر نباشد هیچ رنگ

زردرویی غالب آمد بر سیاهان در فرار

بار دیگر از ته بال و پر زاغان هند

بیضه اسلام چون خورشید گردید آشکار

بس که لاش این کلاغان شد نصیب کرکسان

شهپر هر کرکسی گردید لوح صد مزار

The faces of the castle defenders became white like the shah's banners
The Indians were left yellow-faced (i.e. shamefaced) and disgraced

Even though black is above all colors
Yellow faced-ness overtook the fleeing black Indians

Once again, from beneath the wings and feathers of the Indian ravens
The egg of Islam emerged like the Sun

Vultures fed so much on the carcasses of the crows
Each wing of each vulture became the tombstone of hundreds (Ṣā'ib, 3571)

The dead bodies of the Indians are a motif for this piece. The bloody image of the Indian corpses helps to construct the image of the sovereign Safavid king as reminiscent of Tīmūr and the title ṣāḥib-qirān invoked in the beginning of the poem. The legitimacy is grounded not only in his similarity to Tīmūr, but also pertains to his sword, which plays the role of Imam 'Alī's in the fight against infidels:

آنچنان کز آسمان خیل شیاطین از شهاب

منهزم گردد، چنان گردید هندو تارومار

لشکر فرعون را نامد به پیش از رود نیل

آنچه پیش هندیان آمد ز تیغ ذوالفقار

بس که شد آلوده هر سنگی به خون هندیان

کوه بزکش شد سراسر کوههای قندهار

خاک را از بس به خون هندیان آمیختند

چون شفق، از خاک خون آلود می خیزد غبار

گر در آتش کشته خود را نمی انداختند

کوهها از هندوان کشته می شد آشکار

راه خشکی هند را از کابل و ملتان نماند
ریختند از بس که خون هندیان وقت فرار

آنچنان کآیینه می گیرد ز خاکستر صفا
شد قتل هندیان افزون جلای ذوالفقار

Just as the army of demons is crushed by meteors in the sky
The Indians were vanquished

The army of Pharaoh did not suffer in the Nile
What the Indians suffered from the blade of Ẕulfiqār

The stones were all bloodstained by the blood of the Indians
To the extent that the mountains of Qandahar became like the Buzkush mountain[50]

The soil was blended with the blood of the Indians
To the extent that the dust above the bloody soil resembles the twilight

Had they not burned their dead in fire
Mountains made of dead Indians would appear

There is no longer a land route connecting Kabul and Multan to India
After they spilled the blood of so many of the fleeing Indians

Just as ash can make mirrors shine more brightly
The brightness of Ẕulfiqār intensified by slaying the Indians (Ṣā'ib, 3571)

In general, Ṣā'ib blends all the possible sources of legitimacy to demonstrate that his patron was in absolute control of the realm religiously and politically. He shows that the king's authority comes from the spiritual genealogy of his Sufi forefathers or his connection to the House of Prophet, and that, like the pre-Islamic kings of Persia, he possesses *farr*. These legitimizing patterns are represented in the form of light in all his panegyrics for the kings, especially for his main patron, Shah 'Abbās II. Ṣā'ib does not hesitate to make extreme claims for the legitimation of the Safavid king. 'Abbās II was described with qualities such as eternal knowledge and

---

[50] Mount Buzkush (Buzgūsh) is in East Azarbayjan province of Iran. The appellation of this mountain is the shape of the mountain which is similar to the ears of a goat. The scholars are saying that Buzkush in Turkish means the grey bird, which refers to the mountain's color during the winter. I could not find any sources that submitted the name of this mountain in the same way as Ṣā'ib. Probably, because the pronunciation of *qūsh*, *gūsh*, and *kūsh* are similar, the poet preferred the last version as in a derogatory way it implies that Indians are goats which were killed in the mountains of Kandahar.

infallibility that were exclusive to the Imams. While most of the kings pay tribute to their fathers for being kings, Ṣā'ib asserts that 'Abbās II is better than his father because he came last and therefore, he is more developed personally and politically.

V. Conclusion

As I demonstrated, Ṣā'ib's approach towards the Safavid kingship and legitimizing the rule was different from the earlier poets of the Safavid reign. Ṣā'ib combines Shi'i doctrines with ideas related to Persian forms of kingship and Sufi expressions in order to legitimize the Safavid kingship. In addition to the aforementioned notions of Persian kingship that frequently appear in Ṣā'ib's panegyrics, Shi'i terms and expressions are also frequently applied to refer to the king's role in distribution of Shi'ism and control over Muslim lands. In the process of legitimizing the kingship, Ṣā'ib pays attention to both Sufi and Shi'i lineage of the Safavid kings. He compares the Safavid kings to Imams and Sufis for being sinless, infallible, and a source of miraculous acts and attributes. (See Table 7, 8, and 9 for these patterns). These themes and images are integrated in a coherent manner within a poetic structure that benefits from *radīf*s which tie up the images and motifs of each line together. This coherency emphasizes religio-political legitimacy of the Safavid kings through the very strong religio-political metaphor, "the king is light", which reinforces the idea of sacred kingship for the Safavid monarchs.

Table 7 (Patterns of Persian Notions of Kingship in Ṣā'ib's Panegyrics for Kings)

Persian Notions of Kingship				
Titles	Comparisons	Symbols		
		Farr	Light	Falcon
*	*			
		*	*	*

Table 8 (Patterns of Shi'i Legitimacy in Ṣā'ib's Panegyrics for Kings)

Shi'i Legitimacy					
Lineage	Servitude	Distribution of Twelver Shi'ism	Reference to Imām Mahdī	Similarity to Imāms	Karbala
*	*	*	*	*	N/A

Table 9 (Patterns of Sufi Legitimacy in Ṣā'ib's Panegyrics for kings)

Sufi Legitimacy			
Lineage	Titles	Miraculous acts	Comparison to Sufis
*	*	*	*

Description of cities and their monuments also serve Ṣā'ib in his desire to give

legitimacy to the Safavid king. The freshness of the gardens in Mazandaran, the

greenness of that region, the glory of Isfahan and its monuments (Ḥasan Ābād bridge

and Zāyandeh Rūd)[51], and the beauty of the king's palace all refer to the rightful

kingship of the Safavid king. The fact that Ṣā'ib had interest in praising the king

through descriptions of the cities and palaces supports the argument that Ṣā'ib had

different perspective about kingship in comparison to the other qaṣīdeh writers.

Praising the kings through descriptions of objects close to the kings was not a common

approach for the authors of Safavid qaṣīdehs who preceded him, although poets of the

Mughal courts such as Kalīm Kāshānī (b. 1581 – d. 1651) and Ṣaidī Ṭihrānī (b. 1616 –

d. 1659) did display significant interest in portraying the Mughals' gardens in the

---

[51] To read about the representation of Ḥasan Ābād bridge in Ṣā'ib's poetry see Paul Losensky, "The Equal of Heaven's Vault: The Design, Ceremony, and Poetry of the Hasanabad Bridge." In *Writers and Rulers: Perspectives on Their Relationship from Abbasid to Safavid periods,* edited by Beatrice Gruendler and Lousie Marlow, (Wiesbaden: Reichert, 2004), 195-216.

qaṣīdeh. The Persian poets, mostly inspired by their rivals at the Mughal court, showed interest in praising the royal gardens and palaces to celebrate the kingship in the *masnavī* form. The *masnavī* form became a tool for this representation, which I study in the next chapter.

CHAPTER FIVE:
MASNAVĪ: DEVELOPMENT OF A NEW TOOL OF LEGITIMACY

I. Introduction

In Chapter Two, I examined the patterns of Safavid legitimacy in the state-sponsored materials that were widely accessible to the broader 16th and 17th century audiences. I investigated coins, inscriptions, and charters of charitable trusts (*vaqf*) to demonstrate the variety of legitimizing discourses, which appeared through the Safavid history in public places. In these materials, the ideologies of those groups that formed the basis of the Safavid dynasty, that I categorized them as Sufi-Persianate-Twelver Shi'i ideas, blend together to provide the Safavid kings with political and religious legitimacy. Then, in Chapter Three and Four, I demonstrated that representations of the Safavid ideology in *qaṣīdeh*s of the Safavid period are multi-faceted and diverse, and not working in the same way as other materials of time. I established that most of the court poets of the Safavid period gave less attention to the Twelver Shi'i elements of the kingship. I argued that poets in the *qaṣīdeh* focused instead on the awe-inspiring features of the rulers and their kingly manners, specifically the kings' military abilities. Sufi ethics and characteristics were also evoked to give Sufi legitimacy to the kings. In general, the poets highlighted the Persian and Sufi aspects of the kingship.

In this chapter, I explore the ways in which the poets responded to the kings and their system of reigns through *masnavī* works. By studying the trajectory of legitimizing patterns in courtly *masnavī*s, I demonstrate that Shi'i doctrines appear more emphatically in *masnavī* form in Shah Ṭahmāsb's time; but they disappear again from Shah 'Abbās I's

period (b. 1571 – d. 1629). I establish that moving from Shah Ismā'īl's time to Shah

Ṭahmāsb, the poets moved away from depicting the Safavid king as the head of Sufi

order. Instead, they focused on Shi'i ideas and concepts; an idea which was dropped later

during the reign of Shah 'Abbās. I establish that Shah Ismā'īl is portrayed as Sufi saint

who at the same time looked for power in early *Shāhnāmeh-masnavī*s (by Qāsimī and

Hātifī). Shah Ṭahmāsb (b. 1514 – d. 1576) is portrayed as a Sufi-Shi'i king in *masnavī*s

written for him. 'Abdī Beyg (d. 1590) compareed the king with all twelve Shi'i Imams to

emphasize the similarities between the king and Imams. 'Abdī Beyg also portrayed the

king's palaces and cities under his governance as spiritual places that could reflect the

king's spiritual power. While Zulālī (b. 1607 – d. 1627/8) portrayed Shah 'Abbās I as a

Sufi leader, the later *masnavī*s written for praise Shah 'Abbās II (b. 1632 – d. 1666) and

Ṣafī II (b. 1646 – d. 1692) mainly represented these two kings as pre-Islamic Persian

kings or heroes of *Shāhnāmeh*. These pre-Islamic representations undermined the weight

Shi'i and Sufi legitimacy had previously. This is also echoed in images of kings in

panegyric *qaṣīdeh*s (see Tables 5 and 6).

By building upon the "three pillars"[1] of legitimacy, this chapter sheds light on

new techniques that poets employed to portray the kings' power. The poets were not

limited themselves to the use of titles and expressions but heavily relied on elements of

nature and places to aggrandize royal power. I argue that the Safavid *masnavī*s paid more

attention to places related to the kings such as palaces, gardens, and the monuments

rather than describing the kings' individual characteristics. These spatial references

---

[1] See Introduction.

conjoined with traditional patterns of legitimacy (i.e. Sufi genealogy and the kings' piety) to symbolize the patron's imperial and spiritual power.

By explaining the fine structure of the cities under the king's supervision, temperate climate, gardens, and diversity of plants in conjunction with the pre-existing claims of prophetic lineage, the images of kings become a "combination of the embodiment and characterization"[2] of the patron and his achievements and successes. My study demonstrates that poets focused on the concepts that underpin the kings' sacred right of kingship through descriptive representations of what was known as spiritual and sacred. The kings' special practices of piety, and mystical power (*karāmāt*)[3] associated with them were evoked to give Sufi legitimacy to the kings in addition to the political legitimacy the kings enjoyed by virtue of their lineage and *farr*. Shaykh Ṣafī al-Dīn (d. 1252 – d. 1354) and later Safavid kings (mostly Shah Ismā'īl and Ṭahmāsb) were depicted with special Sufi power in their social and religious life through depiction of their *karāmāt*. Furthermore, this Sufi legitimacy conveyed a celebration of the kings' material power through detailed description of their palaces. In the later years of the dynasty, the Safavid kings were compared to the other prior kings of the world, and their palaces found a vivid image that helps identifying them as sovereign.

This chapter continues in four parts. In Part II, I study the *Shāhnāmeh*s about Shah Ismā'īl. The Safavid kings had a special interest in the Firdawsī's *Shāhnāmeh*. As

---

[2] Richard Brilliant, "Portraits: A Recurrent Genre in World Art," in Likeness and Beyond: Portraits from Africa and the World, ed. Jean M. Borgatti and Richard Brilliant (New York: The Center for African Art, 1990), 14. Akiko Sumi by borrowing the terms of "iconic portraits" and "emblematic portraits" from Brilliant in order to explain the *mamdūḥ*'s portrait in Arabic *qaṣīdeh*s. Akiko Sumi studied the animals, wine circles and architecture of 'Abbasid courts as different forms of representation of 'Abbāsid power. See Akiko Motoyoshi, Sumi, *Description in Classical Arabic Poetry: Waṣf, Ekphrasis, and Interarts Theory.* (Leiden: Brill, 2004).

[3] See Introduction, 23.

this book dealt with the issue of power, authority, and monarchs, writing new

*Shāhnāmeh*s was a good tool for representing the Safavid kings and legitimizing their

reign.[4] The *Shāhnāmeh*s of Qāsimī Gunābādī (d. 1574) and Hātifī Kharjirdī (b. 1454 – d.

1521) elaborated Safavid ideology and helped shaping the image of a sacred king with

special charisma. These two poets attempted legitimizing Shah Ismā'īl by connecting the

Shah to the pre-Islamic Persian kings and by emphasizing the Sufi elements of the lives

and characters of Safavids' ancestors (e.g. their assiduity in praying or their ability to see

their future time of death). The story of Karbala is evoked in the introductory sections of

both *Shāhnāmeh*s to indicate the sinlessness of the king. The *karāmāt* of Shah Ismā'īl's

Sufi ancestors were compared with the innocence of Imam Ḥusayn to give a Sufi

legitimacy to the Safavids. The image of Safavid kings in these two *Shāhnāmeh*s is a

Sufi-Persian portrait (see Tables 11, 12, and 13).

In Part III, I focus on the works of 'Abdī Beyg Shīrāzī, famous as Navīdī, at Shah

Ṭahmāsb's court. I demonstrate that 'Abdī Beyg refrained from straightforward

statements that declared Shah Ṭahmāsb's sacred authority. The poet focused on the

embodiment of royal legitimacy in concrete objects such as the city and gardens. The

prosperity of the city and the glory of the palaces and gardens served his purpose.

Therefore, paying attention to the architecture and construction of the city became a new

tool for praising the king and kingship while still being described in their spatial form.

'Abdī Beyg connected the prosperity of a city and its heavenly sphere to the unique

power of the king as a friend of God. 'Abdī Beyg also wrote in praise of the twelve Shi'i

---

[4] To read about the reception of *Shāhnāmeh* from Timurd period at the court of Mughals and Safavids, read Gabrielle Van den Berg, Charles Melville, *Shahnama Studies III: The Reception of the Shahnama: Studies in Persian Cultural History*, vol.12, (Leiden: Brill: 2018).

Imams and compared them to the Safavid king to legitimize the religio-political power of the king. To see sources of legitimacy of Shah Ṭahmāsb see Tables 13, 14 and 15.

Part IV briefly looks at *masnavī*s dedicated to Shah 'Abbās I (b. 1571 – d. 1629) and 'Abbās II. The language and thematic of the seven works of Zulālī Khwansārī (b. 1607 – d. 1627/8) are close to what usually *ghazal* form presents in history of Persian literature. The king is presented similar to Sufi leaders rather than an imperial king. While the poet demonstrated that he was familiar with the main religio-political discourses of his time (e.g. writing in refutation of famous Sufis and philosophers of the time), he did not make a connection between Shah 'Abbās and his Shi'i identity. Similar to *qaṣīdeh*s of his time, these *masnavī*s refrained from using the titles and benedictions found in other contemporaneous cultural products that, as discussed in Chapter Two, represented the king as a sovereign ruler. While Zulālī's *masnavī*s portray the king as a Sufi leader, Mullā Rafī' (d. 1678) praised the beauty of cities under Shah 'Abbās II's supervision without mentioning any other aspects of the life and character of this monarch.

Part V is dedicated to the works of Muḥsin Ta'ṣīr Tabrīzī (d. 1717), who was patronized by Shah Ṣafī II (b. 1646 – d. 1692) and Shah Sultan Ḥusayn (b. 1668 – d. 1726). Inspired by the earlier poets of the 16th century and the poets of the Mughal courts, he emphasized the king's power by paying special attention to the architecture of cities, buildings, and gardens. Earlier *masnavī*s of Safavid reign, for example those written by 'Abdī Beyg, portrayed the heavenly and beautiful gardens and palaces spatially, but during the reign of Sultan Ḥusayn, descriptions of palaces and gardens are described by their design, layout, color, as well as the materials used in construction.[5] This referential

shift in describing the palaces started from Shah Ṣafī II and continued to Sultan Ḥusayn's

reign. The poets who wrote *masnavī*s for the last Safavid kings envisioned the kings as an

imperial leader.

II. *Shāhnāmeh-Masnavīs*: Qāsimī Gunābādī and Hātifī Kharjirdī

The Safavid reign is marked by frequent reproduction of the *Shāhnāmeh* of

Firdawsī (b. 935 – d. 1020 CE) and writing of new *masnavī*s.[6] Firdawsī's *Shāhnāmeh*

deals with the stories of kings; therefore, it was a good means to demonstrate Safavid

kingly power. The *Shāhnāmeh*s of Ṭahmāsb's period, written by by Qāsimī and Hātifī,

narrate the history of Shah Ismāʿīl's reign, explaining the political circumstances

surrounding the king's decision to leave Gilan to occupy the throne. By describing the

king's lineage and emphasizing his spiritual forefathers, these *Shāhnāmeh*s attempted to

legitimize the Safavid kingship and further to manifest Safavid power.

In legitimizing Safavid kingship, these two *Shāhnāmeh*s paid special attention to

the Safavid lineage. Sufi lineage and the genealogy connecting the Safavid kings to the

family of the Prophet played an important role in justifying the right of kingship in these

two epics. The poets' main endeavor was to demonstrate that Safavid kingship was

destined by God. Therefore, the poets' primary goal in writing was to create a Sufi

legitimacy either through description of the Safavid's ancestors or as considering special

---

[5] To read about writing the description of gardens and in the influence of Mughal court poets on the Safavid poet read Sunil Sharma, *Mughal Arcadia: Persian Literature in an Indian Court*, (Harvard University Press, 2017).

[6] Because the main focus of this section is on the *Shāhnāmeh*s, which were composed during the Safavid period, I did not talk about *Shāhnāmeh-yi Ṭahmāspī*. For more information on this book, see Welch, Stuart, *a Kings Book of Kings*, (New York: Metropolitan Museum of Art), 1972.

karāmat (e.g. Shaykh Ṣafī al-Dīn's special power in praying) for the king. Declaring *farr*, the sacred right of kingship, for the Safavid kings, served the same function.

The two famous *Shāhnāmeh*s written about Shah Ismāʿīl, both patronized by the court system, are good examples which demonstrate the divinity of Shah Ismāʿīl formed based on Sufi and messianic claims, and not Shiʿi religious affiliations. In these two *Shāhnāmeh*s, the poets emphasize the Sufi lineage of Shah Ismāʿīl by claiming similarity between his forefathers and the Sufis of Ardabil. Ismāʿīl's ancestors have been depicted as Sufis with special unique power in praying and knowledge. Innocence, sinlessness, death in path of seeking truth through paying special attention to the battle of Karbala are among the features that the poets emphasized in order to first demonstrate Shah Ismāʿīl as embodiment of sacred and further to legitimize the rulership of this dynasty. In both *Shāhnāmeh*s, the battle of Karbala and death of Imam Ḥusayn, which in the modern Imami discourse is perceived as a battle that happened in defense of Imam ʿAli's right in substituting the Prophet Muḥammad, represents innocence of Safavid Sufi ancestors. The association of the battle of Karbala and death of Sīyāvash, Keykāvūs's son in *Shāhnāmeh* of Firdawsī with death of Safavid Sufi forefather is the innocence. Imam Ḥusayn, Sīyāvash, Junayd, and Ḥaydar decided to go to war and occupying the throne while they did not have a promising military prowess.

Hātifī's *Shāhnāmeh*, famous as *Ismāʿīlnāmeh*, *Shāhnāmeh-yi Haẓrat-i Ismāʿīl*, or *masnavī-yi Futūhāt-i Shāhī*, is Hātifī's last work and was written on the order of Shah Ismāʿīl himself. The book is remained unfinished as the poet died before the end. Based on the original manuscript housed in the National Library of Russia in Saint-Petersburg, the book has only 1137 lines. Qāsimī's *Shāhnāmeh* is inspired by Hātifī's *Shāhnāmeh*.[7]

This *Shāhnāmeh*, which describes the life of Shah Ismāʿīl and Ṭahmāsb, is longer and it

consists of 4300 lines. In both *Shāhnāmeh*s, the lives of Shah Ismāʿīl's forefathers were

discussed after the opening sections in praising God and the Prophet. The poets present

Ismāʿīl's fathers as spiritual leaders with qualities (Karāmāt) such as those of *awlīyā*

allāh (friend of God) to claim Shah Ismāʿīl's sacred personality in the future.

Like chronicles of the Safavid reign that include the Safavid genealogy in their

prefaces, *Shāhnāmeh-yi* Hātifī and Qāsimī include information about Shah Ismāʿīl's

forefathers. Hātifī started with Shaykh Ṣafī al-Dīn's life and establishes his connection to

ʿAlī's family through Imam Ḥusayn.

ز آل علی وز نژاد حسین

که هم عین نورند و هم نور عین

He was from the family of Ali, and he was from the race of Ḥusayn,
They were the exact light [8] and they were the light of eyes (Hātifī, 655)[9]

Qāsimī's position regarding the king's lineage was ambivalent; nevertheless,

Qāsimī prioritized the king's military power over his lineage. Qāsimī only discusses the

king's relationship to the family of Prophet when the issue of "power" is involved. For

example, when the Uzbek king claims his own genealogy to show its nobility to Ismāʿīl,

---

⁷ To read more about *Shāhnāmeh* Qāsimī and how he was inspired not only by Hātifī's work about Shah Ismāʿīl but also his work about Tīmūr, see Michele Bernardini, "Hātifī's Tīmūrnāmeh and Qāsimī's Shāhnāmeh-yi Ismāʿīl: Considerations for a Double Critical Edition", in Society and Culture in the Early Modern Middle East: Studies on Iran in the Safavid Period, edited by Andrew Newman, (Leiden & Boston, 2003), 3-18. Barry wood, Wood, Barry David. "The Shāhnāmeh-yi Ismāʿīl : Art and Cultural Memory in Sixteenth-Century Iran." PhD diss., Harvard University, 2002.

⁸ The first *ʿiyn* in line is double entendre, referring to a spring of water. Therefore, the line could be translated as: They were a spring of light, and they were the light of eyes.

⁹ Hātifī Kharjirdī, *Shāhnāmeh-yi Hātifī Kharjirdī: Ḥamāseh-yi Futūḥāt-i Shāh Ismāʿīl Ṣafavī*. ed. ʿAli Al Davud. (Tehran: Farhangistān-i Zabān va Adab-i Fārsī, 2008), 57-58. (hereafter cited in text and footnotes as Hātifī).

Ismā'īl portrayed to be interested in talking about his lineage and claiming affiliation

with the Prophet and Imām 'Alī:

ستانم ز شاهان عالم خراج

دهم ملت احمدی را رواج

ز آل پیمبر منم یادگار

منم اختر برج هشت و چهار

گل گلشن آل پیغمبرم

جگر گوشه حیدر صفدرم

منم غنچه باغ شاهنشهی

منم سرو بستان فرماندهی

صف آرای میدان شاهی منم

سزاوار ظل الهی منم

Heaven informs me of triumph
That I shall clear the world of foes

I shall receive tribute from the kings of the world
I shall spread the faith of Muḥammad

I remained from the Prophet's family
I am the star of the twelve zodiac houses

I am the flower of the Prophet's kin
I am dearest to the triumphant (lit. line-breaker) Ḥaydar

I am the bud in the garden of kingship
I am the cypress in the orchard of leaders

I mobilize ranks in the battlefield of monarchy
I deserve the title "shadow of God" (Qāsimī, 186)[10]

The seminomadic Turkmen devotees of Shah Ismā'īl had special respect for the

Sufi Safavid *shaykh*s whom they called "Lords of Ardabil". To them, they were saints

who had been martyred for a divine cause.[11] The Safavi house originally was among the

---

[10] Qāsimī Gunābādī, Muḥammad Qāsim. *Shāh Ismā'īlnāmeh*. Edited by Ghaffar Shuja' Kayhani, (Tehran: Farhangistān-i Zabān wa Adab-i Fārsī, 2008).

[11] Abbas Amanat, *A Modern History of Iran*, (New Haven and London Yale University Press, 2017), 40.

landowning nobility of Kurdistan with affinity to *Ahl-i Ḥaqq*. Ṣafī al-Dīn (d.1334 CE),

the patriarch of the Safavid house and Ismāʿīl's ancestor was a respected Sufi leader

admired by the people of his region and the rulers and ministers of his time. Shaykh Ṣafī

al-Dīn was living in a period that the Sufis enjoyed popularity because of a more personal

and intimate form of religion they offered the people.[12] Hātifī presented Ṣafī al-Dīn as a

Sufi who was not inclined towards worldly matters. His tomb was a prominent site of

Sufi veneration with its doors open to the angels. Like other Sufis, the time of his death

was announced to him. When it was time to pass away, his soul, which appeared in the

shape of a dove, a symbol and metaphor for innocence and peace, flew to God. His death

is described to have been as other-worldly and magical as his life and personality. The

poet compares the *shaykh*'s tombstone to the *Ka ʿbeh*, describing it as twice as large as the

Ka ʿbeh. His mausoleum became a place for private and mystical gatherings for his

followers; a place that was believed to reveal the secrets of the world to his followers.[13]

These features are reminiscent of *karāmāt*, the unique power of *awlīyā allāh* (the friends

of God) who could trespass time and space by the will of God. This similarity between

Sufi and the Safavids' forefathers draws on Shāh Ismāʿīl's lineage to present him as the

head of Safavid Sufi order and potential of sacredness which was believed exist among

his forefathers. This claim had the potentiality to dismantle the borders between

monarchs, Sufis, and Imams, that eventually allowed the Safavids to claim the right to

rule in the absence of an Imam.

---

[12] Ibid.

[13] Hātifī, *Shāhnāmeh*, 51.

Ṣafī al-Dīn's son, Ṣadr al-Dīn Mūsā (b. 1305 – d. 1391 CE), was portrayed as Sufi and a saint impossible to committee a crime. Hātifī mentions that Ṣafī al-Dīn had spiritual knowledge and knew science to argue that appointment of Junayd to the leadership of the community could not be illegitimate:

درون و برون ماه ناکاسته
به انواع دانش برآراسته

قوی باطن از دانش معنوی
برون نیز از علم ظاهر قوی

پسر را نشانید در مهد خویش
به دستور کردش ولی عهد خویش

سپرد آن امانت به دست جنید
که در دست او از پدر بود قید

His inside and out was a full moon,
It was designed by different forms of knowledges

His inward (intention) was strong because of spiritual knowledge
His external (actions) was strong because of his scientific knowledges

He seated the son into his own seat,
With his order he made him (son) his own substitute

He secured what he borrowed into the hands of Junayd,
As it was given to his hands from his father (Hātifī, lines 745 – 749)

Royal family, wisdom, knowledge, and brevity are concepts that legitimizes kingship for Junayd in his statement for raising to power:

مرا سلطنت در نسب نیز هست
خردمندی و عقل و تمیز هست

بود ملک گیری به فرزانگی
به جمع دلیری و مردانگی

In my lineage, I also have sovereignty
I have wisdom, logic and recognizing ability

Occupying a throne is possible through prudence
in collecting bravery and courageousness (Hātifī, lines 780 – 781)

However, Junayd was unsuccessful in his attempt as he was killed in a war with

Shirwānshāh an associate of Jahānshāh, the ruler of his time. To explain Junayd's death,

Ḥātifī referenced the battle of Karbala to legitimize Junayd's attempt at rebellion against

Jahānshāh. Ḥātifī compares Junayd with Imam Ḥusayn and gives him the title "martyr" to

associate Junayd with Imam Ḥusayn through the same innocence that is associated with

Ḥusayn and his death in this battle. To emphasize the idea, the poet called Jahānshāh's

army, an army with *Yazīdī* nature and identity.

ز بد مهری چرخ ناسازگار
صف صوفیان را شد از دست کار

گرفتار شد آن حسینی نژاد
به دست گروهی منافق نهاد

شهادت نصیبش در آن شور و شین
حسینی بر آمد به رنگ حسین

یزیدی نهادان بر آورده سر
شده مبتلاشان حسین دگر

From the unkindness of the unkind fate
The lines of Sufis lost their control (over the war)

Who had the lineage of Ḥusayn got captured
by the hand of a group with hypocritic natures

His share of that blaming war was martyrdom
A Ḥusayn raised in the same color as Ḥusayn

People with nature of Yazid raised up
Another Ḥusayn was in trouble by them (Ḥātifī, lines 806 – 810)

     Ḥātifī exemplifies the legitimate right of Junayd's rebellion against Shirwānshāh

by referencing both Sīyāvash's story from Firdawsī's *Shāhnāmeh* and the incident of

Karbala. In Firdawsī's *Shāhnāmeh*, Sīyāvash fled from his father's Persian court and

settled in Turan where the Turanian emperor Afrāsīyāb offered him refuge. Afrāsīyāb

grew to distrust Sīyāvash and ultimately ordered his assassination. Unable to return to the

safety of his father's court and unable to oppose Afrāsīyāb, who had offered him refuge,

Sīyāvash got captured by the Turanian army and beheaded. Junayd being a hostage in the Aq Qoyonlu's court in Tabriz, apparently inspired the poet to make this connection between Sīyāvash and Junayd. Moreover, similar to Sīyāvash who got married to the daughter of whom he sheltered at, Afrāsīyāb, Junayd married Uzun Ḥasan's daughter. Nevertheless, because of this growing distrust, a common theme for both stories, Junayd decided to leave Lebanon and go to war with Shirwan's ruler. Similar to Sīyāvash and Imām Ḥusayn's situation in Karbala, Junayd only had small number of fighters and this lack of support resulted to his death. Similar to Sīyāvash, Jahanshāh's army that was compared to Yazid's, beheaded Junayd. From his blood drops, similar to Sīyāvash's, a plant grew, which in the case of Junayd, became his son.

Qāsimī also referred the battle of Karbala to portray the unjust death of Ḥaydar, Junayd's son. It was under Shaykh Ḥaydar that the Safavids became known as a political movement with Twelver Shi'i identity. The death of Ḥaydar was compared to Ḥusayn's death and the army of Shirwānshāh was compared to Yazid's. Death, in the pursuit of truth, is considered as rebellion against "suppression" and "corruption." Therefore, Ḥaydar was a martyr.

حسینی گرفتار آل یزید

ز روی جفا و ستم شد شهید

A Ḥusayn was captured by the family of Yazid
He became martyred because of (their) suppression (Qāsimī, line 885)

As mentioned earlier, in both *Shāhnāmeh*s, the Sufi lineage of Shah Ismā'īl and its representation has dominance over religious arguments that historically are known to be part of Shah Ismā'īl's claim in power. While changing the state religion to Shi'ism and educating the people with the Twelve Imami doctrines were at the core political propagating system of Shah Ismā'īl, no form of Imami intentions of the king is represented in these two works. Praising a Knowledgeable spiritual king with the strongest military prowess is a poetic convention. Nevertheless, the poetic context of praise, the economics of court stage and the social relationship had changed by the reign of Shāh Ismāʿīl and it is expected to see the religious Shiʿi themes, not if references to Shiʿi doctrines, for example insertion of ʿAlī's name into *azān,* appear. The most relevant Shiʿi theme in both *Shāhnāmeh* is the Battle of Karbala and vengeance for Imām Ḥusayn's murder. Nevertheless, Qāsimī presented the battle as a regional issue that only the people of Shām should be responsible for, and not the entire Sunni believers.

In general, these two *Shāhnāmeh*s attempted forming the sacred charisma for the first Safavid king through spiritualization of his charisma through paying special attention to his Sufi ancestors. Special knowledge, unique power in praying, popularity among students, unique death, connection to the other world, the desire to seek truth even through standing against the powers of time and being killed innocently in this path are the themes both praised the Sufi ancestors of Shah Ismāʿīl with.

Table 10 (Patterns of Sufi Legitimacy in Safavid Shāhnāmehs)

Sufi Legitimacy			
Lineage	Titles	Miraculous acts	Comparison to Sufis
*	N/A	*	*

Table 11 (Patterns of Persian Notions of Kingship in Safavid Shāhnāmehs)

Persian Notions of Kingship				
Titles	Comparisons	Symbols		
		Farr	Light	Falcon
*	*	*	N/A	N/A

Table 12 (Patterns of Shi'i Legitimacy in Safavid Shāhnāmehs)

Shi'i Legitimacy					
Lineage	Servitude	Distribution of Twelver Shi'ism	Relationship to Imam 'Alī	Karbala and Imam Ḥusayn	Comparisons to all Shi'i Imams
*	N/A	*	*	*	*

III. 'Abdī Beyg and Writing *Khamseh*

Like his father, Shah Ṭahmāsb was interested in supporting *masnavī* writing. His

interest in *masnavī* is evident in his support for the works of 'Abdī Beyg. Although Shah

Ṭahmāsb was not a great supporter of panegyric *qaṣīdeh*, his support of Abdī Beyg, who

served as his accountant, demonstrates the significance of *masnavī* writing for this

Safavid king. In his many *masnavī*s, 'Abdī Beyg portrayed the king's special power in

running state affairs, his spiritual influence on the prosperity of the city, and his piety in

religious practices. Indeed, in five of his *masnavī*s, 'Abdī Beyg attempts to legitimize

kingship by presenting the king's influence over different spaces including the city,

palaces, and gardens. He moves the reader's attention from abstract presentations of kingly spirituality such as light and *farr* to more concrete elements such as the cities that, because of the king's successful revitalization efforts, experience prosperity. In this way, the poet employs the prosperity of the cities to embody abstract concepts such as the king's spiritual charisma. This *Khamseh* by 'Abdī Beyg has been praised for documenting the architectural layout and history of Sa'ādatābād. As scholars such as Ehsan Eshraqi, Maria Szuppe, and Losensky demonstrate, this *Khamseh* is an important source for understanding the social life of the Safavid society, politics, and culture. While the praising sections for Ṭahmāsb in 'Abdī Beyg's *Khamseh* indicate developments in Safavid religious and political ideology, the interest the poet showed towards documenting the palaces and city layouts as well as the wall paintings and inscriptions indicates that the king's attention and interest lay not only in patronizing architecture and painting, but also poetry.[14]

'Abdī Beyg applies different techniques through which his works became a unique example of a panegyric. Losensky in his paper about Garden of Eden discusses the significance of 'Abdī's description of buildings, cities, and places at length. By discussing the importance of ekphrasis in 'Abdī's description of objects, places, persons, and times, Losensky argues that 'Abdī Beyg used buildings and cities as a force of order, prosperity, and civilization to depict a legitimate king in power. Although The archetype of building and city as a symbol of a monarch's dominion has been a traditional element of Arabic poetry frcm 'Abbasid time. Nevertheless, it gained fresh momentum during the reign of Timurids in Persian poetry. Under the influence of the poets of the Deccan and

---

[14] Paul Losensky, "The Palace of Praise and the Melons of Time: Descriptive Patterns in 'Abdī Shīrāzī's *Garden of Eden*." *Eurasian Studies 2* (2003), 2.

the Mughal Empire, Persian poetry from the 15th to 18th centuries witness the development of what has been called an "urban-topographical" poetry.[15] In general, 'Abdī Beyg has been known as the first Persian poet who, throughout his descriptions, insisted that Ja'farābād, its buildings and their inscriptions, and its ornamental and agricultural gardens "represent the cosmic and political authority of the Safavid shah, as both poem and place participate in a "monarchitectonins" of imperial ideology."[16]

Losensky, however, correctly cautions us that "for all its documentary value, *Jannat-i 'Adn,* is first and foremost a work of literature, and its factual content is organized and inflected by a complex poetic construct."[17] A comparison of using the force of ekphrasis in describing the royal palaces and cities after Shah Ṭahmāsb, specifically during the reign of last two Safavid kings (e.g.in the works of Muḥsin Ta'sīr Tabrīzī), demonstrates the differences in representations of palaces and cities. In 'Abdī Beyg's works, the capital city Qazvin has a spiritual relationship with the presence of Shah Ṭahmāsb (d. 1576), and the buildings and their components which are described by their location in gardens and in relation to each other represent a second heaven on earth. The focus of poet in representing the palaces are the trees of gardens, fruits, vaults, and pools. This imagery in 'Abdī Beyg's works along with the representation of Shah Ṭahmāsb, as a king with Sufi and Shi'i lineage and with the characteristics of his Sufi forefathers and the Shi'i Imams, presents both places and the ruler spiritual and other-worldly. However, the buildings in works of Ta'sīr Tabrīzī dedicated to Shah Sultan

---

[15] Sunil Sharma, *Mughal Arcadia: Persian Literature in an Indian Court,* (Harvard University Press, 2017), 94-95.

[16] Losensky, "The Palace of Praise", 6.

[17] Ibid, 3.

Ḥusayn (d. 1726), symbolize a temporal king in power. These places present themselves

and not the spiritual world. Ta'sīr Tabrīzī notes the construction of buildings, the layout

of palaces, colors, and textures of the building materials without emphasizing their

similarity with gardens and palaces of the heaven

'Abdī describes the king as having the ability to revitalize his surroundings. in

Zīnat al-Awrāq, where 'Abdī Beyg describes the beauty of Qazvin and its vaults, the poet

describes the king with the ability to revitalize places around him, a unique ability that is

reminiscent of Sufi *karamāt*.[18] 'Abdī Beyg conceptualizes the king's spiritual power by

referring to the power of king's footprints in rebuilding the world:

پی شاهان آفتاب اثر

از خرابی دهد به خلق خبر

پی این شه ز عین پرنوری

هر کجا تافت یافت معموری

شاه ما خسروی خجسته پی است

همه معموری از قدوم وی است

The feet of [other] glorifying kings
bring the news of desolation to the people

The bright feet of this king
Where they shine, they revitalize

---

[18] *Karāmat* in singular form and *karāmāt* in plural form are the qualities available to *awlīyā* (friends of God). *Karāmat* is an action or a quality which contravenes the norms *(naqiż-i 'ādat)*, and it is available for those who are *ṣādiq* (truth-teller/honest) and who are known as *valī* (guardian/intimate friend). Receiving food upon request from God, passing through the boundaries of place and time, finding water where it was not available before, or hearing a voice from absence are among the most famous *karāmāt* which were frequently ascribed to the friends of God. *Karāmat* is for *awlīyā*, and *mu'jizāt* is for the prophets and it demonstrates their authenticity of *wilāyat*. The Safavid poets frequently, and especially through the epic *masnavīs* pictured the ancestors of the Safavid kings with such qualities. Through poems, the Sufi Safavid *shaykhs* were usually portrayed in connection with the other world, because they transgress the temporal and spatial dimensions, and they talk to Imams in dreams. The great ancestors of the Safavid kings could guess their times of death, their bodies would become doves to fly to the other world. Their tombs were sacred places where the angels hovered and talked to them. These tombs were the most similar to the heaven pictured in the Quran. By ascribing these divine qualities, Safavid poets portrayed the Safavid kings as spiritual Sufi-leaders to give them an aura of divinity.

Our king is a ruler with auspicious footprints,
His every step rebuilds the world[19]

In *Rawżat al-Ṣifāt*, the poet makes a direct connection between the prosperity of Qazvin and the king's presence in this city. Magically, by his sudden presence, Qazvin's weather and its scenery change positively. There is more prosperity and more crops. The relationship between the king and the city's prosperity is portrayed in a cause and effect relationship:

خسروی والاگهر دین پناه
خطه قزوین چو شدش تخت گاه

رونق این خطه به حسب مراد
گشت به یمن قدم شه زیاد

خاست نوای فرح از خانه ها
یافت عمارت همه ویرانه ها

کشت وی از خاک بر آورد سر
خشتش از افلاک برآورد پر

خوشه هر کشت شد از دانه پر
دانه اش از دولت شه گشت در

شاخ درختانش به فصل بهار
جای شکوفه درم آورده بار

The great king of pure lineage, the shelter of religion
When the city of Qazvin became his throne,

The prosperity of this region, agreeably
was transformed by the emanation from the king's footstep

Sounds of happiness rose from the houses
all the desolate houses were rebuilt

The crops poked their heads out of the earth
The bricks took to the skies like the birds

Each bunch of seeds fully blossomed
They became diamonds because of the auspicious king

---

[19] Zayn al-ʿĀbidīn ʿAbd al-Mūʾmin Navīdī , *Jannat al-Asmār; Zīnat al-Awrāq; Ṣaḥīfat al-Ikhlāṣ,* (Moskva: Izd-vo "Nauka, " Glav. red. vostochnoĭ lit-ry, 1979), 163 lines 2742 – 45. (Cited hereafter ZA)

In the spring season its trees
grew coins instead of blossoms[20]

In *Zīnat al-Awrāq*, the poet compares the city of Qazvin with the other famous cities to demonstrate that the differences in the cities' natures are due to Shah Ṭahmāsb's special characteristics as a king. 'Abdī Beyg compares Qazvin with different regions to conclude what makes Qazvin different is its ruler. For example, Egypt was given as an example immediately after Qazvin where the poet argues that the splendor of the greenery in Qazvin is due to its ruler:

چه عجب گر ولایت قزوین
شود از شاه مثل خلد برین

مصر هر چند خطه ای عالی است
لیکن از باغ و بوستان خالی است

باغ و بستان و لاله زارش نیست
رستنی یک خلال وارش نیست

It should not be surprising if Qazvin
becomes the sublime heaven because of [this] king

Although Egypt is a great region
it is without gardens and greenery

It does not have gardens and tulip fields
It does not have a single tiny growing plant (ZA, 155, lines 2560 – 2562)

The places that 'Abdī Beyg describes are marked by special power because they are ruled by the king, the appointee of God on earth. Similar to most courtly gardens, the palaces and gardens of Shah Ṭahmāsb represent heaven on earth and receive God's special attention. In *Jannat al-Asmār*, the Eastern vault of Ṭahmāsb's arcadia is blessed by the other world and Bāgh-i Ja'farābād was described as a forever-secured place

---

[20] Zayn al-'Ābidīn 'Abd al-Mū'min Navīdī, *Rawżat al-Ṣifāt*, ed, A. Ragimov, 'Ali Mina'i Tabrizi. (Moskva: Idārah-yi Nashr-i Dānish, 1974), 30, lines 102 – 108 (Cited hereafter *RṢ*).

because of God's special support.[21] The gardens and their palaces are an actual heaven on earth full of other-worldly angels. They are claimed to have been built by God[22] and guide people to the real heaven.[23]

In general, *Rawżat al-Ṣifāt, Zīnat al-Awrāq,* and *Jannat al-Asmār* pay specific attention to the gardens and palaces under Shah Ṭahmāsb's governance. Instead of focusing on the king's personal attitude in kingship, for example the king's generosity or kindness towards the people, Abdī Beyg intensively presents the perfect condition of these places as being the result of the king's special influence over the cosmos. In these works, the king and his bodily features are not the foci anymore. The places, including gardens and the king's residence, represent the spirituality of the special sacred king.

The other source of legitimacy for Shah Ṭahmāsb in this *Khamseh* is the representation of Shi'i doctrines. The introductions of 'Abdī Beyg's works offer an ethical comparison between the Twelve Shi'i Imams and the king. In *Rawżat al-Ṣifāt,* 'Abdī Beyg deliberately emphasizes the close relationship between the manners of prophets and the king. The king is incorporated into the family of the Prophet with expressions such as *muṣṭafavī* (related to Muṣṭafā) and *murtażavī* (related to Murtażā, i.e. Imām 'Alī) while he is also compared to the pre-Islamic Persian kings. The king's personality is depicted as similar to the Prophet's. Like the Prophet, the king's wisdom and rationality help disseminating the Twelver Shi'ism faith, in the sense that Ṭahmāsb, like the Prophet who introduced new religion to his people, help the religion and the state

---

[21] Zayn al-'Ābidīn 'Abd al-Mū'min Navīdī ,"Jannat al-Asmār" in, *Zīnat al-Awrāq; Ṣaḥīfat al-Ikhlāṣ.* (Moskva: Izd-vo "Nauka, " Glav. red. vostochnoĭ lit-ry, 1979), 125 (Cited hereafter *JA*).

[22] Ibid, *JA,* 137.

[23] Ibid, *RṢ,* 34.

to find a new standing during his lifetime. Ṭahmāsb is introduced not as a "messiah" but
as someone who would bring *akhar al-zamān* (final period) of the world with him.[24]

Zīnat al-Awrāq also starts with praise of all twelve Shi'i Imams. The king is praised of
being *tābi'-i khudā va rasūl* (the follower of God and the Prophet) and his manner is
nothing short of the manners and traditions of *a'immeh-yi aṭhār* (the pure Imams).[25] The
introduction of Abdī Beyg in *Ṣaḥīfat al-Ikhlāṣ* is a good example of how the poet
compares the king with Shi'i Imams:

ز روی نسب از رسولش گهر
ز راه حسب سوده بر چرخ سر

از او دیده شرع محمد نوی
چو حیدر از او پشت ملت قوی

حسن خلق شاه حسینی نسب
چو عباد و باقر به علم و ادب

از او مذهب جعفری را ظهور
که در گوهر از موسیش هست نور

منور از او بارگاه رضا
ز دست جوادش یم اندر حیا

ز بس کو مثل در نکو عهدی است
به حق هادی عسکر مهدی است

His lineage extends to the Prophet
And his personal achievements his head touches the fate

Because of him, the legacy of Muḥammad became renewed
Like Ḥaydar, he strengthened the backbone of the religion

In temper he is Ḥasan, and his lineage is from Ḥusayn
In knowledge and learning, he is 'Ubbād [26] and Bāqir

----

[24] 'Abdī Beyg, *RṢ*, 29.

[25] "Zīnat al-Awrāq" in Zayn al-'Ābidīn 'Abd al-Mū'min, Navīdī, *Janna al-Asmār; Zīnat al-Awrāq; Ṣaḥīfa al-Ikhlāṣ*. (Moskva: Izd-vo "Nauka, " Glav. red. vostochnoĭ lit-ry, 1979), 153. (*Zīnat al-Awrāq* hereafter cited as ZA in text and footnotes)

[26] The poet meant Imām Sajjād who was known for being in constant praying. Therefore, the poet applied the word *'ubbād* (from *'ibāda*) which shows the excess of Imam's praying.

Through him the faith of Ja'far is revealed
because he took his light from Imām Musa

Through him the dome of Riża is alight
His generous hand ashamed the sea

Because he is famous for keeping promises
rightly he was compared to Imām Hādī [27]

the *khātimeh* (the final section) of this *masnavī*, 'Abdī Beyg returns to the name

of all fourteen pure imams where the poet prays to God for saving the Shah until the

return of Imām Mahdī. The poet swears to the name of each Imām to convince God to

give everlasting kingship to Shah Ṭahmāsb.[28] The names of all twelve imams are

mentioned one more time when the poet narrates the story of 'Īsā khān (the son of

Lavand, ruler of Gurjistan) and his conversion to Shi'i Islam. While the poet lists the

names and characteristics of the Shi'i Imams, his representation of 'Īsā khān's conversion

argues for his lack of knowledge on Shi'i practices. At odds with the Islamic tradition,

'Īsā Khān mentioned the name of all twelve Imams to note his conversion to Shi'ism (ṢI

226-227). The testimony of faith in Sunnism has two parts: the oneness of God and the

acceptance of Muḥammad as the Prophet. In Shi'ism, the testimony is tripartite as the

acceptances of 'Alī as the heir of Muḥammad was added to the other two expressions. In

narrating the story of this conversion, 'Abdī Beyg portrays Shi'ism as the light and the

previous faith as the darkness.[29] Shah Ṭahmāsb's *lutf* (kindness, favor) is introduced as

the cause of such conversion and 'Īsā Khān's transcendence from darkness to light.[30] The

---

[27] "Ṣaḥīfat al-Iklāṣ" in Zayn al-'Ābidīn 'Abd al-Mū'min Navīdī, *Jannat al-Asmār; Zīnat al-Awrāq; Ṣaḥīfat al-Ikhlāṣ.* (Moskva: Izd-vo "Nauka, " Glav. red. vostochnoĭ lit-ry, 1979), 206. (hereafter cited in text ṢI

[28] Ibid, *ṢI*, 227-228.

[29] Ibid, 222-223.

[30] Ibid.

encounter of ʿĪsā Khān and Shah Ṭahmāsb, which marks the emergence of the

importance of Shiʿi Imams and traditions, recalls the communication between Shah

Ismāʿīl and Sultan Nāmurād when, for the first time, Shah Ismāʿīl was forced to invoke

his Shiʿi lineage to claim authority over the other rulers. I conceptualized the patterns of

legitimacy in *Khamseh* of ʿAbdī Beyg in Tables 13, 14 and 15.

Table 13 (Patterns of Sufi Legitimacy)

Sufi Legitimacy			
Lineage	Titles	Miraculous acts Influence on the cities	Comparison to Sufis
N/A	*	*	N/A

Table 14 (Patterns of Persian Notions of Kingship)

Persian Notions of Kingship				
Titles	Comparisons	Symbols		
*	*	Farr	Light	Falcon
		*	N/A	N/A

Table 15 (Patterns of Shiʿi Legitimacy)

Shiʿi Legitimacy				
Lineage	Servitude	Distribution of Twelver Shiʿism	Compared to all Imams	Karbala and Imam Ḥusayn
*	N/A	*	*	N/A

IV. Zulālī Khwansārī and Mullā Rafīʿ Muḥammad Qazvīnī

Compared to the earlier poets, Zulālī (d. 1615) takes a different approach towards

praising Shah ʿAbbās I in his *masnavīs*. Zulālī wrote seven *masnavīs* that are inspired by

Jāmī's (d. 1492) *Haft Awrang* and are known as *Meykhāneh, Shuʿleh-yi Dīdār, Ḥusn-i*

Galūsūz, Zarreh va Khurshīd, Maḥmūd va Ayāz, Azar va Samandar, and

Sulaymānnāmeh. These seven *masnavīs* are defined by their language that usually was common for the *ghazal* world and their portrayal of Sufi love and human morality. Only *Sulaymānnāmeh*, which is about Solomon and Balqays, is in epic form. Structurally, these *masnavī*s follow the tradition of *masnavī* writing during the Safavid period. After invoking God and the Prophet, Zulālī praises Imām ʿAlī as the only righteous Imam and the only leader after the Prophet's death, and then the main narration starts. Of these seven *masnavī*s, the first two, *Meykhāneh* and *Shuʿleh-yi Dīdār*, are written in sections. The sections are *qadah* (cup) and *shuʿleh* (flame) in reference to the titles of the two books respectively. In both books, the sections eighteenth and nineteenth are dedicated to praise of the king. In the other works of his, the titles of different sections reflect the dominant traditions of *masnavī* writing. From Zulālī's seven works, *Maḥmūd va Ayāz*, *Azar va Samandar* and *Sulaymānnāmeh* have narrative plots and include didactic anecdotes on moral issues. The other four books are descriptive and praise famous figures of the time or the poet's hometown.[31]

All seven works are dedicated to Shah ʿAbbās I. Unlike the dominant image of the Safavid kings in earlier *masnavī*s, which portrayed the kings as deserving their position because of affiliation with the prophet and Imām ʿAlī, the Shah whom Zulālī describes is a Sufi-warrior with only a mere similarity to Imām ʿAlī. The issue of lineage is not hold important for Zulālī. Furthermore, the king's role in promoting Shiʿism is not mentioned. This contrasts with the dominant ideology of Shah ʿAbbās I's time in public places, which regularly introduces him as the slave of Imām ʿAlī or the guard dog of his

---

[31] For more information about Zulālī read the introduction to his *Dīvān* Zulālī Khwansārī, *Kullīyāt-i Zulālī Khwansārī: Sadeh-yi Yāzdahum-i Hijrī Qamarī*. ed. Saʿid Shafiʿiyun, (Tehran: Kitābkhāneh Mūzeh va Markaz-i Asnād-i Majlis-i Shūrā-yi Islāmī, 2006). In this introduction he did not only offer a biography of the poet as was descried through biographies of the time, but also brought a full account of different manuscripts of the poet's works which could be found in the libraries around the world. In details he analyzed each and compare them to each other. Furthermore, the author attempted to identify the poet's style of writing by focusing on the most frequently used literary devices by Zulālī.

threshold. Moreover, for describing his warrior personality, the language that the poet applied does not appropriately demonstrate the king's imperial character. Since most of these works are written with language traditionally is associated with *ghazal* form, the image of Shah 'Abbās as a skillful warrior is not emphasized through this language. The following lines from *Shu'leh-yi Dīdār* describe the Shah's warrior skills through the application of motifs that were usually dominant in the world of the *ghazal*:

شاه عباس ثریا آستان
شاه والا گوهر گیتی ستان

بحر لطف و موج عدل و جوش عشق
شور مصر و فتنه ی شام و دمشق

نوبر نه گلشن فیروزه رنگ
نو امید و نوشتاب و نو درنگ

ادهمش در زیر این نیلی حصار
سایه اندازد به بالای سوار

گر به دریا در خرامد بی شتاب
عکس افتد گاه برگشتن در آب

بر چنین رخشی چنین شیر افکنی
بحر و بر را عافیت بر هم زنی

خنجرش را جوهر خورشید برگ
می فروشد چین پیشانی به مرگ

در بهار خشم و لطفش ز آب و رنگ
یاسیمن و لاله شد نقش پلنگ

Shah 'Abbās, whose palace opens to the Pleiades
The king with pure lineage, and the world conqueror

He is the sea of kindness, the wave of justice, and the surge of love
He causes tumult in Egypt, and turmoil in Syria and Damascus

He is the new fruit of the nine blue heavens
He embodies hope and mastery of war[32]

---

[32] The poet applied *nu-shitāb* and *nu-darang* to show the king's mastery in war. These two adjectives refer to a quality in war that demonstrate the warrior knows when to stop and when to attack.

His horse under this blue sky
Has overshadowed all riders

If he glides to the sea with no haste
his image could only be seen in the water on his way back

On such a Rakhsh, such a lion-killer [is needed]
Who disrupts the peace of sea and land

The sun's essence empowers his dagger
(His dagger) trades death with the wrinkled forehead [of enemies]

In spring, the water and color of his anger and kindness
Makes Jasmin and tulip like leopard's skin (i.e colorful)[33]

The structure of metaphors such as *jawhar-i khurshīd* (the Sun's nature), *chīn-i pīshānī* (the forehead's wrinkles), and *bahār-i khashm* (the spring of anger) invariably represented the dominant form of writing during the 16th and 17th centuries (i.e. Indian/Isfahani style). These metaphors that usually belong to the realm of romance and lyrical writing are not as effective as the metaphors that were used in the *Shāhnāmeh* form for portraying the king's material power. Zulālī regularly uses such metaphors to refer to Shah 'Abbās I. For example, in the section 19th of *Meykhāneh*, the poet starts to praise the king through metaphors of the *ghazal* world that portrays the king as a wine bringer, serving a well-scented wine to his people.[34]

The poet depicts Shah 'Abbās as having authority over the other kings because his soul had been created in the form of a heart,[35] and not because he portrays physical power over the other kings. In *Zarreh va Khurshīd*, the king is praised as being the happiness of the heart.[36] *Falak Awrang* (heaven-like throne) and *gītī bārgāh* (world-like palace) are

---

[33] Zulālī Khwansārī, *Kullīyāt-i Zulālī Khvānsārī*, 241.

[34] Ibid, 289.

[35] Ibid.

[36] Ibid, 343.

among the metaphors that are used to show the king's worldly power. In occasional references to the religious role of the king, the poet employs the word "Shi'i" but the king is never praised for disseminating Shi'ism.

The descriptions of beautiful city, garden, and palace scenes in Mullā Rafī' Muḥammad Qazvīnī's poetry in praising Shah 'Abbās II are not different from the works of 'Abdī Beyg in terms of content. In a poem of travelogue genre, Mullā Rafī' describes Mazandaran, as well as Ashraf and Ṣafīābād palaces. In a very general term, he describes the weather, plants, and birds in Mazandaran and concludes that the magical weather and beauties of the city are the result of Shah 'Abbās II's kingship. Upon reaching this conclusion, he praises the king's generosity and physical attributes. Like other kings, he is described as a great warrior and ideal leader of the empire. In this work, the city is praised for its economic stability and security from invasions, and the king for his just attitude towards the people.[37] There are no references to Shi'i ideas or the Sufi-Shi'i lineage of the king.

V. Mīrzā Muḥsin Ta'ṣīr Tabrīzī and Shah Sultan Ḥusayn

Muḥsin Ta'ṣīr Tabrīzī (b. 1650 – d. 1717) also manipulates the ekphrastic force of the description of courtly palaces and gardens. Ta'ṣīr Tabrīzī was the accountant-poet of Shah Ṣafī II. He spent most of his time at the court of Shah Ṣafī II in Isfahan working as his accountant. Also, he worked for the local governor of Yazd until Shah Sulṭān Ḥusayn dismissed him from the position. He was well educated in the religious centers of Isfahan. He learned theology, Quran, and hadith from Āqā Ḥusayn Khwansārī (d. 1688) and was

---

[37] Mullā Muḥammad Rafī' Vā'iẓ Qazvīnī, *Dīvān-i Mullā Muḥammad Rafī' Vā'iẓ Qazvīnī.* (Tehran: intishārāt Akbar 'ilmī, 1980), 652-660.

well trained in Shi'i legacies. This familiarity with Shi'i learning highly influences his poetry, and his many *qaṣīdeh*s in praise of Shi'i Imams demonstrate his Shi'i intention. Nevertheless, his praise for Shah Sultan Ḥusayn does not make an affiliation between the king and Shi'ism.

While the architecture of the courtly palaces in 'Abdī Beyg's works mostly represents an idealized place with frequent references to the heaven, the buildings in Ta'sīr Tabrīzī's poems embody a real place, a glorious place appropriate for a king whose power is similar to the other empires of the world. For 'Abdī Beyg, the palaces and gardens compete with the sky and stars and ultimately they surpass the celestial bodies. In his poems, while one element of the comparison is concrete (the palace), the other part is abstract (for example the heaven as portrayed by Quran or hadith). However, Ta'sīr Tabrīzī describes the palaces and gardens as real and imaginable without being compared to abstract ideas. In the poems of Ta'sīr Tabrīzī, the palaces and courtly gardens are described precisely with attention to their layout, color, paintings, and more important of all, their function. Ta'sīr Tabrīzī gives the readers sufficient detail to distinguish each building from any other monarchical places. For example, the following lines that describe Shah Sultan Ḥusayn's residence in Sa'ādatābād argue for the king's sovereignty and enable readers to visualize the palace with its detailed description in a realistic manner:

به هر صنعت هنرمندان ماهر
کمال خویشتن را کرده ظاهر

مصور بسته در نقاشی او
کمر محکم به رنگ خامه مو

شود تا دلنشین آن کارنامه
ز مژگان نکویان کرده خامه

به نقش دلکش آن نقش ارژنگ
مصور کرده گل را کاسه ی رنگ

منبت کاریش در قصر و ایوان
نکو چون جبهه پرچین خوبان

به رنگ آسمان پر ستاره
طلا و لاجوردش بی شماره

بماند تا مصون از چشم اختر
به طرح چارقل دارد محجر

به هر یک در مقام جانسپاری
پری کرده است گویا شیشه کاری

به روی فیض کانجا بی شمارست
در دولاب او آیینه دارست

به چوب صندل و عود قماری
زبان هر درش درچوب کاری

مه نو چفت بیرون در او
دو پیکر سینه چاک از پیکر او

ز هر حوضش خجل چاه زنخدان
لبالب آبش از سر چشمه جان

از آن طرح بخاربهای دلکش
عبان گلزار ابراهیم و آتش

در آن گلشن چمن پیرا نشسته
بخاربهای چون گلدسته بسته

درون او یکی فرخنده منزل
مکان مسند سلطان عادل

میان گلشنش از چوب مرغوب
دو تا زیبا بنای دلکش و خوب

اساس خوشتر از طرح سفینه
قرینه با هم اما بی قرینه

به طرح دلنشین بی شبه و مانند
قفس آسا ولی بی بست و بی بند

from each field of art, the artists
showed their perfect skills

To start painting, Muṣavvar[38] [for painting the palace]
tightened his belt and dipped his paintbrush in the color

To make that work of art pleasant
He made his brush from the eyelashes of beautiful beloveds

To paint favorable images of Arzhang
Muṣavvar turned flowers into colors

The carvings in the palace and the verandahs
Are fine like the dimpled foreheads of beautiful beloveds

In the same color as the star-filled sky
It (i.e the palace) was full of gold and turquoise stones

In order to remain unharmed from the evil eye of the stars
The four protective prayers) are carved in there (i.e. palace)

(The carvings are very beautiful as if) they (fairies) sacrificed themselves in
crafting the intricate glasswork

By the grace of blessings that are found in abundance
Even the door of his storage is adorned in mirrors

Because of the fine sandalwood and the *qamārī* wood
Each panel of the door boasts about itself

The door knocker is a new moon
And the Gemini is passionately in love with that moon

The beauty of the garden's pool shames the dimples [of the beloveds]
The source of water is from the soul

From the design of those elegant fireplaces
One can see Abraham's garden and fire

In that beautiful garden a gardener is seated
Who designed those fireplaces like a bouquet of flowers

In this garden there is a blessed house
Which is the place of the just king

In this garden from the fine wood
There are two elegant and magnificent buildings

Their design is better than a ship
They are symmetrical but without parallel[39]

---

[38] Mu'īn Muṣavvar was one of the most famous Persian miniaturists and painters of the Safavid
period. He experienced the reign of last four Safavid kings (Dehkhoda).

[39] The word in Persian is *bī-qarīneh* which means unique.

Their elegant designs have no equal
They [the buildings] resemble cages without locks (Ta'sīr, 177-178)

Ta'sīr Tabrīzī briefly discusses the palace's paintings and wood carvings. He describes the inscriptions on the walls and the materials of the doors. Four *surah*s of the Quran, each starting with *qul* (Say), are written on the walls. In popular Iranian Shi'i belief, reciting these four *surah*s in crucial moments of life helps individuals to go through difficult times and gain success. Ta'sīr Tabrīzī's description extends to include such a high level of detail that even the shape of the door's handle (*chift*) is not overlooked. Further, the poet mentions the pool and fireplaces in the garden. Then, he describes the twin palaces standing in the garden. His description of the palace and the garden remains reminiscent of heaven, but it shows evidence of a transition towards a realistic image of what actually existed at the time as they are described in detail and with attention towards the color and objects that were applied in their construction.

In another example, the poet portrays a Safavid garden where the building known as "Musamman" was located. The portrait of the main building, the structures within this palace, the garden, its trees, and the water fountain reminds the readers of heaven and its beauties while also embodying the power of kingship in constructing and maintaining the beauty and glory of such buildings. In the following verses, the palaces and the gardens are represented in their ideal form to stand for the king's power and glory:

دگر در وی مثمن آسمانی
به طرح هشت خلد او را نشانی

سخن ساز جهان در دلنشینی
ندارد شاه بیت این چنینی

عماراتش چو جنت ذوالمراتب
چراغ منظرش شمع کواکب

به سر از قبه آن عرش منظر
شه خورشید را چتری مدور

گلستانش فرنگی دستگاه‌هست
که بر سر این بنا او را کلاه‌هست

میان باغ فرش از خاره دارد
سراسر جدول فواره دارد

پی فواره نهری با طراوت
مرتب از عمارت تا عمارت

چه جدول برج آبی مایه دارش
ز دلو چرخ ریزد آبشارش

قد فواره در وی بی شماره
کشیده میل بر چشم ستاره

Another (building) is the heavenly Muṣamman
Which resembles the eight heavens

Even the best orator in the world, with such elegance
Could not compose such a Master Verse[40]

Its' buildings have multiple floors like heaven
Its torch is brighter than the stars

On the roof of this building that meets the sky
The sun [king] spreads its light like a parasol

The garden has a foreign appearance
This building rests on its head like a hat

There are marbles spread like a rug in the middle of the garden
There are channels of water winding through the garden

After the fountains there is a fresh river
Which moves from one building to the other

What a channel that a tower of water supplies it
As though their waterfall pours down from the water pail of the sky

The height of the fountains is incalculable
They block the view of the stars (Ta'ṣīr, 172)

Then the poet turns to the Pool of the Mirror in the middle of the garden and continues with the description of small water channels and water fountains within the garden. Although 'Abdī Beyg describes the same objects, Ta'ṣīr Tabrīzī does not

---

[40] The best verse of a poem in terms of beauty and coherence that usually connects the different ideas of a poem together.

represent them as other worldly. These channels go between one palace to the other and

they only represent themselves. There is no special magic beauty or spirituality involved

with this imaging. The description moves next to the west pavilions which has a square

for playing polo. His depiction of the square's orientation in relation to the main palace,

its function, and the other three pavilions helps readers to vividly imagine these places

without making an affiliation between the objects and the heavens:

دگر در سمت غرب آن گلستان
یکی میدان برای گوی و چوگان

به عالم در بزرگی اتفاقش
لوای آسمان چوب قبافش

دهد می شاه دین پرور به بازی
از این میدان به سرمستان غازی

به آن وسعت که بعد از صد شنیدن
به لطف نام او نتوان رسیدن

در آن میدان یکی تالار عالی
دو عالم از جلالش یک جلالی

چنان از رفعتش نقشی نشسته
که دست چرخ را تخته بسته

در آن جنت دگر عالی نشیمن
سر دریاچه ی گلشن معین

سه تالار آن عمارت را به زینت
یکی را بر یکی آیین رفعت

به الوان شیشه ها دورش مطرا
رشیدا خانه گویا کرده مینا

به چرخ نیلی و خورشید زردش
دهد خجلت طلا و لاجوردش

On the west of the garden
There was a square for playing polo

The world agreed on its greatness
The sky was on its center[41]

The king during the game serves wine
to the happy warriors from the square

The square is very huge that even after hundred times hearing of it
one cannot grasp the reality of its area

There is a lofty pavilion in this square
By whose magnificence the two worlds are but a paltry coin.

Because of its elevation it is such a beautiful place
That it tied that hands of celestial fate

There is another elegant palace in this heaven
It is right by the garden's lake

That building has three pavilions
Each on is higher than the other

The color windows adorned the pavilion
(as if) Rashīdā[42] designed the buildings with enamel

the blue sky and its golden sky
are ashamed in front of the gold and turquoise of the building (Ta'sīr, 173-174)

The relationship between the palace and king is not a spiritual one. As mentioned

earlier, the poet in this work does not show interest in Shi'ism to praise and legitimize the

king. Nevertheless, the poet emphasizes the king's sovereignty by comparing him to the

other well-known, respected temporal kings of the world in a section entitled *dar madḥ-i*

nuwwāb-i kāmyāb-i ashraf-i aqdas-i a'lā (in Praise of the Prosperous Deputies of the

Eminent and Most Sacred) in a *masnavī* known as *Ḥusn-i Ittifāq*. In the opening lines of

this section, the king was compared to the Persian king, Darius, and was depicted as the

---

[41] *Qubāq* was a tall and thick pole that was erected in squares. It was a tradition to put a golden or silver ring on the top part of the pole. In playing games such as polo, the horse-runners of each group running towards the pole, tried to aim the ring. Whoever could hit the ring would own it. (Dehkhoda)

[42] Rashīdā is one of the famous Iranian calligraphers of Iran during the Safavids. He was the Mīr 'imād's nephew, who was also a great calligrapher. In 1638, he passed away in Kashmīr (Dehkhoda) Why did the poet apply the verb "mīnā kardan", which was not involved with calligraphy, for a non-painter? Is it possible there was another Rashīdā who was a painter? I could not find any other person as a painter during the Safavids or before. There was a Rashīdā Qazvīnī who was mentioned by Naṣrābādī under the class of poets. There is no mention of his life period (*Tazkireh-yi Naṣrābādī*, 312).

designer of Solomon's throne. The poem includes a comparison of the king to other famous rulers of the world by mentioning the names of many famous and glorious kings of different empires cne after another in consecutive lines, relating each of them to the Safavid king in different ways while also representing all as subservient to the Safavid king. Ta'sīr Tabrīzī lists Kīumars and continued with Ṭahmūris, Jamshīd, Żaḥḥāk, Firīdūn, Manūchihr, and other kings of pre-Islamic times. Bahrām, Parvīz, Kasrā, and Faghfūr of China were mentioned as slaves of the king or as soldiers of the Ḥusayn's army. The kings of the Samanids, Ghaznavids, Timurids, and Khwarazmshahids are also mentioned as kings who accepted the Safavid king as their lord. Further, the poet mentions the Mughal kings Salīm and Akbar, who deferred to Safavid power. Toward the end of the piece, the poet praises the king for giving him the position of the vizierate when he was in Yazd (Ta'sīr, 201-204). In general, the Safavid king in these lines represents a powerful sovereign who does not have any characteristics of a spiritual leader like the Safavid Sufi ancestors.

VI. Conclusion

In this chapter, I demonstrate the different ways through which the poets attempted to legitimize Safavid kingship. I argue that the early *masnavīs* contain the main ideological aims of the Safavids. The power of Safavid kings was claimed through emphasizing Ismā'īl's relationship to his Sufi forefathers and their innocence. This relationship allowed Ismā'īl and the future kings to claim spiritual leadership of the Muslim community.

I demonstrate that both poets applied the motive of place to legitimize their monarch patron. Nevertheless, the representation of places in the works of 'Abdī Beyg Shīrāzī whose *Khamseh* belongs to the middle years of the 16th century and Muḥsin Ta'sīr Tabrīzī whose work was probably written sometime between 1668 to 1715 demonstrate referential differences. I argue the relationship which 'Abdī Beyg envisions between the royal places and his patron is a spiritual one, portraying both place and the king as sacred entities affiliated with the other world. However, Ta'sīr Tabrīzī presents the buildings as they are, without making any definite connection between the royal palaces and gardens with the other-world. The king who possessed these buildings was similar to other emperors of the world whose power, although destined by God, was not perceived other-worldly. This shift in reference to places and buildings from a spiritual entity to a semi-political place in *masnavī*s of Shah Ṭahmāsb to Shah Sultan Ḥusayn represents the influence of modernity in its early stages on poets and poetic discourses.

CONCLUSION

This dissertation responds to the Safavid poets' reflection upon the Safavid ideology. By analyzing *qaṣīdeh* and *masnavī* throughout different Safavid courts from the early establishment of Safavid power to the fall of the dynasty, this dissertation argues that most of the panegyrics produced during this time did not propagate Shi'i ideology; and therefore, did not have ceremonial function. My analysis demonstrates that the panegyrics did not reinforce the twelve Shi'i Imami ideology, especially after the ascension of Shah 'Abbās I (b. 1571 – d. 1629) to the throne. Instead, they focused on legitimizing the kingship through Sufi discourses and describing the kings with Persian notions of kingship.

The Safavid period is famous for its many poets who did not belong to the court system, but who, wrote and presented their work for a public audience in bazaars, coffeehouses, and their own homes, free of court supervision. Because of the diverse venues available for writing and reading poetry during this period, the genres and the forms appeared differently from one place to another; they were also different from the Persian literary past. In the first chapter, I explain the changes which occurred in writing poetry under the different circumstances of this period. Building on earlier scholarship concerning the problems of categorizing the literary history of Persian poetry regions of literary production, I suggest limiting the scope of Safavid poetry to specific themes and images, i.e. images of kingship, within the specific genres to construct a common ground for drawing conclusions about the socio-historical circumstances of the period.

In Chapter Two, I set out the historical background for my literary analysis in the next chapters. In this chapter, I demonstrate the dominant ideology of the Safavids in the cultural materials of time including coins, inscriptions, enthronement orations, and the charities of charitable trusts. This representation demonstrates the trajectory of Safavid ideology and the different combinations of its elements throughout history. Since my main material, poetry, is a linguistic medium, in this chapter I have only focused on those visual and cultural materials that verbally represented the Safavid ideology. I demonstrate that the emphasis of Safavid ideology changed from Shiʿism to discourses related to Persian forms of kingship and Sufism , which is specifically visible in cultural materials produced during the reigns of the last two Safavid kings, Shah Sulaymān and Shah Sulṭān Ḥusayn.

In Chapter Three, in order to analyze the poets' responses to the Safavid ideology and its different elements, I look into the *qaṣīdeh*s of the Safavid period. I demonstrate that the poets approached the Safavid kingship differently from the other cultural materials. Shiʿi doctrines for most of the Safavid period were not central notions for poets and their poetry. Instead, they focused on those aspects of kingship and spiritual leadership which helped the Safavid kings to be perceived as sacred.

In Chapter Four, I examine the work of the celebrated Safavid poet Ṣāʾib, an outstanding exception to the trend noted in Chapter Three. Unlike the other poets of the Safavid period, Ṣāʾib brought in all available legitimacy patterns, from Persianate notions to the Shiʿi responsibility of the kings into dialogue with each other in a very coherent and systematic structure to establish the religio-political legitimacy required for shaping the public imagination about the Safavid polity. Ṣāʾib brought the idea of light emphatically into his representation of the Safavid ideology and also takes advantage from this concept in the structure of his works to portray the king and Shiʻi kingship as sacred entities necessary for political leadership. By studying his poems written after the defeat of the Indians in Qandahar by Shah ʻAbbās II, I draw attention to the poetry of triumph, which has not yet been examined as a separate literary genre. Studying these poems is important, as they show how the people of medieval Iran saw themselves in contrast with the people of other empires and how they constructed their cultural "others."

Finally, by studying the *masnavī*s in the final chapter, I attempted to further analyze the Safavid ideology in poetic form. The *masnavī*s, which were patronized by the court system, also portrayed the Shiʻi kings differently from the dominant religio-political discourse of the time. Shiʻism was not at the center of *masnavī* discourses, even though the public actions of the kings and other court-sponsored media. The same trajectory of Safavid ideology discovered in *qaṣīdeh*s is evident in *masnavī*s. While the *masnavī*s of Shah Ṭahmāsb drew ethical comparisons between the king and the twelve Imāms to give Shiʻi legitimacy to the king, the later poets of the Safavid period emphasized the similarities between the pre-Islamic Iranian kings and the Safavid kings in order to claim authority for the latter. In this chapter, I demonstrate that the depiction of palaces from the beginning of the Safavid dynasty to its end had the same trajectory as the representation of patterns of legitimization. During the reign of Shah Ṭahmāsb, the palaces were voids which, by being similar to heaven, became open for any possible spiritual interpretations. The poetry of Shah Sultan Ḥusayn's period though, portrayed the palaces in accordance to their architectural layout, colors, structure, and function, to manifest the special power of the king in the construction and maintenance of the prosperity of a palace.

I would like to broaden the scope of this study to other forms or genres of poetry to investigate whether the representation of kingship without Shi'i characteristics is due to the form of the poetry or being rooted in the poets' socio-political mindset about kingship. One area that I did not touch on is the *manqibat* genre, which became dominant in some works of poetry. In this genre, the poets expressed love for the twelve Shi'i Imāms. Some poets wrote about all twelve Imāms in one specific *qaṣīdeh*, and some poets wrote twelve *qaṣīdehs* in praise of each Imām. Examining these works could demonstrate how the poets thought about the Imāms and Shi'ism, as well as how Shi'i poetic discourse could make distinctions between the Imāms and the kings. Another important point that needs more exploration is the arc of historical development in Shi'i ideology. The field is much explored by Safavid historians through analyses of the treatises of Shi'i scholars; however, there is still a need to understand what Shi'ism was when Shah Ismā'īl first announced it as the state religion and how it would develop further.

At a broader level, the Persian poetry of the 16th and 17th centuries, its themes, and the poets' engagement with the religio-political discourses of its time can be globally contextualized in a comparative mode among the three imperial histories of the Mughals, the Safavids, and the Ottomans. Although the field of Safavid studies has grown within the last decades through the time and effort dedicated by historians, and despite the growth of interest in studying Safavid poetry, the field of the Persian *qaṣīdeh* remains relatively unexplored. This lack of attention to the Safavid *qaṣīdeh*s is mostly due to the language used in these poems. In this literature rhymes are more complicated than earlier

poems so the forms of similes and metaphors. A primary aim of this dissertation,

therefore, is to increase interest in Safavid literary history and to show that the Safavid

literature should not be seen merely as literary texts but as sources which could provide

Safavid historians with more information about Safavid ideology and its forms of

kingship during the late medieval and early modern period.